THE GRAMMAR
AT WAR

1914 - 1918

Richard Lewis Campbell Dargie

The Grammar at War 1914-1918

Published by
The Aberdeen Grammar School Former Pupils' Club

First Published 2014

ISBN 978 0 9930123 0 3

Printed and bound by
Imprintdigital
Upton Pyne, Exeter

Cover design by Sarah Judith Dargie

Contents

Preface

Thanks are due to a number of people who have had a hand in the origin and the development of this book.

Arthur McCombie, Principal Teacher of History, Deputy Rector and historian of Aberdeen Grammar School first inspired the idea for this book many years ago in the early 1970s. His belief that pupils best understood History by researching historical sources resulted in my first glimpse of the wealth of material to be found in the Grammar magazines from the Great War period. Although more than forty busy years passed before I had the time to examine those sources again, the idea for this book was planted long ago in Room 4 by an inspiring teacher who encouraged a lifetime's interest in History in many Grammarians.

I also wish to acknowledge the part played in this project by Dr Theodore Watt, my 'virtual co-writer' though perhaps ghost-writer is a better description given that he died in 1946. A full appreciation of Dr Watt and his contribution to the life of the School and the City of Aberdeen throughout the first half of the last century concludes this book. Suffice to say here, that without the many thousands of hours that he gave to researching his fellow Grammarians, much of the rich history of the school would have been lost forever.

Thanks are due to Douglas McAllister, Jock Hendry, Brian Crookshanks and Alan Hamilton of the FP Club Executive Committee for their positive response to the idea of a book that would commemorate the Grammar FP cohort of the Great War. They are also to be thanked for the diplomatic way in which they periodically enquired about the slow progress of a book which, like the war itself, took a lot longer to complete than first envisaged. Grant Hamilton has been very helpful with the online arrangements for publicising and selling the book.

The staff of Aberdeen City Libraries were, as ever, helpful and generous with their expertise when it was requested. Special thanks are due to the staff at the Central Library which continues to be, in difficult and changing circumstances, one of the treasures of Aberdeen's civic life.

I also wish to thank my uncle David Rennie, a former Gordon Highlander and volunteer medalist at the Regimental Museum at St Luke's, for his interest in this book and for showing me something of the work that goes on behind the scenes at the museum and a little of its fascinating collections that cannot be displayed for reasons of space.

Two conventions of the School Magazine have not been adopted in this publication. These are the practices of identifying FPs by their complete set of names and by their years of attendance at the school. This has been done to make the text easier to read without the complication of unnecessary detail. The full name of an individual has been given on occasion, when it is of interest in itself or where several FPs share the simple version of the name. For a similar reason, certain aspects of military terminology have been simplified eg in many instances full details of the battalions in which FPs served have not been identified. This will doubtless infuriate enthusiasts of military history but hopefully enhance the flow of the text for the general reader.

Period names for territories have usually been retained; thus Nyasaland rather than Malawi etc. In places, the language in source extracts reflects the attitudes of the Great War period rather than those of our own more sensitive age. On grounds of historical authenticity, these instances have been not been amended.

Errors are inevitable in a book of this scope, and all errors are of course the sole responsibility of the author. Readers who spot inaccuracies are asked to contact the author through the publication's email address on the AGSFP Club website so that they can be amended within a planned future digital edition.

The current author has faced a similar dilemma to that which confronted Arthur McCombie and Brian Lockhart when writing their magisterial history of the school, *Bon Record*. Given the number of Grammar FPs who distinguished themselves in the Great War, it has simply not been possible to mention them all in this book. To do so would have resulted in a list, rather than a book aiming to illustrate and explain the experiences of FPs in the context of the times. Inevitably, men who made a significant contribution in their field of operations have received only a brief mention, and in many cases none. The author takes solace in the fact that almost all of the Great War FPs already have their place of honour in Theodore Watt's Roll of Pupils published in 1923.

In the course of researching and writing this book over the last three years, I have taken to 'chuntering on' a great deal about the Grammarians of 1914-1918. The principal targets of this artillery barrage of Great War trivia have been a few friends at the FP Club Centre, and my family who were in the front-line trenches without any possibility of retreat. Fortunately for them all, with the publication of this book, an armistice has been declared and the chuntering guns will hopefully fall silent.

Chapter 1

The Spirit of the School

At first light on Tuesday 11th July 1916, two figures slipped out of their granite homes in the West End of Aberdeen, met at a pre-arranged spot, and headed out of the city towards Donside. As dark clouds were gathering in the early morning sky, they cycled like demons to get as far from Aberdeen as fast as possible in case the coming rain tempted them to turn back home. Despite losing time to technical mishaps, they cycled almost seventy-five miles that day, finally making camp at 10.30pm amongst the midgies in a wood near Nethy Bridge. Up at five the next morning, they covered another seventy-five miles past Loch Laggan and the Spean, reaching Fort William in time for afternoon tea. Still full of bounce, they immediately headed up Ben Nevis and reached its summit at 9.30pm where they were rewarded with a glimpse of their ultimate destination, the mountains of the West. Respite that night was taken in the hut on top of the Ben. It had to be a short rest in order to escape the morning toll collector who charged walkers using the summit path. By daybreak they were cutting down the mountainside and wading the river Ness to avoid having to pay for their pleasures.

Thus began a two week tour of the Western Highlands by two Grammar pupils, biking and hiking over the roughest countryside in the British Isles. Making their way across Glen Shiel, Torridon, Assynt and Skye, they covered more than 700 miles by bike and boots, climbing some of the best mountains in the land. They took their nightly shelter in sheds and abandoned cottages, none more desolate than the isolated ruin at Camasunary beyond the shadow of the Cuillin. Their one night in a civilised bed was at the manse in Glenelg where they enjoyed true Christian hospitality, a fine supper and breakfast. Otherwise, breakfasts of tea and eggs were negotiated from crofters' wives. 'Enormous suppers' were enjoyed at Highland establishments such as the Sligachan Inn, incurring a daily expense of around three shillings. Throughout the expedition, the boys

1

navigated using a Bartholomew's tourist road atlas, although the constable at Edinbain on Skye kindly lent them a more suitable map for the wilder parts of the island, once he had assured himself that they were Aberdeen Grammar schoolboys and not German spies.

Grammar FPs of the era were equally adventurous. In spring 1913 the newly-formed FP Motor Cycle Section went ahead with their initial meet in the teeth of a blizzard, managing forty miles or so before a quick stop for tea at Banchory. In May they set off for a weekend run to Loch Ness. They faced a number of obstacles; incessant rain, at least one collision with a telegraph pole, frequent mechanical failures and at Nairn, the preference of 'the local for conversing with his fellow agriculturalists in the middle of the High Street'.

In the upper sections of the route, the neglected roads were 'more like a scenic railway than a turnpike' with lower stretches often completely washed away. At Invergarry and Spean Bridge, the road was 'poisonous' while at Dalwhinnie it resembled 'nothing so much as a bunker after the passage of a party of earnest golfers'. Along these tough Highland miles 'much unparliamentary language was heard' although the group cheerfully mucked in to carry out repairs to each other's vehicles.

They faced worse disappointments than punctures; at Laggan they discovered that their arranged accommodation was 'limited'. Pushing on to Dalwhinnie, they found that a party of 'lively Aberdonians' had invaded the only hostelry there after being blown off Ben Alder. These drouthy hillwalkers had 'exhausted the hotel's possibilities'. There were no rooms, no food and not a single drop of drink to be had. Now eleven on the Saturday evening, the motorists had no option but to saddle up and head on to Pitlochry, another thirty uncomfortable miles away. Sanctuary and some supper was eventually found at an early hour in the morning at Fisher's Hotel, thanks to the obliging hostess. After negotiating the Devil's Elbow, the group returned home on Sunday evening with one machine empty of petrol and under tow for the final eleven miles. The whole party was agreed; the weekend had been 'one of the best ever'.

In winter, FPs found other ways to challenge themselves. Several were pioneer members of the Scottish Ski Club and formed a group that set out at dawn from Ballater in January 1913, intent on a expedition to Mount Keen. As the sun began to tinge the snows of Lochnagar in pink, the party were already enjoying 'a splendid run down to the upper waters of the Tanner'. The icy summit of Mount Keen was reached by one o'clock where they enjoyed a clear winter's day view that stretched all the way to the Ochils far to the south. The descent homewards was fast, 'rather too fast, for the least expert member of the party had several falls' but the group believed they had probably enjoyed the finest ski run yet made in Scotland. Arriving back in Ballater around five, they had covered twenty-four miles and climbed an estimated 5,000 feet: 'an ideal day's sport'.

These three expeditions, recounted in happy detail in the school magazine, tell us much about the spirit of the Grammar community in the years before and during the Great War. They reflect the belief of its great rector Henry Fyfe Morland Simpson that the school was 'no mere crammer or exam-shop' but an institution that encouraged boys to live a full, confident life and to push themselves to take advantage of all its possibilities, mental and physical. Classroom learning was clearly important but so was being involved in school activities and sport. In modern jargon, Simpson was an advocate of 'educating the whole child'. In the language of the Grammar of the time, he hoped to build *mens sana in corpore sano*. Tales such as these three expedition reports perfectly illustrate the values of effort and endeavour that Simpson hoped to instill in his pupils.

These intrepid Grammarians with a taste for adventure had attended a school that was changing, and growing, quickly. In Simpson's twenty-seven years as Rector, the pupil roll grew from around 270 to over 700, while the curriculum expanded with greater emphasis upon the 'newer' subjects such as science and modern languages. The 1863 buildings had been extended, so the school enjoyed the new facilities of a technical workshop and a gymnasium as well as added classrooms.

The heart of Simpson's school however was the Hall, or Valhalla as it was known by those who appreciated the Rector's interest in Norse and Germanic legend. For long a bare, dusty space, it had been used only occasionally for the annual distribution of prizes and the like. In Simpson's rectorship, it was transformed into the heart of the school, both a shrine to the long centuries of Grammar tradition, and a place where the school came together on a daily basis. More than sixty portraits of illustrious FPs lined its walls and the names of former Rectors were picked out in gold lettering on a dark oakwood board. Valhalla was the perfect setting for morning assemblies, the high moments in the school year such as Empire Day, and many less formal moments such as dramatic performances and the popular sing-song evenings. Simpson had done well to convince the penny-careful School Board of the Hall's value to morale, persuading them to leave it alone when they had eyed it as potential classroom space.

By 1914 preparations were also underway for a new playing field at the Bleachfield below Anderson Drive. Full costings for the project had been drawn up and the School Board had approved the plans. All that remained was for the school community in the shape of the Former Pupils' Club to fulfill its promise to the Board to raise a contribution of £1000. The Club managed this, and more, by the following spring.

The FP Club was Simpson's greatest innovation. Already in its twenty-first year by 1914, the Club had over a thousand members, many of whom were scattered around the globe but who welcomed some vestigial bond with home. Three times each year, the school magazine made its way to the letter-boxes of FPs in every part of the world. Members not only appreciated it but contributed in turn, passing on news of their life in the colonies and beyond to the readership back in the Granite City The editor, Theodore Watt, found space in every issue for articles about FP life in foreign parts; Life on a Perak Coconut Estate, From the Lesser Slave Lake, A Day's Sport in India, A Glimpse of California, A Jaunt in Java, Alone in Borneo. These pieces were eloquent evidence of the global reach of the Grammar School, as were the pages of Notes About Old Boys recording their progress towards success and pre-eminence in every walk of life.

The June 1914 issue however carried a tale that was both exotic and chilling for it concerned the violent death of an FP caught up in the chaos as Mexico disintegrated under revolutionary pressures. William Benton, originally from Keig, had emigrated to Texas in 1879. He did well and invested his riches in cattle farming in northern Mexico. By 1914 the Benton haciendas ranged over 100,000 acres and were stocked with prime cattle, many bred from Scottish beasts. The millionaire Benton was on good terms with Mexico's President Diaz which did not make him popular with the revolutionaries. In a quarrel with the rebel Pancho Villa, Benton was stabbed and killed, possibly by Villa himself. The murder was widely reported in the scandalised British press. Questions were asked in the House. The Foreign Secretary Sir Edward Grey sought clarification from the US and Mexican Governments. Such was the interest in Benton's murder throughout Britain, let alone Aberdeen, in the summer of 1914.

Benton's demise was not the normal stuff of the Grammar School Magazine. Then as now, its pages were devoted to the normal round of school events; staff retirals and appointments, prizes awarded, match results and the doings of the school societies and the FP Club. Yet Theodore Watt devoted six pages, including a full-length photograph of the unfortunate Benton, to the shocking Mexican events. He would have thought it incredible that in forthcoming issues, he would soon be reporting the violent deaths of dozens of Grammarians.

Also prophetic was a short piece sent in by a uniformed FP serving in Bengal entitled Military Manoeuvres in India. The writer described how the army was developing new methods of communication, replacing the heliograph and flag signals with field telephones. The artillery innovations that the writer witnessed at a field camp near Dacca were ominous. He noted the accuracy of modern ordnance capable of 'plugging the target after one or two sighting shots'. Illuminator shells were used for night gunnery practice. These 'burst like a firework and lit up the country for miles around' allowing the gunners to follow up with real shells. The writer noted the power of these newer guns: 'when you think that one of these pieces can blow a hundred or so men to pieces, it makes you realise what terrible things they are'.

Magazine readers probably paid little interest to this paragraph, moving on instead to enjoy the rugby report or the humorous summary of the Literary & Debating Society's programme of events. But the very next issue would report many more tales of Grammarians caught up in equally explosive events. This time they would be much closer to home.

Chapter 2
The Outbreak of War

The Grammar School magazine of October 1914 was the first to appear after Britain's declaration of war on August 4th. It contained three new features: a Muster Roll of FPs known to be serving in HM Forces; a list of FPs who had been 'Mentioned in Dispatches' which would soon begin to record the many honours for exceptional service and gallantry awarded to Grammarians; and a section titled *Pro Patria Mortui*, notes on those who had fallen in the conflict. It also contained a great deal of informal information that demonstrated how, in little more than two months, the war had already impacted on the school community and the lives of FPs in Aberdeen and throughout the Empire.

The first and most obvious change wrought by the war was the presence of strangers on the school campus. The buildings of the Central School [later Aberdeen Academy] were quickly requisitioned for hospital use and its pupils, male and female, were 'billeted' upon the Grammar. The two schools shared the Skene Street buildings on a 'shift' basis, with the truncated Grammar School day now running from 8am to 1.30pm. While some Grammarians struggled with the enforced early rising, the free afternoons created by the new situation were universally popular. Most pupils were happy with the new arrangements, partly because the new school day was half an hour shorter and because, as one remarked in the magazine, 'that bun at 11 o'clock is a great attraction'. The wartime innovation of a mid-morning canteen selling milk and cakes was popular but it was a rowdy place, packed with scholars who 'maddened by hunger and privation, were frantically waving their pennies to the two over-worked waitresses and imploring to be served'. The early closure however had an impact on the Grammar's after-school activities and it was some time before school clubs adjusted to the new conditions.

The normal sporting routine of the school was badly affected: the magazine gloomily announced that 'as there are no other teams to play, there will be no matches this year'. The gymnasium in the Westfield building, later the Lower School and then 'Language Block', had become a Red Cross hospital. The annual Sports, held in the late summer period in those days, were deferred until the following spring. The project to create a new recreation field was already underway but most of the school's sporting activities still took place on the field facing Whitehall Place immediately to the north of the school buildings. But that piece of land, the editor lamented, 'is constantly in use, in winter is more or less a sea of mud, and in summer cricket is hopeless'. Now, even this limited facility had been commandeered for the martial drilling of pupils and recruits, and 'our studies are disturbed by the somewhat spasmodic utterances of the drill sergeants. In the early afternoon they are heard far off - tramp, tramp, tramp; then they come nearer and nearer until they eventually pass under the Sixth's window and take up their position on the field. Daily, unmelodious and disagreeable noises greet the ears of the Sixth as they sit with their beloved (!) Cicero or Demosthenes - Quick march - Halt - Mark time - Form fours. The six stalwarts who compose the Sixth are wondering how they will be able to form fours'.

The small number of pupils languishing in the Sixth was the result of enlistment: ten others who would have been completing their school studies that session were eligible to volunteer for service and had already done so. Numbers in the school were also depleted by the fact that thirty-three Scouting pupils were often away from Skene Street, engaged in war work 'at the various coastguard and military stations, hospitals etc in Aberdeen and the neighbourhood'. The staff of the school were also beginning to be called to other duties. George Dawson, an FP and Maths master, was the first from the Grammar staffroom to fill the ranks, joining the Royal Scots in October 1914 before being transferred to the Special Brigade of the Royal Engineers a year later. Inevitably, the normal routine of the school year was disrupted in all kinds of ways and its rich extra-curricular life, so carefully nurtured by Morland Simpson over many years, was in danger of withering away. As one despondent pupil noted in that first winter of the war: 'no debating society, no football team, no anything'.

The war also affected the activities of the FP Club. The AGM scheduled for April 1915 was cancelled as 'a very large proportion of the members of the Club are serving with His Majesty's Forces and it would therefore be impossible to obtain a representative meeting'. The sports sections were 'dormant as practically all their members have either enlisted or received commissions'. The rugby fixtures for 1914-15 were cancelled but, undaunted by the Kaiser, the Badminton Section determined to arrange at least one evening's play in the week. Almost every member of the Hockey Section was in the Territorials. Several were already in France while others were training at bases in southern England. However enough Hockey FPs were serving with units stationed in the Aberdeen area, or were medical students at Aberdeen University and thus required to graduate before enlisting, that a scratch eleven could be cobbled together for the occasional friendly. The FP Club programme of social events was postponed and the Club Executive decided that 'if the European War is not brought to an early conclusion, the Annual Dinner and the Annual Ball will not be held'. On a more positive note, by February 1915 the recreation ground fund totalled £1186, 13 shillings and sixpence, allowing the FP Club to pay its promised £1000 to the School Board with quite a bit to spare for games equipment. The work of enclosing and laying out the future Rubislaw was soon well advanced with the contractors reporting good progress 'under the wartime circumstances'.

If FPs at home in Aberdeen were going to have more time on their hands, FPs elsewhere already had their hands full. From the very first war edition, the school magazine proved an effective medium for letting the Grammar community know what FPs were doing for the imperial war effort. In pre-war days, the magazine section Notes About Old Boys had announced the routine news of career appointments, promotions and retirals. These were now eclipsed by more gripping tales and from the outset, this section of the magazine featured snippets of news about Grammar FPs involved in key moments of the war.

The German war plan had long hinged on defeating the French quickly and decisively before the Russians could mobilise their vast manpower. Everything depended on taking Paris before the winter set in. The Allies' successful defence of Paris in September 1914 was therefore the key turning point in the war. There would be no quick German victory in the West as in 1870. The German High Command soon began to look east for a breakthrough and the Western Front settled down into four years of mud, tedium and hell.

Grammar FPs were present in the first frantic days of panic in the French capital and witnessed the scrambled response to invasion as reinforcements were hurriedly carried to the line in the only vehicles available, Parisian taxis and buses, with the incoming wounded deposited in the only beds available, those of the big Parisian hotels. Ian Thomson, an Aberdeen medical student, served as an orderly in a motor ambulance unit carrying the wounded the worryingly short distance from the Front back to the emergency hospitals that had been set up across Paris. Two other Aberdeen FP medics, Thomas Robson and Gordon Key, acted as medical dressers in the Scottish Section of the Red Cross Hospital installed in the Hotel Astoria. And already there were dispiriting messages from France: Capt Alexander Fraser, Royal Army Medical Corps, reported missing. Fraser in fact emerged from the chaos of those early days to serve throughout the war winning the DSO, MC and the French *Croix de Guerre*.

By October 1914, Grammar FPs were already in the armed forces in large numbers. The Muster Roll, the list of FPs 'taking a worthy part in the defence of the Empire', contained almost 500 names in October 1914 and over 600 by February 1915. There were however serving FPs who were not yet included on the roll. At this early stage in his information-gathering, Watt could not know the details of all the Grammarians throughout the Empire who had volunteered since August 1914. Nevertheless his figures were the best possible, given the circumstances.

In the first Muster Roll in October 1914, Watt listed twenty-two FPs serving in the Royal Navy and Royal Marines: of these eight were medics ranking from Fleet Surgeon to Deputy Surgeon-General in charge of the RN Hospital Malta. Watt was also able to identify 408 FPs in the Army of whom 225 already held a commission at this early stage in the proceedings, forty-one at the rank of Major or above, and sixty-one at the rank of Captain. While the largest contingent of FPs [169] were serving in the Gordon Highlanders, an astonishing ninety-two FPs were already in the ranks of the Royal Army Medical Corps and the Indian Army Medical Service, almost all of them commissioned medics. Thirty-four FPs were already serving in the Royal Engineers, and forty in the various artillery formations; not a bad effort from a school with a tradition in the classics rather than modern sciences.

In the next edition of the Muster Roll printed in February 1915, Watt noted that many FPs had 'given up good appointments and come home in order to offer their services to the Country'. One member of the club came 'from China travelling steerage all the way; another came from the Argentine, another from British Columbia, yet another from the Straits Settlements'. By this stage Watt had listed 42 FPs who were serving in colonial units. Most of these were Canadians, reflecting the large number of FPs who had gone to Canada to seek their fortune there in the decade or so immediately before the war. It also illustrated how the war was developing from a European into a global conflict. And one entry on the Roll, Alexander Spence Donaldson Royal Flying Corps, hinted at the new forms of warfare that were already evolving above the fields of France and Flanders.

Chapter 3
The First Fatalities

The deaths of six Grammar FPs were reported in the first two war-time issues of the magazine published in October 1914 and February 1915. The differing circumstances in which these men died tell us much about the global spread of Grammar FPs whilst signalling that the events unfolding in northern France and Belgium were only part of a burgeoning world war.

The case of the first FP killed in action made this point clearly for his death occurred far from the fields of Flanders, still bearing their late summer harvest and not yet turned to mud. In 1914, Thomas Peppé Fraser was a thirty-four year old FP and Aberdeen University medic who had entered government service under the wing of the Colonial Office. When war broke out he was serving as a member of the West African Medical Staff in Nigeria. Neutralising the small military contingents that the Germans had deployed in their collection of overseas colonies was an early priority for Britain. The German forces in these colonies posed no substantial military threat to the Empire but they did offer the potential for developing into an on-going nuisance. Extinguishing them quickly would secure Britain's lines of communication, and snuff out the German potential for trouble making. In line with this policy, in late August 1914 a detachment of British troops was sent on reconnaissance along the north-eastern frontier of British Nigeria with German Cameroon. On 29th August, in an action against German colonial forces, Dr Fraser was killed and buried in the hot dry sands close to the German fortress at Mora.

Another of these first six fatalities to be recorded in the magazine underscored the point that the 'short war in Europe over by Christmas' had consequences that stretched across the British Empire. Angus Legge, son of one of the most popular and longest serving of teachers at the Victorian Grammar, was also a medic in the colonies. Legge held posts at the Hospital for Infectious Diseases in Singapore and in that city's Municipal Health

Department. Since the outbreak of war in August however, he had also been serving as a lieutenant in the Singapore Volunteer Medical Company.

In February 1915, a detachment of Indian Muslim troops mutinied and killed a number of Europeans, both officers and civilians, male and female. On the evening of the 16th, with the mutineers loose in the bush and the colony still on edge, Angus Legge volunteered to lead a unit of stretcher-bearers on a night detail. He and his sepoys were required to carry medical equipment up to a rural location that was now deemed at risk of attack. In the darkness, Legge and his men were outflanked and ambushed by the mutineers. He was shot in the thigh and his femur splintered. By the time the sepoys, under fire themselves, could reach him, Legge had suffered severe haemorrhaging and shock. He died on arrival at hospital. Legge's death caused great sorrow amongst the FP community in Singapore, almost all of whom had been tutored by his father. The incident also highlighted the fact that the war, by encouraging dissident elements to believe that Britain's energies were diverted elsewhere, threatened to disrupt the certainties of the pre-war age and loosen Britain's grip on Empire.

The first FP fatality at sea occurred on the first day of 1915. It was a reminder that, though the attention of the British public was fixed from the outset on the battlefields of France and Flanders, the fundamental struggle for victory would take place at sea against the threat of the German U-boat. Herbert Shinnie was a professional seaman with experience in the Merchant Navy and the Royal Naval Reserve, and he had served on the battleship HMS *Formidable* since August 1914. After covering the speedy transportation of the British Expeditionary Force to France in the first days of the war, *Formidable* had been based at Sheerness and Portland supporting the long-term British plan to blockade the Channel, seal off the North Sea and so hem German shipping back into its ports.

At 2.20 on the morning of New Year's Day 1915, a sailor on middle watch on board HMS *Formidable* reported a white wake rapidly approaching from a south easterly direction. It was too late for the great ship to take evasive action. The dull thud of torpedo contact on its hull was almost immediately followed by an explosion. The *Formidable's* engines were damaged by the blast, rendering the ship unviable. Captain Loxley gave the order to launch the boats from his badly listing command but darkness and worsening weather added to the onboard chaos. A second German torpedo hit home at 3.05. No assistance was available to the *Formidable*. The other capital ships in its squadron had rightly steamed away from the danger. Two light cruisers that remained closer to the stricken ship had to adopt evasive manoeuvres to avoid being hit themselves. They could render little meaningful assistance. Sub-Lieutenant Shinnie supervised the lowering of the quarter deck lifeboats, ordering the married petty officers to board first and take command of them. When the final order came for all men to look out for themselves, Shinnie was seen by survivors to be checking that each one of the men around him had something that could float to hang on to. At approximately 4.45, the *Formidable* disappeared. Shinnie was one of 547 officers and men out a complement of 780 who were sucked down with her. He would not be the last FP to suffer that fate.

The three remaining FPs on this first list of fatalities all served on the developing Western Front. Their deaths were typical of many more reported in the Grammar Magazine over the next four and a half years. Sydney Goldsmid, a lieutenant in the Worcestershires, distinguished himself in the early days of the war and was mentioned in dispatches by the British Expeditionary Force commander General Sir John French. Goldsmid was reported 'wounded and missing' in October and then 'missing believed killed' in December 1914. Sergeant George Duncan, the son of a long serving Grammar 'jannie', was a professional soldier in the Gordon Highlanders who had served in India and Egypt before the war. He was killed in an action between Dixmude and Ypres, just three weeks after landing at Zeebrugge in October 1914. His commanding officer wrote a short obituary letter in a tone that was to be repeated over and over again: 'He was a most painstaking NCO and a man of sterling worth. On 29th October he died at his post, doing his duty in war as he did in peace. While in charge of his men he was shot; his death was instantaneous and he suffered no pain'.

The sixth of these fatalities was Major Alexander Robb of the Durham Light Infantry, a decorated officer who had seen active service on the North West Frontier and had also served as a Lecturer in Military Subjects at Durham University. On 20th September 1914, Robb's unit were near Troyon on the banks of the river Aisne, pinned down by sniper fire and shelling from the Germans who, as ever, held the higher, drier ground. After repulsing a German infantry assault, Robb ordered his platoon to advance uphill with bayonets attached. The charge faltered under a hail of German bullets and shrapnel from German, and friendly French, artillery fire. The Durhams took heavy casualties and many of the surviving men were pinned down, flat to the ground. Fifteen yards short of the enemy line and with signs that the Germans were under pressure and retreating, the Durhams were ordered back to their own trenches.

Major Robb however was missing but had been seen lying wounded in front of the German trenches. To rescue the major, Pte John Warwick of the 2nd Durhams crawled uphill, unarmed, attracting the full attention of the German riflemen. He eventually found his wounded officer, lying less than 30 yards from the German firing line. Robb ordered Warwick to leave him and go back, an order which Warwick of course ignored. They were both pinned down by snipers for some time but a French artillery barrage offered a chance to escape while the German riflemen took cover. Warwick supported Major Robb back down towards the British line where a comrade, Private Nevison, rushed out to help. Nevison sustained a fatal shot in the head when the three men were just 15 yards from safety. Warwick was shot in the back and the right shoulder, but survived. Major Robb died later that night. Warwick was recommended for the Victoria Cross but was ultimately awarded the Distinguished Conduct Medal for 'gallant conduct in voluntarily rescuing a wounded officer under heavy fire'.

This tale of a small action on the Western Front in autumn 1914 contains nothing that would surprise any modern reader familiar with the Great War and the countless books and films that have depicted its horrors. In fact little in it would have surprised the Grammar readership just a few months later, for the general public in wartime Britain soon became inured to tales from the Front. But much in this story was still novel, unfamiliar and exciting to readers of the school magazine in the early months of the war. And it would also have given them some understanding of the trials that so many other Grammarians were about to encounter and endure.

Chapter 4

Training Tales

The Grammar School was getting ready for war long before the Kaiser invaded 'plucky little Belgium', thus breaching the 1839 Treaty of London designed to defend Belgian neutrality. Numerous senior pupils and FPs were already members of the School's own detachment of Gordon Highlanders - D Company of the 4th Territorial Force Battalion. In March 1914, another twenty senior pupils had enrolled in the 'School Company', encouraged by two persuasive FP recruiting officers, Major Thomas Ogilvie and Capt Charles Peterkin, and perhaps by the thought of a long summer camp at Tain which promised to offer 'a great time'. Some of those camping in Easter Ross that July would soon find themselves undergoing more serious training at the major army base in Bedford later that year.

In the early months of the war, several Grammar FPs penned humorous descriptions of their time at Bedford for the school magazine. They describe the horrors of 'the dawn rouse' when raw recruits were woken less by the piper's six o'clock overture than by the exposure to the chilling blasts that followed their sergeant's resort to 'the ancient and never-failing device of pulling off the blankets'. The army recruit's day was punctuated by parades, drilling and long excursions into the English countryside 'at the double'. Preparations for each coming parade prepared the men for the routine and precision of army life: 'buttons have to be brassoed, spats and rifle sling blancoed, rifles cleaned and shoes brushed. After we have been subjected to a critical inspection by the captain, we are marched off to the tune of the pipes and arrive in slightly over an hour at the place where our manoeuvres are to start'. Discipline, regular food, fresh air and an abundance of exercise soon had an effect on even the least muscular FP recruits; 'it would surprise those who remember the unathletic ones amongst us to see how well we stand 'doubles' of over a mile in length'.

Concerns about food have always loomed large in solders' letters home and FP missives to the Editor were no exception. In the first weeks of the war the diet at Bedford was dull, consisting of 'the customary stew provided by the Government'. If FPs wanted something more appealing, they had to provide it themselves: 'tins of sardines or pineapple chunks are a favourite delicacy for this purpose'. By February 1915, things had clearly improved, for a subsequent FP cohort at Bedford enjoyed breakfasts of tea, kippers, sausages, mealy puddings, porridge and milk. Afternoon tea, taken *al fresco* after long marches or mock skirmishing, was a simple meal of tea, bread, butter and jam with occasional cheese. Stew and potatoes still appeared on the dinner menu but roasts offered some variety. Plum pudding 'known as duff' and tinned fruit were the usual desserts.

Such was the diet of FP Gordon Highlanders en route to the Front - if they could get their hands on it. For these Scottish soldiers, mostly privileged and well-bred sons of Aberdeen's bourgeoisie, soon discovered that army meals were 'most unlike our home life. It is hardly usual in civilised society to have to line up for each meal, or to enter into a sort of scrum round a 'dixie' and emerge a few minutes later grasping a kipper firmly by the tail, or with a sausage impaled on a fork'. Most of the FPs sending messages back to Theodore Watt had grown up in the large granite homes of Aberdeen's West End. In 1914, families in these comfortable residences continued to employ a small complement of domestic servants. For many an FP, the first shock of army life was having to do things for oneself: 'it is a new sensation to think that as soon as one has finished eating, dishes have to be washed and laid by for the next meal. There are some who will never be reconciled to having to take their turn of cleaning up the mess-rooms after the meals are finished'.

Some free time was available in the evenings, if all necessary duties had been completed to the army's satisfaction and one was not down for night duty. Some FPs inevitably took the opportunity to explore the Bedfordshire environs. The army training base lay next door to a girls' Physical Training college but the writer of one article was at pains to reassure his readers back home that the proprieties were being maintained: 'be not alarmed, we are staid and aloof…the more serious-minded of us stay in camp to write letters or play billiards while the light-minded go down town to frivol about in the cafés or picture houses'. There was also time for sport, with three FPs representing the Scottish Territorials against an English Territorials XV in a scratch international.

Training young civilians to kill other human beings has always been a serious and brutal business but FP correspondents were at pains to make light of their experience and emphasise the funnier moments of army life. Officers were always the favoured butt of jokes amongst the other ranks: 'Our captain is now mounted and issues his commands from the back of a fiery charger. He has been remarkably free from accident so far, but other commanders are occasionally to be seen retreating from their companies at the gallop when their steeds happen to have urgent business in the far distance'. The trainees in the Gordons were also quick to laugh at their own peccadilloes: 'On the whole, we in the Fourth have been remarkably free from disease. Perhaps the most prevalent form is a fungoid growth on the upper lip. The victims of this disease are, as a rule, very sensitive about it'.

These articles from the early months of the war also hint at the way in which Britain's Great War soldiery was to form its own very distinct view of the war, one that was often at odds with civilian sentiment. *It's a Long Way to Tipperary* enjoyed a renewed popularity amongst British civilians in 1914 but not amongst the 4th Battalion at Bedford or many other army units for that matter: 'it is a popular belief that soldiers are always singing *Tipperary*. No impression could be more erroneous. If anyone starts singing it on the march he is greeted with stony silence and soon desists. A much more popular song is that whose chorus ends with *It's just like bein' at hame*. You will note the intentional irony of that last statement'.

Hundreds of Grammar FPs made their way through Bedford during the war. One correspondent even noted that 'the place swarms with Grammarians. Hyslop is at the piano as I write. Captain Peterkin is poring over the mess accounts; Rose and Valentine are discussing golf close by, and in the offing are Slessor, Saunders, Kelly, Williamson etc'. For all that Bedford gave them a short, sharp introduction to the army and its ways, from the later perspective of the trenches, many were to look back at their time there with fond nostalgia.

Bedford was something of a holiday camp in comparison with the training that some Grammar FPs endured in preparation for the Front. In early 1915, Robert G Combe, who was later to win the Victoria Cross, wrote a typically positive note to the school magazine from his base at Melville, Saskatchewan: 'Training conditions here are sublime. I had fifty recruits out the other morning for a route march with the thermometer at

18° below zero. I froze my chin and one cheek. Several of the men had frozen noses and cheeks. We all feel very fit however and the cold is most invigorating'. Like many of the further-flung FPs, Combe was looking forward to the chance to return to Scotland, having been away from Aberdeen since 1907. Some of his men were Canadian Scots by descent only and had never seen the old country. Combe was also keen that his wife, who planned to accompany him to Europe, should see the 'old School' and he hoped that 'it will come up to my boastful accounts'. Nor was there any doubt in Combe's mind how the war would end, for like many migrants to the New World, he had drunk from its deep wells of optimism: 'I just noticed one of my old class in the first list of volunteers - Hugh F Mackenzie. I hope that I shall meet many more and that we have a chance to have a little reunion - preferably at Potsdam!'

Chapter 5

En route to the dug-outs

In October 1915 and June 1916 the school magazine published a narrative penned by an anonymous FP serving with the 4th Battalion Gordon Highlanders [Territorial Force] in Flanders. It was put together from letters that the FP sent home plus excerpts from a diary he kept while at the Front. The pieces are a vivid, frank but good-humoured description of one Scottish soldier's introduction to modern war. They also represent a very readable summary of the typical experiences faced by dozens of Grammarians who served in the trenches. An edited version of this narrative is reproduced in the next two chapters.

The first article described the writer's arrival in France and his acclimatisation to the unfamiliar routines of life at the Front, and the devastation and carnage he encountered there. It ends with a description of his first experiences in the firing line as the 4th Territorial Gordons moved ever closer to the enemy in support of the regiment's Regular battalions.

The voice of this anonymous FP is a simple, direct one and it tells the tale of the trench-dweller as clearly and honestly as any other Great War diarist. Like most of his generation, he makes little public complaint about being sent into the horror of the Western Front. In places however, he points the reader to other thoughts and feelings, as when describing the relative luxury of life at HQ, which is done in a positive tone devoid of rancour but in detail nonetheless. The pieces that the writer sent home obeyed the letter of the military censor's regulations but evaded their spirit. The names of military units and strategic locations are duly omitted [in most cases but not all] but there is a stark candour in the casual descriptions of combat and death that must have horrified readers opening the school magazine at the breakfast tables of the granite villas back home. Theodore Watt received many such pieces from FPs and often included a page or two of eyewitness news from a distant battlefield. However it is clear that Watt sensed the special quality in this correspondent's communiques; he devoted an unprecedented twenty-seven pages of the magazine to them. Watt also revealed the writer's identity when he penned his obituary in 1918.

Lt Douglas Meldrum Watson Leith MC, was killed in action on the first day of the Ludendorff Offensive, 21st March 1918, aged 26. Born in Old Meldrum but living at 4 Carden Place when he entered the Grammar, Douglas was an athletic blue and a double graduate in Arts and Science at Aberdeen University. Before the war erupted, he hoped to enter the Indian Forest Service. He enlisted in the Grammar Company of the Gordon Highlanders in September 1914 and served on the Western Front for seven months in 1915. After an officer training course in Blighty, he was back in action 'over there' in January 1916, later serving as Intelligence Officer for his battalion and his brigade. In three years of war, he fought at Ypres, Beaumont Hamel, Arras, Cambrai, and Passchendaele. He was found dead after the prolonged bombardment that heralded the last big German offensive of the war on the Western Front. His commanding officer recorded that 'a large shell splinter struck him near the heart...death must have been instantaneous'.

March 1915. We had a rather hurried departure from England, and it was not very long before we arrived within the hearing of the guns. The passage across the Channel was accomplished in safety. An escort of about 15 destroyers saw us over from Southampton to Le Havre. At the latter we spent three pleasant days under canvas. On the way to the camp a crowd of French youngsters yelled at us for souvenirs and made amusing remarks about our 'skirts'. The skirl of the pipes afforded them huge delight.

It was cold at night and we slept fully dressed. In fact, for a fortnight after my arrival in France I had not off my clothes. We got served out with sheepskin coats and look like a battalion of teddy bears. Under my tunic I wear a rabbit-skin vest, and while I was washing one morning, a little French girl came in about and, holding my vest, remarked as she pointed to a herd of goats on the road 'Frère, Frère'.

It was funny watching some of our fellows who knew little or no French trying to flirt with the French girls with the aid of phrase books. They seemed to get on quite well in spite of their limited vocabulary. A coffee and cigarette shop stood close by the camp and one Scot was anxious to procure cigarettes of which two kinds were being sold. To his request for cigarettes the French girl answered, 'Ce paquet-ci ou ce paquet-là?'. 'Well, I'm d---d' said he to his chum, 'I never heard them called by that name before'.

From Havre we had a 26 hours' train journey to a place about 10 miles from the firing line. It was a slow and wearisome journey. One would have thought that the train had square wheels. We were billeted in a vineyard in hot-houses. They may have been hot once on a time, but I never slept in a colder place. Snow and hail, thunder and lightning, sleet and rain, all had their turn, and the place was a perfect sea of mud.

At Havre there was not much to suggest that a war was going on in France, but at Bailleul ambulance trains and Red Cross wagons, aeroplanes hovering overhead, mud-stained soldiers returning from the trenches, the roar of the big guns, and on a still calm day, the crack of the rifle fire, brought the whole thing vividly before us, and we knew that before very long we would be right in the thick of it too. Every evening just after turning in for the night we got served out with rum, just like the Regulars.

From Bailleul we advanced 7 miles still further on our way to the trenches and arrived at La Clytte, where we are billeted in huts, 20 men occupying one hut. These huts are much warmer than the so-called hot-houses. Each hut has a brazier, and in the evening with several candles for light and the brazier for warmth, we are quite jolly and comfortable. We have been attached to a certain brigade of a certain army division of a certain army corps, and are now doing our turn in the trenches with the Regulars.

The 4th Gordons have been going into the trenches in companies. The company that I'm in received its baptism of fire ten days ago. We spend 48 hours in the reserve trenches and another 48 hours in the firing line. The former are about 1,200 yards behind the latter and are fairly immune from rifle fire, though easily within the range of shells. Bullets occasionally find their way past. I shall always remember our first tramp from the huts to the trenches. It is a distance of about 4 miles and we start at dusk so as to get into the trenches at dark. None of these movements, of course, are carried out during the day.

Preparatory to starting we were inspected by the Brigadier and by that famous soldier who saved the British Army at Mons, General Sir Horace Smith-Dorrien. Our Captain then gave us a cheery lecture on the crimes punishable by death on active service. The most trivial offences seem to come under that category. At 6 o'clock we joined the Regulars who were to be with us in the trenches, and all marched off in the gathering dusk as quietly as possible. Snipers' bullets occasionally pinged overhead. The landscape was lit up by the light balls which the Germans send up at night to show any movement.

At 7am the next morning we took our place in the trench, as the Germans start shelling about that time; but they seemed to be resting that day, so after four hours we got back to our more comfortable quarters and did some cooking and sleeping. Next morning we had to bolt into our holes like rabbits. Shrapnel shells began to burst overhead. One burst while I was rushing from the barn to my part of the trench and I can tell you that it was not long before I flopped in the mud. One is not particular about clothes on such occasions. The Germans kept up the game till late afternoon, and all that time we had to remain huddled up in the mud at the foot of the trench.

At 8.30pm we set out for the firing line. We marched on our way through a village that had been destroyed by shells. Never have I seen such desolation and devastation. It was just the skeleton of a village. The walls had gaping holes torn in them; above them stuck up the beams and rafters. That was all that was left. A stretch of about 800 yards of open country had to be crossed before we got into the firing line. Bullets whizz about all over the place and you have simply to trust to luck to get safely across that fire-swept zone. I must admit that I felt decidedly shaky going across these fields for the first time The fellow in front of me got hit in the leg but he was the only one hurt. Victor Bisset was immediately behind me carrying his mess-tin on his back. Next morning on taking it out for his tea, he found that a bullet had passed clean through it. Narrow squeak, wasn't it?

The trench where I was, was only 80 to 100 yards from the Germans, and their snipers were constantly potting at us, but it was quite safe as long as we did not pop our heads over the parapet. At night one man watched an hour, while the other sat under his rifle and then took his turn again. No sleep was allowed. During the day we saw the British big guns making a sorry mess of the German trenches. They in their turn sent over a few souvenirs to us, but the nearest one to me was fully 50 yards away when it burst. Our spare time was spent in filling sandbags, improving our trenches and cooking our grub. All that has to be done by oneself.

There is one thing that we have all learned since coming out here, viz., to look after No 1. There would be little fear of my being unable to look after myself now. It is ludicrous seeing us, on entering a new trench, hunting about in the dug-outs for any braziers, sticks, coke etc which may have been left behind. There is little here that we don't make use of. Water is our chief difficulty and it is very scarce.

I dug up three French rifles and a bit of a French tunic. They lost a great many men in the trench where we are. In a field 200 yards to our left I saw the bodies of about 50 Frenchmen lying in extended order (about two yards between each) who had been mown down by the Germans. There they have lain for three months with their officer in the rear. No one has been able to bury them. Dead horses and cattle lay near the ruined farms. The only living thing seems to be the cat. Such is war.

May 1915. The brigade has been moved northwards to a most important part of the line. The town, from which we are only half a mile distant, is too well known to mention, besides the censor would be on my top for it. Suffice to say that the British call it the Kaiser's key. Fighting here towards the end of last year was tremendously severe, and heavy fighting took place again not so very long ago. I hope we are not here longer than a week; things seem a bit too lively.

We marched the few intervening miles that afternoon. We halted for tea in a lovely grove where an Indian native battery was stationed. It was a most picturesque scene. Overhead there was leafy greenery, while underneath were the small but scrupulously clean dug-outs which the Indians occupied. We 'parley-voused' with them till nightfall, and watched them preparing their own grub which looked most appetising.

We arrived at our destination about 11pm. Being the only Territorial battalion, we were put into the supports. Our 1st Battalion went into the firing line. Being supports, we are about three-quarters of a mile distant and liable to be called forward if a severe attack is made. But we get the hard work. We rest through the day but when darkness comes down we are sent off to dig trenches, carry rations, water, sand bags, respirators etc. down to the firing line. This goes on until dawn.

Our men are not in trenches but in dug-outs along a railway embankment which is like a rabbits' warren. It is all tunnelled with dug-outs and you see the men crawling in and out like rabbits from their holes. Some are comfortable, some are not. Booth, Victor Bisset and I occupy a comfortable one with room for three. We crawl into it on our hands and knees and can't stand up inside. It has rained fairly heavily for a day or two and the place is a fearful sea of mud.

Today I visited some dug-outs in order to get some wood for ours. They were 200 yards distant from our own at the side of a wood and were most elaborate. Our men had been shelled out of them, and the stuff left lying about would have equipped a battalion - rifles, ammunition, equipment, personal belongings, bayonets etc. Shell heads and fragments were lying about thick, and a souvenir hunter would have a profitable time there. When we get back to our huts, we shall need a couple of days to clean ourselves I'm afraid. It is next to impossible to get shaved or washed here and we shall be worse than navvies in a short time.

The town was in flames when we arrived and had been burning for days. It must be quite uninhabitable by now; about three church spires remain upright, although pierced with shell holes. We saw the Germans shelling the place with incendiary shells. I am awfully curious to see inside that town but no one is allowed.

I was called away on Friday to visit with our officer a village close by behind the firing line. Shells and shell noses lay thick. One dead man was lying in the street; dead cows and horses lay scattered about the square. The houses were in ruins. In most of the houses were little odds and ends just as the people had left them. In one I saw a table with wine glasses on it untouched. The church interior was full of debris. The vaults in the churchyard were torn and rent by shell fire and the coffins and bodies exposed. Curiously enough, the big crucifix at the door was untouched. This is no exaggeration or hunting after effect on my part.

It was last Sunday night that the Germans made a big attempt to gas our troops at _____. Our battalion was having a few days rest in huts several miles away but several of us felt the effects of the fumes, chiefly a soreness of the eyes. On Monday night we should have occupied our usual trenches but owing to this attack we got urgent orders to move where the Germans had pierced the line. All of us have been provided with respirators.

I received orders to appear next day for an interview about my commission. The town I had to reach was thirty miles down the line but no trains were available until I had walked six miles. The countryside was beautiful and the roads lined in usual Flemish fashion with big trees. Single soldiers and battalions of soldiers of all nationalities were moving about, while wagons, ambulances, motor cars flew to and fro without end. Soldiers are all 'hail fellow, well met'. As I trudged along, I never lacked company. They come in about and chat away, after the usual salutation of 'Hullo, Jock!'

At the end of the six miles was the town with the station - a good deal shelled but with little appearance of damage. Most of the inhabitants had fled however. After some difficulty I found an inn, ordered coffee and eggs, bread, jam and butter. It was great, sitting in civilized fashion again on a chair at a table with a white cloth. The hostess had fled from Ypres and had set up a house in this less lively town. I managed to chat away in French with her quite well.

I really feel my French has improved because at the station I was complimented very much. As I was waiting the train, two officials came in and spotted the kilt. French and Flemish have a great affection for the kilt and bestow lots of little favours on the wearer, un-bestowed on those who wear the 'breeks'. For instance, one French woman pressed sandwiches on me for my journey; another gave me a big glass of coffee and rum and I simply had to drink it to please her, although the stuff made me almost sick. Well, the two officials spoke away for some time and I chatted back, every now and then excusing my French. 'Dear monsieur', I was amazed to hear one say, 'you speak French fluently with the right accent. Some English officers speak very well, but with such an English accent'. I was greatly 'bucked' about it. All the same I don't suppose Max Mackie would agree! I used to sit very near the bottom of his French class.

Next morning I took a stroll round the town which is the Headquarters of the BEF. It is a beautiful town, of course untouched by shell fire being so far away from the firing line. At 11 I had my interview, the usual thing - another signature for my paper. At 12 I resolved to have a decent dinner again so I entered a restaurant and had soup, roast, potatoes, vegetable and wine. There is nothing in this sort of life like doing oneself well when you have the opportunity.

At 2.30 I had the great good fortune to witness a meeting between Generals Joffre and French. Sir John French wore the usual field service khaki. Two motor cars arrived. Out of one came Joffre in his blue tunic, red knickerbockers and brown leggings. He shook hands with French; both stood chatting for a few minutes, and then entered a motor car and drove off together for a tour of inspection, I suppose.

I left for my own Headquarters about 4. Next evening I expected to rejoin my company in the trenches, but no; I am still at Headquarters. It consists of the Battalion sergeant-major, office staff, tailor, shoemaker etc also some pioneers about 20 in all, who seldom go into the firing line but stay a mile or two or even more (it is six just now) behind. At present I am in a wood; five of us are in a small tent made of a waterproof sheet and life is quite pleasant here. On Sunday last, an English regiment gave a band performance and it was most enjoyable. I spent four or five very pleasant days here. We went for eggs, loaves etc to the neighbouring farms and lived well but two days ago I got orders to rejoin my company in the trenches.

I reached the firing line at 10pm and was immediately sent off with a digging party. Getting back at 1am, I was on sentry till the 'stand to arms' at 2. From 2 to 3 I had a snooze, and then we were wakened by a fearful din a little to our right. The Germans had begun to bombard our trenches. About 3,000 shells came over during the day, and still they say the Germans are short of ammunition.

Our First Battalion had about 100 casualties. The shells landed right in the trenches about 70 yards from us. They fell in front, above, behind; the whole ground heaved and the debris and fragments were flying all around. Two or three little bits struck me, several of our fellows were wounded; not one was killed. It was simply marvellous. A kind Providence must watch this Battalion. Some of our fellows got half-crazed with fear, but we stuck to our trenches and got congratulated on it later.

The recent hot weather has made a most unpleasant 'dead man' smell. There must be heaps of dead lying about, some buried a few inches under, and others lying exposed, or at the bottom of shell holes and on the surface. If one side does not move on soon, there's bound to be pestilence here in summer. The Germans had been using that frightful gas of theirs here about ten days ago, and these poor fellows had been overcome by the fumes. One lay with his jacket pulled over his head as a shield. His hands were both gripping his collar. On each side of the line crosses and mounds mark the graves of those whom our men had time to bury. One gets accustomed to these sights. At first I was horror-struck; nowadays I am simply curious. But these things make you realize what an awful sin and what a horrible delusion war is. However, in a way it is all interesting and an experience which, in happier days, we shall think much on.

Chapter 6

In the thick of things

In the high summer of 1915, the Belgian village of Hooge was the scene of intensive fighting. Hooge lay on the twelve mile long road from Ypres to Menen [English Menin], a key artery for Allied communications but one that was visible to the Germans who occupied the higher ground in the area. The road was well within range of their guns. Even at relatively quiet points in the war, Allied casualties in this sector were high due to periods of almost continual German shelling. Both sides launched significant offensives throughout the summer of 1915 hoping to gain or retain key strategic points in the landscape.

The conflict around Hooge saw the use of huge amounts of underground explosives which created some of the largest craters on the already pock-marked Western Front. It also saw the introduction of a new weapon - flamethrowers. Douglas Leith's description of these events is packed with small details that bring his memoir alive; an officer wounded while celebrating the offensive's initial success, German prisoners fearing that they might be shot, an airman falling from his burning plane to certain death, the continual disposal of the dead. And the almost callous summary of the action in a one line communique from GHQ.

Leith's memoir mentions two fellow Grammarians who had become his trench comrades; Bisset and Booth. Victor Bisset, originally of Albyn Place, saw action with the Gordons and later with the Royal Field Artillery with whom he was wounded in 1917. When he was demobbed in 1919, he held the rank of Acting Captain. The second comrade was John Lyon Booth MC who lived in Mile End Avenue when he joined the Grammar in 1904. Graduating MA with a First Class Honours in Classics from Aberdeen in 1914, Booth had just begun a career in journalism with the *Aberdeen Daily Journal* when the war broke out. He served in the 4th Gordons until August 1915, at which point he was commissioned in the Seaforths, and won his MC in November 1916. In April 1918 Captain Booth was in acting command of his battalion. His men had just repulsed a

German attack near La Bassée to the south-west of Lille. Booth was on the enemy-held side of a canal, firing at the foe in order to cover the withdrawal of several of his men across to the Allied bank. His Colonel recorded that he was less than 100 yards from the enemy when he was killed.

June 1915. A British attack at Hooge. One hundred years ago we were on the eve of great events in Belgium. The same things seem to be happening again today. The Battalion has been hard at work digging communications trenches, hidden trenches, carrying trench boards, trench and parapet ladders, boxes of ammunition, grenades and all the hundred and one things that soldiers need in attack. Why? We shall see soon.

Well, on Sunday night we entered the trenches. Most of the company went out digging but I was put in charge of a rifle battery. This consisted of eight rifles set on a stand; 7 or 8 inches between each rifle. All were aimed at a crossroads in the German lines 1800 yards away. My duty was to load and fire these rifles pretty frequently all through the night and once or twice through the day. It was a soft job and interesting. I managed to scare quite a lot of fatigue parties as I rattled off the eight all at once when a fatigue party approached. The noise was rather startling when close in.

At 7pm on the 15th it was read out to us in orders that tomorrow was the anniversary of Quatre Bras, that two British brigades were coming up to make an attack, that we were to be in the reserve, that it behoved us to be courageous and accomplish what British soldiers accomplished 100 years before. As I was sitting at my battery between 10 and 11pm, the attacking brigades moved up to prepared positions in front. They streamed over our parapet in the moonlight, all bright and cheery, though all of them knew it would be the last night for many. He's a wonderful cheery person, however, the British Regular Tommy.

The attack was going to begin with an artillery bombardment timed to start at 2.50 and last to 4.15am. Our guns were to fire for an hour and twenty-five minutes, then our soldiers were to advance. 2.50 was drawing near and one or two guns put in a few ranging shots. We waited with our watches - the grey dawn was beginning to break and there were signs in the sky of a glorious day. We thought of the Germans in the wood and trenches beyond, all unaware of the hail of death which was soon to be launched on them. Bang! Bang!! Bang!!! And the shells were screeching through the air. Prompt to the second the guns had started. The din was something terrific. Never in my life have I heard anything like it. You can imagine 150 guns all firing together, many of them not half a mile behind you. In front of us the wood was hidden by smoke and flame. A regular line of flame showed over the German trenches as our shells burst. Soon we could see nothing for smoke. Then out of the ground our men seemed to jump. Line after line we could see advancing through the smoke to the German trenches with bayonets fixed - and it was all done so coolly. The British just walked into the first German trench. One man lost something on the way and went back for it, others were smoking cigarettes. The first trench was carried with little or no opposition. In the reserve we were so excited that many of us jumped on the top of the parapet and cheered and cheered. One of the officers was hit while doing this.

Half an hour later we learned that two lines of trenches had been captured, and later the word was passed that the British had advanced two miles and were still going strong, so Booth and I settled down to make breakfast. At 8am the first batch of about 30 German prisoners in their grey-blue uniforms were escorted through our lines. The fellow next to me was handling his rifle and some of the prisoners, thinking he was going to shoot, held up their hands. Some were wounded, but I expect all were jolly thankful they had escaped with their lives. It seemed an irony of fate that these fellows had to dodge their own shells - once through our lines they came within the danger zone of their own guns and one shell landed very near to them.

At 9.50 the order came along to us to fix bayonets and file out of the trench. We thought we were in for a charge. We went on to the road, and wading through a trench of water were posted in an advance post or 'redoubt' much nearer the Germans who were shelling like fury. We had simply to stay there and await their counter-attack which was sure to come. One big shell burst on our parapet and half buried us with debris. Shrapnel was bursting all over the place and the big shells were coming in fours: one, two, three, four, all in a row. Through that inferno we could see our soldiers, some advancing to augment the lines, others in ones and twos carrying messages, the stretcher-bearers rushing hither and thither to pick up the wounded. 'D' Company of our Battalion suddenly appeared in the midst of it and advanced nobly to do their bit, which was to dig trenches and strengthen our new position. They lost 4 killed and 27 wounded but they did not flinch.

About 3pm the counter-attack came. It was heralded by a fiercer bout of shelling during which gas shells were used and some of us had to use our respirators; then we heard the crack of rifle-fire getting louder and then dying down. Later it was passed down to us that the British had repulsed the attack and were still holding the gained ground. It was magnificent. The way our men stuck in was grand.

Evening was coming down and we were longing for relief. 9pm had come and there was still no relief, so our officer called me to go with him to HQ to make enquiries. We had a mad dash down the road, over shell-felled trees and through mud. Several times we had to throw ourselves flat to lessen the risk of getting hit but we escaped and gave our message. 10pm and the shells were getting nearer our trench. There had been a slight lull but the row started again. It was most nerve-trying to hear these big shells coming toward you, their droning noise getting louder as bursting point approached. At 3 am we got orders to shift and right gladly did we do it.

I noticed in the daily papers for 17th June the following in Sir John French's Official Dispatch: 'The British succeeded in taking two lines of trenches at _____ near _____. All counter-attacks were repulsed'. Such was the bald report. What a lot was never mentioned! How very little does the public really know!

Sunday - we marched through fields that had been cultivated once but were scarred all over with trenches and shell holes. Rank grass and wild poppies formed the growth above. A few hundred yards away there were fire and support trenches but whether German or British Lieutenant S did not know. He resolved to risk it and walked on in the open. A few bullets did whistle over our heads but did no damage. After wandering over fields and through a maze of trenches for a couple of hours we reached our destination in the firing line. A Major, on being informed how we came, remarked, 'You're cool devils; you were asking for bullets by walking there'.

We had tea there and a jug of boiling rum. The hours were passing and still no wounded had arrived, but several German prisoners passed us. Unfortunately they had no helmets by the time they came our length. Otherwise you might have been receiving a souvenir from me.

At present we are in dug-outs in a pretty wood with rather a pretty name. There are small ravines and a burn trickles through. There is undergrowth of ferns and young trees. The wood is a regular warren of dug-outs. In fact you are hardly safe to walk in places for fear of falling through a roof. There is an open space in the wood, a sort of grove, with mounds dotted about, most of them marked by simple little wooden crosses. It is an ever-growing graveyard. There are so many around here but this is the prettiest I have seen. As I write here in my dug-out I can see an officer reading the service over some poor chap.

July 1915. About ten days ago we left for the trenches and did a spell of four days. A mine exploded in front of us and the regiment on our left did the charge afterwards. Our company supported them and helped them to bomb back and shoot down the approaching Germans. Several fellows got German helmets and souvenirs. Next day the Germans shelled us terribly. It was perfect hell while it lasted. The trench was blown-in in several places and the dead and wounded were still lying about. We lost about sixty men killed and wounded. The German trenches opposite me were only 25 yards away. We could hear the Germans shouting and singing and could see the smoke rising from their cooking fires. We have never before been in trenches in such close proximity to the enemy. There is some advantage in being so close - shelling cannot be effectively accomplished.

The only excitement happened on the third afternoon, when the Germans threw over trench mortar bombs. These are beastly things but in the day time they can be seen falling. So we had some warning of their approach and could dodge. One chap in this platoon was sitting a few yards away from me making tea. A mortar bomb landed beside him, blew the mess tin from the fire, wrecked his equipment and buried his rifle. The fellow himself was not scratched. There are some really marvellous escapes. On the afternoon after the mine explosions, four members of the battalion were standing chatting together. A shell landed in the middle of them; two were killed, one died of wounds later, while the fourth was absolutely untouched.

We saw rather an interesting sight the other day - a German aeroplane brought down by one of our own airmen. Our airman either dropped a bomb or fired a shot on the petrol tank. The aeroplane burst into flames and a man fell out from an enormous height. Then the machine turned upside down and descended, a mass of flame, flashing on its downward journey.

We were in ripping trenches the last three days. They were all named - Bond Street, Regent Street, Shrapnel Corner, Whizz-Bang Avenue etc. Several weeks ago the 4th Gordons dug some fire and communications trenches which we occupied for 26 days. The main trench is called Union Street while a smaller trench off it is called Union Terrace. At one corner there was a small sign-board sketched out on a white sand bag. One finger pointed up the communication trench which led to behind the firing line. The other finger pointed to the German trench. Written on the first finger were the words 'To Blighty'. On the other finger were the words 'To Hell'.

After our spell in the trenches we return some distance behind the firing line to what is called our rest camp. There is really little physical rest because we are kept busy with platoon and company drill, musketry, bayonet fighting and all the odds and ends that annoy a soldier out of the trenches; but there is a great relief for the nerves. There is no longer the unpleasant sensation of hearing shells and bullets and wondering if any of them are for you. There is not the 'stand to arms' at daybreak. In short, we have not the same worry. Our tempers improve and once more we begin to enjoy life.

Chapter 7
Gallipoli

By early 1915, it was clear to strategists in London that there was no easy solution to the stalemate on the Western Front. Churchill and other 'Easterners' believed that Britain should use its naval reach in the Mediterranean to find another way to defeat the Central Powers. An expedition to capture Constantinople offered several game-changing opportunities; to install a pro-Allied government in Turkey, open a secure supply chain to Tsarist Russia and use the Balkans as a platform against Austro-Hungary. The initial naval phase of the campaign in February-March 1915 aimed at sailing straight towards Constantinople, where morale was low and elements in the government were already secretly negotiating with the British. The Allied naval attack foundered thanks to a combination of minefields in the narrow Dardanelles sea channel and resolute defence by the Turkish howitzer companies along the coast which harried British minesweeping craft. The Allies' Plan B was to occupy the Gallipoli peninsula and march northwards to the capital. The military invasion of Turkish soil began on 25th April. It was a day of confusion, ominously ending with beleaguered imperial forces struggling to retain a slim toehold on the beach at Anzac Cove. The Allies were to spend the next eight months in desperate efforts to penetrate the Turkish lines on battlefields that were now every bit as deadlocked as those in France and Flanders.

Most Allied troops in Gallipoli found themselves in precarious places, pinned down on the beaches and at the mercy of Turkish snipers and artillery sitting in secure defensive positions in the cliffs above them. Not only was the geography of Gallipoli against the Allies. Turkish resolve had been stiffened by the arrival of German military advisers and German equipment. The campaign commander Sir Ian Hamilton was soon well aware that 'every modern appliance of telescope, telegraph and wireless was at the disposal of the enemy.' In his dispatches, he noted that the entire Allied operation 'lay open to the view of the Turks upon Achi Baba's summit and Battleship Hill. Enemy aeroplanes could count every tent and every ship'. A letter by one ANZAC FP, Patrick Margetts of Alford and Melbourne, described the hopeless situation facing the Allies: 'we haven't much view from our parapets. Ridge after ridge of brown earth, inoffensive looking, but field glasses reveal Turkish trench after trench, strongly reinforced with sand bags and overhead cover. Abdul knows his work'.

And the weather didn't help. The troops amassed for the Gallipoli campaign had sunny weather when sailing from the Antipodes and India or through the Med from Blighty. Weeks of training in the hot Egyptian summer had followed, characterised by one FP contributor as 'awful - sun, sand and flies!' It was good preparation for the unrelenting heat of a Turkish summer. However, at Gallipoli the temperature and the inevitable build up of poorly buried corpses and body fragments generated a plague of flies and severe outbreaks of the 'Turkey Trots', violent dysentery that contributed to the deaths of several wounded and ailing FPs. And in the autumn and winter, the Dardanelles experience the same cold, damp weather that blows down from Russia towards Constantinople. Capt James Clarke described the realities of a Mediterranean winter in a letter home, written at Suvla Bay in December 1915: 'I am at present on old Gallipot and it's not exactly a health resort, what with torrential rain, snow blizzards with 15 degrees of frost and high explosives coming at you all the time. I don't think I have seen worse weather in Aberdeen'.

In places, Turkish riflemen and bombermen were very close to the Allied line but they enjoyed the advantage of height in well chosen and well protected spots in the cliffs. By contrast, Allied riflemen returning fire had to take chances in order to try and keep the Turkish heads down. Patrick Margetts described the deadly duels between riflemen which dominated the squaddie's life at Gallipoli: 'Our front trench is very close to theirs: from 10 to 30 yards the distance runs. Plenty chances for bombing and we get our share - especially at night. During the day it is mostly sniping work. We get a glimpse of a figure ducking quickly past an open trench or a head bobbing over a parapet…not much to fire at. We've had fourteen weeks of trench warfare now and have earned the title of old hands. Our post, Lonesome Pine, was a pretty hot corner'. Avoiding the snipers and the blast from Turkish mortars whilst going about one's business on the crowded beaches became the all-important survival skill as Capt Clarke reported: 'It is useful in these days to be a 100 yards man. I know exactly what I can do it in with an offshore and an onshore wind when the high explosive begins'.

Private Margetts soon joined the ranks of Allied casualties and the exchange that led to his wounding was typical of many in this coastal combat between riflemen: 'Haven't altogether escaped myself. One morning I located a sniper in a rear trench and I'd my rifle up ready when a bullet hit my rifle and I got a few splashes of lead in my head and shoulder. Had a few days of glorious rest in the beach hospital so I didn't mind very much after all'. Margetts recovered but suffered a second, more severe wounding at Pozière on the Somme. He was discharged in 1919 with the rank of Sergeant but died of his wounds back in Sydney in 1920.

The battle between the Turkish snipers in the craggy hills above and the Allied infantrymen in the sandy trenches below was a cruelly unequal one. FPs killed by sniper soon featured on the lengthening casualty lists. Dr Arthur Kellas, a major in the RAMC and commander of the 89th Field Ambulance at Gallipoli, was 'hit in the head by a sniper while making final arrangements before an action'. Cecil Ratcliff-Gaylard, another ANZAC FP, was also killed by a sniper's bullet to the head in one of the many struggles over Gaba Tepe, the prominent headland from which Turkish artillery delivered shells onto the ANZAC positions below. An assistant manager on a sheep station in New South Wales, Ratcliff-Gaylard had been one of the first 200 men to enlist with the Australian Imperial Force when the war sparked to life in 1914.

Several FPs also fell victim to the almost continual shelling and mortaring from above. Lt William Ward found himself in the Cable Signal Company of the Royal Engineers thanks to his pre-war experience as an employee of the National Telephone Company. His specialist skills had taken him to Constantinople once before, during the 1913 Balkan War, and he volunteered for the Gallipoli expedition two years later as he believed his local knowledge would prove useful. At 12.30am on August 1st 1915, Ward was on duty on Beach Q [Lancashire Landing] when his signal tent was hit by a high explosive shell, killing seven of his comrades and wounding six others. A piece of shrapnel embedded itself in Ward's brain. Although he was evacuated to a nearby hospital ship and operated upon, he never regained consciousness and was buried at sea two days later.

Five days later, the imperial forces made their final attempt to break away from the beaches and win the higher ridges that dominated the central ground of the Gallipoli peninsula. From the outset, this initiative was mismanaged. A new landing at Suvla was as confused as the first at Anzac Cove in April. Fresh troops were poured into the fray but met tough resistance from the Turks and were badly mauled. One of the few Allied successes in this mess was the temporary capture of Chocolate Hill on 7th August by the Royal Irish Fusiliers. Lt John Chalmers led his men of the 5th Battalion in the uphill charge and took his objectives at bayonet point. Chalmers was wounded in the action but his efforts were in vain as the offensive petered out. Chalmers later won the MC in France but was killed in the great German onslaught of March 1918.

Over seventy FPs are recorded in the school records as having taken part in the Gallipoli adventure. Of these, almost half served in ANZAC units. The others mostly served in British Army units such as the Scottish Horse while a few, like Alexander Gordon engineer aboard the Aberdeen Line steamer *SS Themistocles*, were present as members of the merchant navy and did their work for the campaign by ferrying wounded men in and out of the battle-zone to the safety of the hospital ships lying out of range of Turkish guns. Capt Edwin Macleod, a nautical surveyor, was the Ship's Navigator in the vessel responsible for laying the anti-submarine defences at Suvla Bay immediately prior to the Allied landing. Macleod also contributed to the success of the Allied evacuation in early 1916.

One FP in particular distinguished himself in the Gallipoli campaign. Major-General Andrew Skeen was one of six sons of Dr and Mrs William Skeen of 13 Westfield Terrace, all of whom went to the Grammar. Four of Andrew's brothers were medics, but the fifth was Oliver St John Skeen, who served with distinction in South Africa, Egypt and Persia. Andrew, who served on the ANZAC General Staff and later as Aide-de-Camp to King George V, was twice mentioned in dispatches from Gallipoli - in particular he was commended for his meticulous planning which ensured the successful, silent landing of reinforcements at Anzac Cove in August 1915. Over three nights, ANZAC units were smuggled into 'their prepared hiding places' under the noses of the Turks who could see across the entire landscape from their vantage points and who were less than thirty yards from the Allied lines in places. Sir Ian Hamilton doubted whether 'any more pregnant enterprise than this of landing so large a force under the very eyes of the enemy and of keeping them concealed is recorded in the annals of war'. Skeen also played his part well in the ultimate phase of the campaign, helping to organise the effective departure of the badly battered Allies in December 1915 and January 1916. He was appointed a Companion of the Order of St Michael and St George and later knighted.

Churchill's original plan to attack Turkey and create a new Front in the Eastern Mediterranean was visionary and could have shortened the war by many months. Instead Gallipoli took its place in the long list of British military disasters. Yet again, over-confident senior commanders failed to accord their enemy sufficient respect. Shambolic planning and weak, long-distance leadership completed the fatal recipe. The campaign achieved nothing and was a murderous waste of lives and resources. The Allies sustained 56,000 fatalities, with over 130,000 men wounded and 7,500 taken prisoner. One of the few good things to come from the fiasco was the fact that some later US commanders studied the campaign very carefully and learned lessons that helped to save American lives in amphibious landings in their Pacific war against Japan after 1941.

Chapter 8
The War at Sea

On November 1st 1914, British and German warships clashed in the Pacific Ocean off the coast of Chile. This engagement, remembered as the Battle of Coronel, was the first significant naval action of the war and naturally Grammar FPs were involved. At the outbreak of hostilities, George Scott and Charles Lawrence were both mobilised as midshipmen in the Royal Naval Reserve. Their first posting was to the auxiliary armed cruiser HMS *Otranto*. Originally a merchant steamer carring passengers and mail, the Otranto was requisitioned and beefed up with six naval guns, then sent to help the Royal Navy patrol the southern oceans. It was the *Otranto* that first spotted a German battlegroup steaming southwards at speed along the coast of Chile. Having lost their base at Tsingtao, the Kaiser's toehold in northern China, this powerful squadron of five fast and modern German cruisers had crossed the Pacific with the intention of raiding the coasts of the Americas and disrupting Allied shipping before returning home to the Reich.

The British force that encountered this powerful warband was a motley collection of ageing and obsolete craft, some of which were largely manned by inexperienced reservists. The squadron consisted of the flagship HMS *Good Hope* [which had been mothballed before the war], the light cruisers *Monmouth* and *Glasgow*, and the *Otranto*. On sighting the German contingent, the British vessels assembled in battle order with the lightly armed *Otranto* taking up rear position. The British had hoped to delay engaging with the German cruisers as long as possible, playing for time in the hope that HMS *Canopus*, a slow but powerful battleship further away on patrol, would turn up to equalise what was an unfair match. With no sight of *Canopus* however, the British under the pugnacious Rear Admiral 'Kit' Cradock, twice attempted to engage their more powerful adversary. The German commander Reichsgraf Von Spee was conscious that his ships were a long way from home and that their stocks of ammunition could quickly be depleted but not replenished. He knew it would be easier to range and pick off the British ships on the horizon in the light of the setting sun. Von Spee therefore avoided combat and waited.

Just before 7.00pm the German ships finally opened fire. Within minutes, events confirmed that the British were hopelessly outgunned: their 4 and 6 inch guns carried around 10,000 yards at best. With their superior armaments and better gunnery skills, the Germans could stay out of range at 12,000 yards or more, and still hit the British craft. Cradock, who had known that the situation was hopeless from the outset, ordered the *Otranto* to depart the scene and carry the news of the action to port. HMS *Good Hope* was soon ablaze and the fire quickly spread to its magazine. Midshipman Scott saw the flagship first go up in the air and then sink down into the sea. The *Monmouth* sank some minutes later.

In a letter home, Midshipman Scott described the feeling of powerlessness that he and his shipmates felt as they watched their comrades scattered to the Pacific waves. They also knew that they could share the same fate at any moment: 'the worst of being on an armed merchant cruiser is that if a shell gets into us, we shall immediately catch fire and then *finis*... for the first two or three minutes that I was under fire my knees felt like India rubber and a cold sweat broke out on my forehead'. Scott had particular reason to feel apprehensive for his battle-station was the fire-control for the *Otranto's* forward guns which he ironically described 'as the best place in the ship to get hit, as it is the custom to knock out the gun controls first'. Nevertheless, the *Otranto* made it to safety. After coaling and provisioning at Rio, it eventually received orders to join a new and more powerful battle group that was being put together with the aim of clearing all German shipping from the southern seas, or in Scott's words 'to fork them out'. The German squadron was duly destroyed at the Battle of the Falkland Islands in December 1914. The toll of almost 1900 German dead included Von Spee and his two sons. Midshipman Scott later transferred from the Royal Navy to the RFA and died in 1918 after being wounded and gassed in France.

Scott's letter home made mention of 'several German merchantmen skulking around dropping mines'. An estimated total of over 190,000 mines were laid in the Channel and North Sea areas alone by both sides during the hostilities. Sweeping the sea lanes clear of enemy mines soon became a routine task for a number of FPs in the Royal Naval Reserve, who found themselves deployed upon requisitioned fishing smacks and leisure craft for this purpose. One contributor to the school magazine serving on the south coast of England described his life as a crewman in a flotilla of minesweepers that helped keep the Channel free of German mines:

'A look round the fleet shows us everyone is getting ready, the crews moving around deck, and the funnels belching out clouds of smoke. At 5.30 in the morning the air is disturbed by six winches heaving up anchor. Single line ahead we lead the gallant little fleet to sea once more, to sweep clear the path of the leviathans of our Navy, so that they, with their crews of 800 men, may not be trapped by one of these diabolical engines of modern warfare. When one considers that at the lightest touch on one of those deadly mines a stout trawler is blown to smithereens and of a crew of thirteen, in cases where a mine has been fouled, rarely have more than three men been saved, one cannot but marvel at the gallant fellows cheerfully doing their work with never a look of fear or anxiety on their faces. No wonder then that when these good lads get on shore they get merry and noisy'.

The anonymous writer of this piece was most probably Lt William Mackintosh RNR who spent most of the war sweeping mines in locations as diverse as Portsmouth, Malta and Peterhead Harbour. Mackintosh hit the headlines in early April 1916 when his patrol ship HM Minesweeper *Olivine* came across an enemy device in the Thames estuary that was much larger than the floating mines he usually encountered. Zeppelin L15 was one of five German airships on a bombing mission over south eastern England on the night of March 31st. Initially damaged by gas shells from land batteries along the Essex coast, the airship was finished off by a lone Royal Flying Corps 'fighter plane'. L15 collapsed down onto the lower Thames estuary and was scuttled by its crew off the Kentish coast near Margate. At 3.30am on a dark and muggy morning, the crew of the *Olivine* spotted the monstrous airship, as it slowly deflated and subsided into the smooth waters of the Thames. The surviving Zeppelin crew of one officer and fifteen men had taken refuge on the top of the airship's crumbling envelope. At some risk to himself and his craft, Mackintosh successfully rescued and captured the beleaguered German aviators before it was too late, receiving the DSC for his thoughtful actions that night.

Despite the best efforts of the forces at the Royal Navy's disposal, the sea lanes of Empire could never be entirely cleared of German mines. A typical result of this was the sinking of the P&O liner *Maloja* at the beginning of its journey from London to Bombay in February 1916. A little over two miles off Dover, the *Maloja* struck one of the many mines laid in the Channel by German submarines. The *Maloja's* passengers were quickly loaded aboard the lifeboats but the degree of list was such that the boats could not be lowered from the stricken liner into the sea. An estimated 155 souls lost their lives as a result. There were not many survivors from this tragedy, but the lucky few did include the FP James Watt who was the *Maloja's* senior purser.

Less fortunate was William Rudolf Center who was on board HMS *Russell* in the central Mediterranean on 27th April 1916 when it struck two German mines deposited by the German submarine U-73. The *Russell* was a large front-line battleship that had played a key role in the evacuation of Allied forces from Gallipoli. It sank slowly allowing most of the 720 men on board to escape. However injuries from the explosions and subsequent fires below deck accounted for over a hundred of the ship's complement including William Center. A Fleet Surgeon and gifted linguist, he died from his injuries at Malta Naval Hospital the following day.

In the decade before the war, the capital ships of the Royal Navy were powerful totems of British imperial power. Each new Dreadnought launch helped bolster the confidence of a British public that feared the superior technological abilities, and ambition, of the German Reich. Popular authors and the sensationalist elements of the Fleet Street press had led the public to expect that any future war would be decided by one great collision between the Royal Navy's dreadnoughts and the Kaiser's fleet of battlecruisers. In fact, throughout the war, the Navy's work was largely confined to more mundane matters such as patrol, minesweeping and blockade. As a result, the expensively assembled Grand Fleet sitting patiently at anchor at Scapa and Rosyth made few appearances in the school magazine. One rare mention in the October 1914 issue serves to illustrate the humdrum routine of navy life in the first months of the war. It concerned Harold Finlayson, at that point a young Surgeon-Lieutenant on one of the busy supply ships provisioning the Fleet as it lay in its northern bases. Doubtless keen to include at least some mention of the Senior

Service, Theodore Watt recorded his one piece of naval news; that young Harold Finlayson was rumoured to have had the honour of dining with Admirals Jellicoe and Beatty, the men it was said 'who could lose the war in an afternoon'.

The magazine had a little more to say about the FPs who did finally participate in the one significant sea battle of the war at Jutland. On the last day of May 1916, Lieutenant-Commander Thomas Wilsone was aboard the Dreadnought battleship HMS *Colossus* which spotted the German High Seas Fleet at 5.51pm. *Colossus* steamed forward and contributed to the sinking of the cruiser *Wiesbaden* and then inflicted serious damage upon the *Derfflinger*. The *Derfflinger* had earlier encountered and badly damaged HMS *Queen Mary* whose magazines caught fire and exploded soon afterwards. The *Queen Mary* was one of the most modern of the Royal Navy's battlecruisers yet it rolled over and sank almost instantaneously, taking 1,266 officers and men with her. One of those lost souls was Lt-Commander John Murray, an FP engineer who had enjoyed a highly successful naval career at sea and then on the staff of the Royal Naval Colleges at Dartmouth and Keyham.

During the battle of Jutland another FP, Major Arthur Troup of the Royal Marine Artillery, was serving on board the cruiser HMS *Shannon*. The *Shannon* played little part in the key moments of the engagement but it spent days afterwards relentlessly searching for survivors in the cold seas off the Danish coast. Troup was subsequently recommended for promotion by Admiral Jellico in his post-Jutland dispatch, and he received the Order of St Stanislaus from the Russian Government. He later served in France with the Royal Marine Howitzer Brigade, a special heavy artillery unit commissioned by First Sea Lord Churchill so that the Navy could 'get involved' on the Western Front.

After Jutland, the main German battle group never went to sea again in search of a decisive battle with the Royal Navy. German surface activity was largely restricted to sporadic raiding as the FP William Buyers discovered in December 1916. Buyers was skipper of the steamer SS *Yarrowdale*, carrying a French Government cargo of shell casings, barbed wire, motor parts and frozen meat from New York to Le Havre. The *Yarrowdale* was surprised by the disguised German raider *Möwe* north of the Azores and taken as a prize to Swinemünde in the Baltic. The ship was re-equipped and sent back to sea under a new flag as the German raider *Leopard*. Buyers and his crew were interned in Germany but the British authorities repeatedly petitioned Berlin for the captain's release on account of his age. He was 66 when eventually repatriated in October 1918.

In the last two years of the war, the main task of the Royal Navy was to throttle the German war effort by maintaining the blockade. Nevertheless the role of the Navy evolved in the latter stages of an increasingly technological conflict with new weapons to hand. Numerous FPs served in the evolving Royal Naval Air Service such as Lt Douglas Capper who undertook work as a seaplane officer in the North Sea, and Alexander Gray who was stationed at one of the RNAS stations in coastal France. Thomas Macintosh served as one of the Royal Navy's first test pilots during his stint at the Marine Aircraft Experimental Station at Isle of Grain in Kent. John Gray, originally of Colaboll Farm near Lairg, first served as an Air Mechanic at HMS *Icarus*, the seaplane station at Scapa Flow in Orkney, before transferring to the Royal Flying Corps in France. Another air mechanic, Robert Tennant, was based at the RNAS School of Special Flying at Redcar in Yorkshire. He probably worked on the squadron of giant Handley Page bombers based there, those 'bloody paralysers' that the Admiralty had demanded so it could exact revenge on German cities for the Zeppelin and Gotha bomber attacks on London.

Thomas Lamb of Broomhill Avenue started 'his' war in the Royal Scots in 1915 and finished it at the RNAS station at Luce Bay in Wigtownshire. Lamb piloted one of the four naval airships based there which provided aerial support for Allied shipping approaching the north channel of the Irish Sea en route for Liverpool. After the war, he served on HM Airship R34 which departed from East Fortune aerodrome near Edinburgh on 1st July 1919 and landed at Mineola, Long Island 108 hours and 12 minutes later, setting a new world record for flight endurance. The R34's journey across the Atlantic and back totalled 7,420 miles in all, with the ship reaching speeds of over 90mph on the return journey.

One sea-faring FP found himself forced to be a land-lubber when he was posted to the 63rd Royal Naval Division in the British Army. This unit originally consisted of surplus personnel at the naval bases and dockyards of southern England. They had been hurriedly shoved together and ferried over to the Front during the panic for Paris in autumn 1914.

Although lightly armed, the unit acquitted itself well in the defence of Ostend and Antwerp in the first months of the war. It later served at Gallipoli, the Somme and Passchendaele, retaining its distinct naval traditions and *esprit de corps* in the face of sustained opposition from several hostile Army commanders. Petty Officer Alexander Ross from Victoria Road in Torry served in the RND's 2nd Hawke Battalion from 1914 until his death three years later in charge of a midnight working party beyond the front line.

Another sailor forced to fight on land was Jameson Boyd Adams, later Sir Jameson, an RNR officer before the war and the second-in-command on Ernest Shackleton's 1907-09 Antarctic Expedition that fell just a little short of reaching the South Pole. Beginning the war as Flag Lieutenant to Admiral Hood, he enjoyed success in several operations along the Belgian coast. He was then put in command of a battery of Royal Naval Siege Guns at Nieuport in the small sector of Belgium that still remained in Allied hands. Badly wounded in 1917, Adams transferred to the Munitions Ministry and received the DSO and French *Croix de Guerre* in 1918.

Other FPs experienced their naval service in ways far removed from the expected clash of Dreadnoughts. Peter Shaw RNR was an officer on the Cunard liners *Lusitania* and *Franconia* before the war but was commanding a patrol torpedo boat in the Channel by 1915. A gallant officer who had saved the lives of hundreds at sea, Shaw assisted his fellow FP William Mackintosh in the capture of the damaged L15 Zeppelin in the Thames estuary. Shaw was mentioned in dispatches, reached the rank of Lt-Commander and had received the DSC by the time of his death aged thirty-six on 21st April 1918. Shaw's demise occurred during the naval assault on the Belgian port of Zeebrugge, designed to block the entrance to the German U-boat base there. The Zeebrugge raid was only a limited, temporary success and cost 583 British lives, including FP Lt-Commander James Young of the RNVR, a rising barrister before the war. A survivor of several Royal Navy night raids on the Belgian coast however was Alfred [Jack] Hayward, a midshipman on the destroyer HMS *Vanquisher* who took part in mine-laying operations off Flanders throughout August 1918.

FP medic Arthur Percy Spark served as Surgeon on board one of the stranger craft built for the Royal Navy in the Great War. This was M23, a shallow draught monitor ship designed for action in river estuaries and coastal bombardment. The M class vessels were makeshift floating platforms that supported large 7.5 and 8.2 inch cannon recycled from older battleships. The monitors carried these guns close enough to shore to hit targets in enemy-occupied Belgium. After the war, M23 long adorned Dundee Harbour in the guise of HMS *Claverhouse*, serving as the RNVR drillship there until 1959.

Spark, one of four FP brothers from the manse at Durris, had an interesting war which began as a private in the Gordons. Badly wounded in 1915, once back in Blighty he completed his medical studies in 1917. He soon found himself in the war again as a Surgeon-Lt in the Navy. After spells with the Belgian Coast Patrol and at the RN Hospital on Corfu, he served as Medical Officer on the naval yacht HMS *Triad* in the early summer of 1919. *Triad* spent several months transporting the members of the British Dardanelles Commission around the key sites in the Gallipoli campaign prior to the publication of their final report on that disappointing debacle. One of Arthur's brothers, Ian, had an equally varied experience of the Great War. He initially served in France in the Special Brigade of the Royal Engineers, a unit formed in 1915 to respond to the German use of chemical warfare. By 1917 Ian was serving as a Surgeon Sub-Lieutenant attached to the Channel Fleet on board HMS *Orcadia*, an anti-submarine destroyer equipped with its own torpedoes.

Chapter 9

War in the Air

'Just as I am writing, an aeroplane has come into sight, so we are nearing the Front evidently'.

By 1916 troops going up the line were left in no doubt that the battles in which they were about to take part were being fought above, as well as on and under, the fields of France and Flanders. By that stage in the war, the individualistic and often erratic exploits that marked the first months of the air war were a distant memory. The Royal Flying Corps was now a key component of British strategic planning on the Western Front and the war in the air was becoming as deadly and as systematised as the land conflict. Planes were now everyday objects in the skies above the Front, spotting for their gunners on the ground, taking ever more precise aerial photographs, carrying ever heavier bombing loads and engaging with the enemy in the choreographed dog-fights that often entranced the trench-dwellers below.

In October 1916, one correspondent to the school magazine graphically described the dramatic scenes he witnessed as a new kind of warfare unfolded high above the men in the mud:

'Several aeroplanes came over but high up, the smoke puffs of the anti-aircraft shells go all around them but never seem to hit. It is a fascinating thing to watch the plane and the puffs of smoke following it. One that went over just now must have had at least 100 shells fired at it, yet sailed home unscathed. A fleet of six planes came overhead. They were huge battle planes and went over to the Hun lines. They encountered a tempest of shells, but seemed to regard these with contempt for they never altered their flight. There was a shout outside and some said that an aeroplane was down; we fixed our eyes on the smoke puffs and in a little, one could distinguish a plane falling like a great gull slowly turning over and over. I'm afraid it must have been one of ours as it was well over the German lines. Yesterday an aeroplane was brought down about two miles behind us. It

was a Hun all right and had two men in it who were in the expressive French term écrasés [crushed]'.

This new aerial war needed men with special skills and aptitudes. The RFC found many of the men it needed from the ranks of Army officers who had a technical background or who had distinguished themselves in the field. Many Grammar FPs fitted the bill. Typical of these new aviators was Alexander Wilson, a solicitor pre-war who served in the Gordons in the first phase of the war until wounded in April 1915. After recovering from his injuries, Wilson returned to the fray, transferring to the RFC in November that year. Flying Officer Wilson enjoyed stratospheric promotion, serving as an Air Board officer in charge of Aerodrome Construction in 1916-17 and as one of the RAF's representatives during the Paris Peace Conference at the end of the war. He commanded RAF Headquarters in Paris in early 1919 and was in charge of the key Aerial Route 1 which linked London to Cairo and to Britain's newly acquired mandated territories in the Middle East. Wilson left the RAF in 1920 bearing the honours of the military OBE and the Greek Military Medal.

Another loss to the Gordons was Alfred Thom MC, an engineer who enjoyed a distinguished pre-war career in various senior technical positions in Rangoon, Sumatra and the Broch. Like Wilson, Thom served in the field until wounded, winning his MC in July 1915. In the RFC he served as Flight Commander and Chief Technical Officer at several home aerodromes. In 1917 he was appointed to the crucial role of Commanding Officer at Kenley Acceptance Park where new craft were checked over before entering service with the RFC.

Like many FPs around the globe, James Wallace, an architect in Buenos Aires, interrupted his career to return home and volunteer. After initial training in the Artists Rifles, he joined the RFC in 1917. Wallace piloted Bristol fighters, fondly known as Biffs, and served in 11 Squadron to April 1918. All previous RFC squadrons had been detailed to perform reconnaissance and artillery support duties but 11 Squadron was the first specifically created to undertake an offensive role. Wallace therefore flew in the oldest dedicated fighter squadron in the RAF.

Some FPs undertook their entire war service in the air such as Reginald Martin who entered the RFC as a cadet soon after leaving the school in 1916. A year later he was in the Independent Air Force under the command of Sir Hugh Trenchard, often described as the 'Father of the RAF'. The innovative IAF was an aggressive bombing unit that carried the war to the enemy by hitting German aerodromes as well as industrial targets inside the Reich's borders. James Reynard flew in 102 Squadron, a night flying unit that specialised in bombing enemy railway infrastructure but enjoyed strafing German troops and transport columns when opportunities arose. The squadron flew over a hundred missions against transport targets in the last year of the war.

Throughout WWI, Grammar FPs performed a wide range of duties in the RFC and RAF from fighter pilot to all the essential backroom jobs. In addition to officers on active flying duty, FPs served as observers, air mechanics, flying instructors, aerial gunnery instructors, wireless operators, strategists and aerodrome planners. James Chalmers joined the Aeronautical Inspection Department at South Farnborough in 1915 which tested the air-worthiness of new models. John Sorley flew with 6 Squadron, originally a forward reconnaissance unit designed to spot enemy offensive manoeuvres on the battlefield as its motto *oculi exercitus*, the eyes of the army, indicated. Behind the scenes, Walter Bulloch, an architect in Aberdeen before the war, worked on the construction staff of the Air Ministry, while James Smith was typical of a number of FPs who undertook important duties as 'back-room boys'. Smith, an academic in political economy, served in the Directorate of Air Organization at the War Office and Air Ministry. His work in Whitehall was recognised with an OBE in 1920.

Although numerous FPs performed acts of outstanding heroism in aerial combat, Donald Fasken Stevenson can lay claim to be the most decorated flying Grammarian of the Great War. Stevenson began the war as an officer in the Sherwood Rangers, a yeomanry cavalry unit based in the East Midlands. By November 1916 he was a Flying Officer in the RFC and commanded 35 Squadron in the final months of the war. Stevenson won the MC and Bar, and the DSO. His citations speak for themselves:

'For conspicuous gallantry and devotion to duty in carrying out three contact patrols in one day in bad weather and at low altitudes. Although attacked by enemy machines in superior numbers, he drove them off, and by his fine reconnaissance work brought back valuable information. He has at all times displayed indomitable pluck and initiative, obtaining photographs which necessitated his flying through our barrage at a

height of less than 1,000 feet. On another occasion he brought down a hostile machine. He was under heavy fire from the ground the whole time, and was eventually forced to land behind lines owing to his petrol tank being shot through. In his patrols, lasting many hours and in bad weather conditions, he attacked enemy infantry, transport and batteries from a low level, using his machine gun and dropping bombs, frequently returning with his machine riddled with bullets. His cheerful spirit, consistent dash and fearlessness have set a splendid example to all in his squadron, and greatly encouraged them at a time when the casualties in it were extremely heavy'.

After the war, Stevenson rose to the rank of Air Vice-Marshal. In the Second World War, his desire to carry the war to the Germans as belligerently as possible resulted in controversial low level operations and heavy RAF casualties in 1941. Donald's son Peter was a Pilot Officer in the Battle of Britain with a number of 'kills' and the DFC to his credit who died in a sweep over Boulogne in 1943.

Stevenson survived the war but inevitably there were casualties amongst the Grammar cohort in the skies. Some never finished their training, for the accident rate amongst new pilots was high. George Cameron died in an accident at South Carlton training base near Lincoln, inexplicably crashing to the ground from 900 feet. James Ross was killed whilst performing his farewell flight from RAF Duxford in Cambridgeshire in July 1918. Arthur Davidson of Don Street in Old Aberdeen survived his training but was ambushed and killed by four enemy planes in September 1917 just weeks after his arrival at the Front. Gordon Hutcheson was wounded in action over Mont Kemmel south of Ypres in April 1918 and died in hospital in Boulogne a month later.

Two FP aviators died late in the war supporting the Fourth Army in its great push towards final victory. William Sellar died in a bombing raid over the German lines at Albert in the Somme sector in August 1918 while Leonard Scroggie simply vanished during an aerial battle over Bruges. He was reported missing on September 25th and is remembered on the Flying Service Memorial at Arras and on his family tombstone in Springbank Cemetery. Edward Willox had better luck. He crashed his Sopwith Camel on the penultimate day of the war, 10th November 1918, but survived to take up rubber planting in Malaya.

The school magazine tells of three Grammarian aviators worthy of very special note. James Simpson of Portree, Cape Town and the Federated Malay States transferred from the Black Watch to the RFC in June 1916. He was an enthusiastic pilot who seemed oblivious to the dangers around him. A large bombing raid on a Hun aerodrome that went badly wrong was recounted in his letter home as if it were of no more consequence than a scratch game of rugby football on the old school field on Whitehall Place. The fusillade of German anti-aircraft shells he encountered was casually dismissed as 'perfect'. Repeated attacks by seriously superior Fokkers were brushed off and Simpson praised the Hun for 'peppering us very successfully'. Simpson's observer was also peppered in the knee and the leg, and their machine sustained a total of seventy-seven bullet holes. It was 'almost falling to pieces': the instrument panel was riddled and the petrol tank had sprung a leak. Miraculously, it had not exploded. Simpson nursed the plane home but his observer 'poor fellow, had to have his leg removed above the knee'.

Back at base, Simpson was hailed as a lucky pilot with the lives of a cat. He himself shrugged off the terrors of aerial warfare: 'I didn't feel the slightest sensation of fear and that is why losing one's life in a game like that isn't really as awful as some may think'. In October 1916, Simpson was directing the fire of British artillery batteries when he was struck by metal fragments from an exploding German anti-craft shell. The splinters broke his left arm and penetrated his abdomen. Mortally wounded, losing too much blood and beyond saving, he managed to retain consciousness and steer his machine and his observer back to a safe landing at base.

Harry Mackay of Duthie Terrace, an observer and machine gunner, is remembered in the annals of the RAF as a tenacious aviator who achieved five definite victories in his Airco DH4 scoring 'one kill and four out of controls'. His last moments are best described in the words of his pilot officer which appeared in the school magazine of June 1918:

'returning from a raid over enemy lines we found ourselves intercepted by three squadrons of German machines, numbering thirty in all. The odds of course were out of all proportion but we decided to, well, do the best we could. It was a splendid fight and we shot down three enemy machines before poor Mac was shot. He was firing over the tail of the machine at four Huns that were attacking close in, when he suddenly fell back. He

looked round at me with a laugh I shall never forget, then dragged himself up by the gun mounting and gripped his machine-gun again. I was at the mercy of the Hun who had shot Mac. He was pouring in a terrific fire at me. Well, Mac took careful aim, and only fired about ten rounds when I saw the German pilot throw his hands to his head and the next instant plunge downwards out of control. We were now being fired on by about ten enemy machines and several of my controls were shot away, so I simulated an uncontrolled spin to earth. I managed to reach the aerodrome safely but poor Mac had only time to shake hands and whisper 'Tell them at home it's all right'. He was actually hit by twelve bullets and how he kept on shooting I don't know'.

George Thomson survived his brush with death thanks to his own 'presence of mind and contempt of danger'. On November 4th 1918, exactly one week before the Armistice, the plane in which Thomson was flying was hit by a German shell. The left aileron control was shot away and the machine began to fall out of the sky. With a fatal crash seemingly inevitable, at 500 feet Thomson climbed out of his seat and onto the right hand lower side of the plane, 'thus enabling the pilot to bring the machine on an even keel and land safely in our lines'. Thomson was awarded the DFC for his exceptional bravery and for saving the life of his pilot.

No field of combat in the Great War experienced such rapid technological change as the war in the air. The flimsy biplanes that flitted above the dry fields of France in late summer 1914 bore little resemblance to the powerful beasts that thundered against the German war machine in autumn 1918. The aircraft that helped bring final victory were not just faster and stronger but they carried bombloads that could not have been imagined at the start of the war. In 1918 Alexander Kellas, Himalayan explorer and brother of Arthur who died at Gallipoli, was already wondering if these new improved aircraft could fly over the highest mountains in the world. The pioneering Australian aviator Harry Hawker had already taken a plane up to 24,408 feet, surely enough to cross the great Himalayan passes with something to spare? Kellas gave a well received lecture on this theme to the Royal Geographical Society in London in March of that year. An older man who undertook scientific work during the war, Kellas had an interest in the use of oxygen at high altitude, a useful field of research for aviators and mountaineers alike. Despite being in his fifties, his specialist knowledge and his pre-war reputation for bagging peaks in Sikkim earned him an invitation to join the 1921 British Everest Expedition alongside the ill-fated George Mallory. Sadly, Kellas died from heart failure in Tibet in June before having the chance to test his belief that Everest could be conquered by men carrying oxygen on their backs.

Postscript

After leaving the Grammar School in 1915, James Crombie served in a Labour battalion but was discharged on medical grounds. He then worked until the end of the war in a large shed that stood at the north-western end of Forbesfield Road. This was Henderson's Scottish Aviation Factory which built 205 Avro 504 biplanes. The Avro 504's greatest moment came in November 1914 when four set off from Belfort near Strasbourg in eastern France and bombed the Zeppelin base at Friedrichshafen on Lake Constance. By the time James Crombie was assigned to the factory in Forbesfield Road in 1918, the 504 had long been obsolete as a front-line plane but they remained useful for training and communications. Contracts for another 245 were cancelled in January 1919 once it was clear that the Armistice would be permanent.

Chapter 10

The U-Boat Menace

For all the thunder in France and Flanders, strategists in London and Berlin knew that the Great War would be won or lost in the sea lanes of the Atlantic. Both Germany and Britain needed to import much of their food and their industrial supplies from overseas. With its vast navy, Britain could maintain an blockade that isolated German shipping from global trade routes. In response, Germany increasingly relied on its submarines to inflict damage upon Allied merchant shipping. As Admiral Beatty observed 'the real crux lies in whether we blockade the enemy to his knees, or whether he does the same to us'.

When the war began, the German Imperial Navy had only twenty-four submarines in service but the threat that these 'invisible ships' posed was made clear early in the conflict. On 22nd September 1914 three British cruisers were sunk by U-9 in less than an hour. Almost 1460 lives were lost and the bodies of dead crewmen washed up along the Dutch coast for weeks. The destruction of this so-called 'Live Bait Squadron' shook the Admiralty and the British public, both complacent after years of jingoistic celebration of Britain's naval might. Countering the U-boat threat now became a key strand in British strategy. Nevertheless, in the winter 1916-17, Allied losses reached a level that cast real doubt on Britain's ability to stay in the war. By November 1918, the U-boats had sunk almost 5,000 vessels, destroying 13 million tons of shipping and taking over 15,000 lives.

The Grammar School can claim to have one of the 'pioneering fathers' of this most terrible naval weapon amongst its FP community. The naval architect Marley Fotheringham Hay gained extensive experience of designing and constructing submarines in the 1890s working in New York as chief draughtsman with the Holland Submarine Torpedo Boat Company. In 1903 Hay supervised the construction of the first US Navy submarine launched on the Pacific Coast. Back in Europe in 1907 he constructed submarines for the Dutch Government at Vlissingen, and then for the

Austro-Hungarian Empire at its port of Fiume on the Adriatic. In the last two years of peace, Hay built submarines for the Royal Navy at Denny's yard in Dumbarton. His popular book *Secrets of the Submarine* was published in 1918. It included a conversation that Hay had enjoyed with the Reich's naval supremo Alfred von Tirpitz in 1913. The German Grand Admiral had casually remarked that 'he was not at all certain that submarines were an essential part of Germany's naval programme'. In the coming years, many Grammar FPs were to wish that von Tirpitz had indeed lost interest in building *Unterseeboote*.

Herbert Shinnie was the first FP to die at the hands of a U-boat when HMS *Formidable* was sunk by two torpedoes off Portland on New Year's Day 1915. Alexander Lamb, an engineer on the troopships *Dunvegan Castle* and *Saxon*, survived several close encounters with submarines but his luck ran out in March 1917. He died on duty in the engine room of His Majesty's Hospital Ship *Gloucester Castle* when it was struck by a torpedo off the Isle of Wight. Lt James Rae RAMC drowned in April 1917 when the troopship SS *Arcaian* went down in six minutes in seas to the northeast of Milos. Over a thousand men were safely evacuated from the *Arcadian* in those few, frantic minutes thanks to the captain's earlier strict insistence on regular lifeboat drills. Dr Rae was amongst the unfortunate 277 who were sucked under the water when the ship suddenly capsized, or perhaps was one of those in the water killed by pieces of the ship's wreckage surging back up from the depths with great force at high speed. Second Officer Herbert Chinn survived the immediate aftermath of a torpedo attack on his transport ship but died several months later from the effects of long exposure in the water.

Another FP victim of the U-boat was James Stuart, chief engineer of the cargo steamer SS *Coquet* sunk in January 1916 by U-34 two hundred miles east of Malta. Although a German ship, the U-34 flew under the Austrian flag and was one of the most successful submarines of the war, sinking 119 Allied ships. To save his valuable load of torpedoes, Kapitan Claus Rücker sunk the *Coquet* with explosive charges after setting its crew adrift on two damaged lifeboats in heavy weather. The steamer's captain protested that it was 'nothing short of murder to send thirty-one men away in winter, so far from land'. Seventeen men made it to the coast of North Africa. Stuart was not among them and had probably drowned with the others in his lifeboat before reaching the Libyan coast. The seventeen survivors were soon reduced in number with three killed by passing Bedouins and ten carried off into slavery.

Captain Charles Davidson RNR had better luck when his London bound troopship *Malda* was torpedoed on the voyage home from Boston in August 1917. The *Malda* was some time a-sinking but any hopes of saving her were dampened by the continued presence of the guilty U-boat. Davidson and his men were forced to set off in boats for the Scilly Isles, over 130 miles north-east of their position. Davidson survived; his boat was spotted by a passing convoy. He and his men were landed safely at Milford Haven and he commanded again in the warmer waters of the Eastern Mediterranean, serving at Milos and Patras throughout 1918. Other FP survivors of U-boat attack were Beddie Stephen, Chief Officer on the cargo ship *Baron Vernon Godfrey* which was shelled and sunk by U-34 off the Algerian coast in 1916; Godfrey Symmers, captain of the steamer *Umaria* sunk by U-boat off the Italian coast in 1917 and George Esson, Chief Officer of the SS A*delaide*, torpedoed thirteen miles off St Kilda in 1917. Alexander McGregor was probably the luckiest FP in the British mercantile marine, surviving three torpedo attacks.

Lucky too were those aboard the Liverpool liner *City of Marseilles* when it came under attack off Sardinia in November 1914. The passenger list included Herbert Sorley, an FP member of the Indian Civil Service on his way east to take up a magistrate's post in Sind. Sorley first realised that the *Marseilles* was under fire when the liner veered sharply, leaving a turbulent wake astern. Seconds later, a shell landed in the water less than fifteen yards from the port side of the ship where Sorley was enjoying a pleasant stroll after breakfast; 'it dropped into the sea like a cocoanut and failed to burst. If it had, I should not be writing this now. It was a shrapnel shell and it would likely have picked off the whole group of us'. A second and third shell from the U-boat failed to hit their mark, but hot metal fragments from these 'near things' clattered down onto the liner's decks.

While the sub re-loaded, Sorley and his companions made their way to the muster point in the dining room, donned their cork and canvas lifebelts, and joined in the prayers rendered up by an Anglican vicar. The two hundred or so mostly British passengers stiffened their upper lips: 'There was no panic. Everyone was cool and collected. The conduct of the women and children was splendid: no crying, no screaming, no pandemonium. Everyone did as he or she was bid, and calmly waited for the worst'. Sorley himself took out his copy of *The Prisoner of Zenda* and settled down to enjoy it: 'I never felt less afraid in my life' he remarked.

Only later was Sorley made aware of the extreme danger that he and his fellows had been in. The submarine's conning-tower had been spotted by the *Marseilles* fifteen minutes before the first shell exploded. At that distance, the liner's captain could not tell its nationality. The *Marseilles'* top speed was only sixteen knots but the surfaced submarine could reach twenty with ease. While Sorley was happily turning over the pages of Anthony Hope's 1894 masterpiece, 'the black speck on the horizon' was gaining on the liner and coming within torpedo range.

Now the *Marseilles* revealed its secret, a concealed 4.7 inch calibre gun manned by trained gunners. Soon the *Marseilles* was rocking from the report of a gun that seriously outmatched the 3 incher on the sub. Then realising that the *Marseille's* gunners had found their line and length, the U-boat slipped under the waves, instantly dropping to ten knots 'while our speed increased by Herculean efforts on the part of the stokers to seventeen'. There was only one minor casualty in this engagement: one of the liner's gunners sustained a facial wound from a splinter. Sorley noted that 'but for the gun there would have been another Lusitanian disaster. The sole result of this dastardly attempt to destroy a passenger ship was that lunch was delayed a quarter of an hour'.

Another fortunate Grammarian who cheated the U-boat was Clement Cobban, captain in the Indian Army in peacetime but in 1915 promoted and attached to the War Office because of his skill in Russian. In 1916 Major Cobban was detailed to accompany Field Marshall Lord Kitchener, the Secretary of State for War, on a secret voyage to Russia acting as his translator. Through circumstance, Cobban was not aboard HMS *Hampshire* on 5th June 1916 when it left Scapa for the northern Russian port of Archangel. About a mile and half off the Orkney mainland, the *Hampshire* struck a mine and sank in a heavy gale, taking almost 650 men to their death. Kitchener and all of his staff perished. For his later war work, Major Cobban received the Russian Order of St Stanislaus. Unfortunately his reprieve from the sea's cold clutches was only temporary. In 1941

Cobban and his wife drowned when the Liverpool steamer SS *Avoceta* was torpedoed by U-203 off the Azores.

Most references to U-boats in the Grammar magazine date from late 1916 and 1917. By then German Naval Command, frustrated by the failure of its battleships to break out at Jutland, was investing heavily in its submarine arm. British Intelligence believed that an additional 100 U-boats were being built to join the fifty or so at sea at any time. With America now finally about to join the war, Berlin hoped that its new longer-range underwater craft could cut Britain's supply lines before the full weight of the USA came into play. In the three months of April, May and June 1917, over two million tons of Allied shipping were lost. At that dire point in the war, when so many Allied ships were being sunk, Watt tried to lift his readers' morale by praising one FP seaman who had managed to make it safely across the pond. George Sinclair first went to sea as an apprentice on the Aberdeen-built wool clipper *Pericles* but was now in command of transports crossing the North Atlantic. Sinclair steamed into Aberdeen in September 1917 and off-loaded his precious cargo at Regent Quay having 'successfully evaded the submarine peril and brought home a large supply of foodstuffs'. After the quickest of visits to his family home, Sinclair 'sailed again into the fog of war'.

Sinclair's success in making it home safely was probably due in part to the improved anti-submarine tactics that the Allies were using by 1917. In the first two years of the war, the Admiralty had put its faith in penning in the U-boats, using boom nets and minefields around the entry to U-Boat bases or across relatively narrow seaways such as the Dover Straits . These strategies were however expensive, time-consuming and ineffective. In 1917, the Admiralty overcame its aversion to convoying. Earlier fears that convoys slowed down shipping and presented U-boats with a concentrated target were set aside. And once America entered the war, US politicians explicitly demanded that their troopships be escorted across the Atlantic by naval destroyers.

The adoption of the convoy system was no magic bullet but Allied shipping losses were stemmed. Escorting warships had a reasonable chance of spotting and taking on German subs. Closer to the British Isles, seaplanes and airships with wireless transmitters and the embryonic aircraft carriers HMS *Furious* and *Argus* rendered more effective support to the convoys. Fast coastal motor boats like those captained by FP Peter Shaw, capable of 30 knots and equipped with torpedoes and depth charges, also made life more difficult for the Reich's sub-mariners. And many ships now had their own Hydrophone Officer, one of several roles fulfilled by Alistair Kinghorn RNR RNAS who served upon minesweepers around Britain's coasts.

Another FP in the minesweeping business, William Mackintosh RNR DSC, described the more aggressive tactics now being employed against U-boats by the small craft of the Dover Patrol: 'Half way from home a light, as bright as a heliograph, flashes out our pendant number. The message arouses our interest to a great pitch; submarine reported 12 miles SE by E of [censored]; open out and search carefully. The signal is semaphored throughout the fleet and our boats are headed for the locality. Everybody is on the alert and a smart lookout is kept. In the distance six destroyers can be made out zig-zagging at a great pace'.

Mystery ships [also known also as Q-ships and Special Service vessels] were another weapon in the struggle to secure the seas. It was well understood that U-boat commanders preferred to surface and use their deck gun against a target rather than use up their small supply of torpedoes. The apparently unarmed Q-ships acted as 'mercantmen bait' to lure U-boats to the surface but they carried concealed heavy weaponry.

The Q-ship HMS *Prize* was successful in its first three patrols in the Western Approaches, damaging several U-boats in early 1917. The infuriated Kaiser had specifically called on his mariners to sink the *Prize* on sight. On its fourth patrol, HMS *Prize* was off the Irish coast, flying the Swedish flag. In theory it was supported by a British submarine but the *Prize* and its escort sub had become detached. Kapitänleutnant Wolfgang Steinbauer, commander of U-48, spotted the *Prize* on 13th August. A survivor of a meeting with the *Prize* earlier that year, Steinbauer saw through its disguise immediately. After an exchange of shells, he withdrew but tracked the schooner till he was able to despatch it with two torpedoes fired at lethal range. The *Prize* sank instantly with all hands lost including Kenneth Macdonald RNR, a student in Arts & Medicine at Aberdeen.

Two other Grammar FPs are known to have served on Mystery ships. Arthur Anderson served on HMS *Redbreast* until its demise in July 1917 when it failed to convince a suspicious U-boat commander in the Doro Channel off the eastern coast of Greece. John Elmslie served as medical officer on HMS *Spiraea*, a disguised naval, throughout the last winter of the war. Elmslie's final posting was aboard HMS *Magic* on American convoy duty until it was damaged by a German mine off Fanad Head in County Donegal in April 1918. Fortunately Elmslie survived to graduate in Medicine in 1920.

Alexander Gordon witnessed the tide turning against the U-boats as Allied ships learned to cooperate in numbers more effectively. His armed steamer left Greenock in convoy, took an evasive course to Ireland and waited there in the loughs until joined by a larger flotilla from Liverpool. Twelve hours into their journey, Gordon recorded that 'a submarine raised her ugly head some four miles abeam. Fortunately we sighted her almost at once and got our 6 inch gun trained full upon her'. The U-boat was soon aware of the accuracy of the steamer's gunners. It ducked below the surface and headed off in search of easier prey which it found in the shape of a slow Spanish transport: 'with characteristic chivalry the submarine turned her attention in this direction'. The Spanish ship looked doomed until a heavily armed American merchantman came to the rescue: 'it was a fine act, finely carried out, and we all raised our hats to the Stars and Stripes'.

Further evidence that the U-boat threat was waning was provided by Ernest Horne, a Senior Wireless Operator who was amongst the last to witness a U-boat attack on Allied shipping in the Great War. In the very last days of the war, a hostile submarine appeared in the middle of his convoy but after torpedoing one ship, it was driven off by the escort destroyers. Horne described the event in a cheery manner and looked forward to the coming Armistice: 'the depth charges must have stirred old Fritz - it did us anyrate! It was rather exciting while it lasted. However I don't suppose I'll have any more such experiences, as by the look of things the end is very near'. Horne died at Liverpool on 25th November 1918, aged twenty years.

The most graphic account of the war at sea to feature in the Grammar magazine described the sinking of the troopship *Aragon* in late 1917. The *Aragon* arrived off Alexandria on 30th December laden with 2,350 troops and 150 VAD nurses. The *Aragon* and its escort destroyer HMS *Attack* were waiting for the signal to enter the harbour when the troopship was hit by a torpedo port and aft. With little cargo in her hold to absorb the explosion and stem the inflow of water, the Aragon was quickly in difficulty. An anonymous FP who survived the disaster described chaotic scenes that were far removed from those of stoic deportment on the *City of Marseilles* three years before.

His report told instead of blood streaming down faces, smashed lifeboats hanging from their davits, the dead lying on deck, insufficient lifeboats for those on board, the sea dotted with people on rafts 'and others like me with a lifebelt only'. Between mouthfuls of lapping oily saltwater, the writer watched the bows of the *Aragon* rise out of the water before it slipped down into the sea. A mighty underwater explosion as the hot metal of the ship's boilers came into contact with the cold Mediterranean left the *Aragon's* escaping lifeboats upturned and useless. Two small trawlers came out to help, but passed by the desperate writer. A nearby lifeboat was crowded with men who 'were all mad evidently, yelling and cursing; men on one side were rowing, those on the other side were backing'.

Seventeen minutes had now passed since the torpedo struck the troopship. HMS *Attack* had managed to save many off the *Aragon* just in time and was now 'black with people'. Most of the rescued were ushered below deck on the *Attack* and thinking they were now safe, they removed their wet and inconvenient lifebelts. At that point, the crowded destroyer took a torpedo in the same location as the troopship. Like the *Aragon*, after buckling a little, it slid under the waves with a terrible loss of life.

The writer was fortunate. He stayed afloat and scrabbled aboard an empty rowing boat that had been launched by a rescue ship. A wave brought a much-needed oar up to his side. Safety on a trawler was a manageable thirty yards away. A few minutes later he was on the quay at Alexandria. Suddenly his problems now were quite mundane; the loss of his kit, an old razor and a beloved Sam Browne belt, plus the fact that he was now wearing the clothes of a man many inches taller than he, 'so the garments were hanging in wrinkles all down my legs'. Whisky and blankets soon raised his morale. He was however suffering from what might now be called post-traumatic shock; 'I was very uncomfortable and could not sleep the first night. Next day I was seedy; jumpy and depressed. I saw the ship go down a score of times. Whenever I shut my eyes I felt the waves swinging about me'. The article concluded; 'I could have said much more about the disaster but it might be objected to, so I had better leave it as it is'.

The unluckiest FP mariner was probably William Rutherfoord who served his apprenticeship with the Aberdeen shipbuilders Hall Russell and then sailed as a engineer with the Union Steamship Company of Vancouver. In 1917 Rutherfoord was on the SS *Norwood*, a freight steamer of 800 tons that plied the east coast of northern Britain. On February 11th the *Norwood* was nearing the end of a journey up from Middlesborough to Aberdeen. It seems that the *Norwood* was refused entrance to its home port because of intelligence reports that a German submarine had just laid a clutch of mines near the mouth of the harbour channel. Later rumours suggested that the steamer was actually denied entry thanks to garbled communications between the two regional naval on-shore commanders at Peterhead and Aberdeen. For whatever reason, the *Norwood* was left sitting off Aberdeen until it fell victim to a torpedo launched by Oberleutnant zur See Ernst Rosenow, officer in charge of the UC-29. With all seventeen of his crewmates, William Rutherfoord drowned within sight of Girdleness.

Chapter 11

The Grind of War

1916 was the year that any Allied lingering hopes of an early end to the war evaporated. It was the year of vast slaughter at Verdun and on the Somme, the failure of the Navy to secure a victory at Jutland, the morale-sapping fall of Kut in Mesopotamia and the disastrous Brusilov Offensive in the East, 'the battle that broke two Empires' and finished Tsarist Russia as an effective ally. At home, the British population found itself fighting a total war in which the State took ever-greater powers to maintain the war effort. In France and Flanders, the war had settled down to grinding attrition with all the elements of industrialised trench combat in place.

In 1916 Watt printed a portion of a letter from an FP captain in the Gordons serving at the Front. Douglas Leith's earlier reports home often betray a fresh-eyed curiosity about the events unfolding around him. By contrast, these remarks from 1916 describe a grubbier war in which the conflict was almost secondary and staying alive, and warm, was paramount. The letter was almost certainly written by James Hay, by 1910 a partner in the Aberdeen legal firm of Adam, Thomson & Ross. Hay was forty-two when he was mobilised as a Lieutenant in the 4th Battalion [TF] in early October 1914. He served in France throughout the first half of 1916 and his acting rank of Captain was confirmed in June. He later served in Palestine from 1917 to 1919 as part of the British force occupying the vanquished Ottoman province. The tone of Hay's letter is resigned and matter-of-fact, no more so than when describing his discovery that German engineers were tunnelling towards his dug-out, intent on blowing him up.

5th March 1916. Base Camp. We got our movement orders. We are sent from one officer to another to report, like animated parcels. I had just sat down in the Mess when the orderly came in with orders to go to the Medical Officer at once for examination. The MO asked a series of very personal, not to say impertinent, questions. He passed me all right and we set out for the train. The four of us got one compartment and drew rations. There was a keen frost and I have seldom passed a more unpleasant night. I was cold to the bone. My legs were frozen until I stripped the cushion of its antimacassar and whipped it round my knees. Then my feet grew frozen and I could not get them warm. The kilt is a rotten dress for travelling in.

Battalion HQ here is a byre with a kilt apron hung over the top half of the door to keep out the draught, and a fine dung-hill just close to it. Preparations for going into the trenches are going on; we are to be in the trenches 12 days - six in support, then six in the firing line. In the afternoon I took a walk along the route we were to travel at night, so as to be able to recognise it. Troops were moving continually along the road, both French with their nice blue tin helmets, and our own. At 8.20 we moved off, walking slowly because the men were carrying a lot. We are met by a bunch of guides, French of course but most talked English quite well.

About 500 yards along I met McK; he told me to come into his dug-out. There was a brazier in the doorway and two candles lit up the scene. The place has plenty of mice which spent the night eating my chocolate. The mice run on the table under our noses. The countryside outside is full of rats; one could see them everywhere when we came up at night.

12th March. At 10 McK and I started off to explore with Geddes who is a bombing officer. We set out along a communication trench that was being repaired. It was very narrow, not more than two and a half feet. The going was awful, knees deep in mud. My gumboots nearly came off with every step we walked. The firing line was not an inviting place - mud awful, fire-steps broken and the parapets so low that the men crouch against them. The enemy were about 100 yards away. I had peeps through periscopes and loopholes but of course did not see anyone. We went out to a sap very cautiously within 40 yards of the Boche but heard nothing.

About 9am the Boche gave us a regular morning 'hate'. He sent over big stuff and a lot of it burst within 200 yards of us. There were also pip squeaks - smaller shells and shrapnel. They screamed, hissed and rumbled right over us for an hour. Dunn comes back and tells us that the colonel of the battalion in the trenches we are going to has just been killed, hit in the head by a sniper. We have had visits from the officers who are to come into our quarters from the front. At this game we play Box and Cox all the time with another battalion. They hold the line while we rest, and vice versa. We have told them about our quarters and the habits of our mice and they tell us about the habits of the Boche on our front.

15th March. While sitting on the top of my dugout steps, some New Zealanders came past. They are engineers and are here to do mining. They give us the pleasant news that the enemy have a mine a long way towards us. They had been on top of it in a counter-shaft and their object is to blow it in. This should lend a certain liveliness to the front, if it comes off.

I do hate this kilt. I never seem warm in it and would like to sit on a brazier all day and night. The cold in my legs wakes me up every night. We have now got steel helmets to wear, flat pans painted dark green. Hitherto I have been wearing the Tammy, or Balmoral. Most officers go about here without belts; the only equipment which must be worn at all times is the gas helmet, and a revolver if one goes in the firing line. One needs to know these subterranean passages or one will soon get lost.

18th March. We had rather a quaint time last night. Our report about the mysterious noise in our dugout was evidently taken notice of, and a mining engineer from the Antipodes turned up and said he had come to investigate. I told him to go into McK's bed, lie down and listen. He did so and I read a book. We were thus disposed when Gillies and McK came in. They were silent as mice, and we all sat dumb and motionless, smoking and listening with might and main. I began to think our RE captain had fallen asleep when his subaltern arrived. He thought he would hear better if he lay on the ground, so he stretched out and laid an eager ear to our earthy floor. It seemed most comical.

The NZ were tough-looking nuts. They looked as if they had seen a lot of the world and plenty of work. I felt great confidence in them. At last they heard it and then there was considerable debate. The sub was sure it was a drill. The captain would not commit himself, agreed it sounded like it, but it had too wide a sweep. Ultimately they arranged to come back in the daytime, and bring what they referred to as 'the Machine'. This turned out to be a microphone. When I turned in I heard the sound again most distinctly. It resembled the noise of boring metal with a brace.

Last night it was lively. The Battalion on our right let off their Lewis guns at 9.30, so we went down to the firing line to hear the display. It came off alright but invoked a tremendous reply. The Boche was roused and shot at us without intermission. Later we heard that the burst of fire had been more deadly than we thought - two cyclist officers had *been hit and one killed.*

Another Engineer turned up to listen. He played bridge with McK and me and the Trench Mortar man, and so heard nothing in spite of 'the Machine'. He returned later and heard it all right. He is sure it is a drill, and was much excited, and crawled over our floor with his ear on the ground.

1st April. I put our trench mortar men into action in retaliation for a rifle grenade which came our way. Their weapon is very formidable. The bomb is like a soccer football with a steel stem on it of 2 inches diameter. It is for all the world like a poppy seed vesicle on a stalk. It popped off behind the German lines and I watched the results through a periscope. You can follow its flight all the way. We had three shots and they all seemed to land in the enemy support line. The resulting explosion was splendid and the noise tremendous even at our distance, 600 yards off. 'That'll learn them.'

8th April. We use our old newspapers as tablecloths here, and when conversation flags, as it does very often in our mess, we read paragraphs as we eat. If one looks up, one sees three necks screwed at different angles reading paragraphs at right angles to the line of sight, or even upside down. One hits upon notable pieces of news this way.

9th April. Last night our artillery had a great strafe. It was quite a sight. It looks finer at night. We could see the flashes as the shells burst over the Hun lines and hear the tremendous 'dunts' of the high explosive. The big trench mortar bombs left a trail of sparks behind like a rocket and came down with a terrific roar. One battery behind us fired salvoes i.e. all the big guns at once and the noise was deafening. All through we could hear the rat-a-tat of the machine guns. When two or three go together it is like the noise of rushing water and the stream of bullets must be tremendous.

28th April. We scored by getting out of the firing line yesterday for our successors came in for a heavy 'ramie'; five mines were blown up at about 2am. Then the artillery broke out everywhere. There was a fiendish row which went on for two hours. The company that took our place were heavily shelled and had eleven men hurt, several with legs broken but none killed.

30th April. Yesterday and today have been days of broiling heat. Moving about the trenches with a heavy revolver on one's belt and a heavy gas helmet on one's back is quite tiring. At night I am too hot, sleeping in my clothes. Yesterday an aeroplane was brought down about two miles behind us. Another was brought down, but fell in their own lines.

1st May. The Huns have put up a big poster in front of their lines saying 'Kut-el-Amara fallen; 3000 prisoners'. It is very conspicuous. It is a bad affair that will hearten them up a lot. H and I went forward to read it and could do so easily with glasses. On returning, we heard a noise like a train whistle when it enters a tunnel, but very prolonged. I suggested it was a gas cylinder escaping, and when we got back we heard that gas was signalled from a sector on our right. I scrambled up the bank in front and saw a cloud just behind the notice board and several of our shells bursting over it.

6th May. At stand-to we had twenty-nine mortar bombs and four salvoes of shrapnel. The former fell between the trenches and the latter were just over us. I got our trench mortar to reply. He gave them five and our artillery did a little, and peace followed. Altogether the Hun must have put over 100 mortar bombs and at least as many shells in our little holding today. Casualties nil, unless he slew any of our rats. Moral and intellectual damage, nil also. The only effect is to hearten up our new recruits who are much interested.

Chapter 12

Eastern Fronts

In eastern Europe a titanic war unfolded. Here the vast empires of Russia and Austro-Hungary clashed and doomed each other to destruction. And it was in the east that the German Empire generally committed most of its land forces, once it decided to hold the French and British in the west in a defensive stalemate along advantageous ground of its choosing. Few FPs were involved in the military side of the war in Eastern Europe for although Britain was allied to Imperial Russia, it committed no significant forces there until 1918. As in the Second World War, British effort was largely confined to sending material support to its Russian ally via the northern seas to Murmansk. Nevertheless, several FPs witnessed events in eastern Europe and sent reports back to Aberdeen, while others ended up fighting in Russia for some time after the guns had gone quiet in Flanders.

William Hunter's business in textiles had taken him several times to Central Europe. At the outbreak of war in 1914 he was in Lodz, then an industrial city in the Russian province of Poland, that busied itself producing textiles and chemicals. In the nineteenth century, British merchants had dominated the Lodz textile trade but as in other areas, they had been ousted by the willingness of their German competitors to invest and lend credit for the longer-term. By 1914 there was only a small British community left in the city, numbering seventy or so according to Hunter.

On the evening of 29th July, Hunter saw Russian Government placards going up on the streets of Lodz ordering the mobilization of men and horses. He also witnessed the shock of the local population on hearing that war with Germany was imminent, for most knew little of the fast-developing events that were plunging Europe into catastrophe. The town was calm for several days until new placards appeared announcing that Germany had declared war. Lodz was less than sixty miles from the German border and panic was inevitable. Rumours that the German army was close spread through the city. Shops were stormed for food. German civilians were rounded up by the Russian police and detained until they could be sent to detention camps further east. On 30th July, all monies and papers in the banks were confiscated by the Russian Government. Investors lost their savings while the city's factories ground to a halt owing to a shortage of credit, and soon afterwards, a shortage of coal.

The leaders of the business community in Lodz were practical men and they hurriedly began to plan ways of keeping the city working, such as printing their own local currency and distributing basic foodstuffs at their own expense to the workers and the poor. Then came more bad news from the local Russian police. Following the withdrawal of Russian troops to a more defensible line nearer Warsaw, the city was being abandoned to the oncoming German army. The police had themselves been ordered to withdraw from Lodz at short notice. There were three prisons in the city, containing over 850 inmates, many of whom were dangerous criminals serving long sentences. The prisons could no longer be manned; they would be left open and the convicts set free. A civil guard, in which Hunter enlisted, was immediately set up to take charge of the prisons and when the convicts rioted, over 200 rounds were fired to restore order. The militia had also to deal with the bandit gangs exploiting the chaos by robbing the city's supplies of coal and flour from the central railway sidings.

Just as order was returning to Lodz, the first German military unit arrived in town. Its commander demanded, and received, food for his 1500 men within fifteen minutes. The city authorities were then required to find food for another 25,000 German troops in just two days – this in a city where supplies had been dwindling for several weeks. The misery of the Lodz citizenry was compounded when a Zeppelin and a squadron of aeroplanes appeared on an exploratory bombing raid. This was one city's introduction to what was to be more than six years of war and insecurity, for civil war and revolutionary terror continued in much of eastern Europe long after the troops had gone home from the western trenches.

Unsurprisingly, Hunter and his wife decided to return to their home in England at the first opportunity and found a place on the last train for Warsaw. Space on the train was strictly rationed and most of their belongings had to be abandoned. There was very little food onboard or at the stations along the way, but hot water was available so tea could be served sporadically. Thus began their long and circuitous overland journey from Warsaw to Petrograd, then on to Finland, Sweden and Norway.

It was far too dangerous to sail directly across the Baltic. A few nights before Hunter left Petrograd, thirty-five British subjects were taken off a Swedish steamer by a German patrol boat. The safer journey by train was long and slow but not uninteresting for the Hunters enjoyed the company of a Belgian lady from Petrograd, a British naval engineer, an Englishman from China, a Russian diplomat en route to the Hague and an American gentleman in the service of the Russian Grand Duke Cyril. Only Hercule Poirot seems to have been missing from their carriage. The last lap from Bergen to Newcastle was the most dangerous, for the North Sea was already awash with mines and their steamer was stopped four times by inquisitive British gunboats. After all the excitement, Hunter noted, 'it was a great surprise to find everything so normal and quiet at home'.

Another FP in this troubled part of Europe was John Campbell, a surveyor representing a London engineering company who spent a total of seven years in Petrograd that spanned the last years of Tsarism and the birth of Soviet Russia. Theodore Watt hinted that Campbell's time in Russia was more interesting than it seemed on the surface but that the Censor would not permit him to say more. So the only comment by Campbell on wartime Russia that reached the Grammar magazine reader was his considered opinion that the condition of the Russian people had improved marvellously since the sale of vodka had been prohibited.

Fredrik Nielsen, an FP of Danish extraction, also seems to have been operating in the Russian Empire at this time. Nielsen was an employee of the Great Northern Telegraph Company based in Copenhagen which operated a network of sub-sea and trans-continental cable routes. By 1907 these stretched from Iceland to Aberdeen and onwards through the Baltic and Russia to Vladivostock, Nagasaki and Hong Kong. Nielsen worked first at the company's Aberdeen office and then at the Baltic port of Liepaja which passed from Russian into German hands, becoming Libau in 1915. Thereafter he was stationed in the Russian capital until December 1918.

The journalist Frederick Rennet was another FP to be found in Petrograd throughout this turbulent period. Rennet worked for the American news agency Laffan's and was stationed in Russia before and during the Great War, writing a number of articles about political developments there. As revolutionary Russia disintegrated into bloody civil war, Rennet was imprisoned by the Bolshevik authorities. Badly weakened by his period of captivity, he died in Lübeck in 1922.

When the Bolsheviks assumed power in Russia in October 1917, peace with Germany was one of the key aims of the new Soviet regime. The war on the Eastern Front formally ended in March 1918 with the signing of the Treaty of Brest-Litovsk. In reality the collapse of the Russian war effort in late 1917 allowed Germany to transfer its eastern divisions to the West throughout the winter in preparation for a massive offensive in spring 1918. Allied governments were desperate to restore a government in Petrograd that would resume the struggle against the Central Powers. There was also, in London, Paris and Washington alike, a deep fear of Bolshevism. Accordingly, the Allies intervened in Russia, supporting the various White groups that were arrayed against the Reds. In all, more than 255,000 troops from sixteen Allied nations fought in Russia in 1918-19 on fronts as far apart as the Crimea, Vladivostock and Murmansk in the north. Forty thousand British servicemen played a part in the campaign and a number of FPs were inevitably involved.

James Meston Reid RE had seen service against the Turks at Gallipoli, Suez and Sinai, and against the Central Powers on the Macedonian Front where he commanded a Greek Labour Battalion. Reid contracted malaria in the course of his Middle Eastern travels. Nevertheless, he volunteered for the North Russian Expeditionary Force in June 1918 and commanded the Allied fortifications at Port Onega near the White Sea. He died from bronchial pneumonia at Archangel on 6th November 1918.

Other Grammarians caught up in this difficult campaign included John [Ian] Innes of Strathdon, house surgeon at Aberdeen Royal Infirmary and a lecturer in experimental physiology at Aberdeen University. In 1918, Innes served as Bacteriological Medical Officer to the 86th General Hospital in Northern Russia and as Medical Officer on board HM Hospital Ship *Braemar Castle* which was lying in the harbour at Murmansk. Hugh Pirie, an engineer in Aberdeen, Canada, Illinois and then with the Army Ordnance Department, had already visited Russia in January 1918 on a special mission to Petrograd. In the North Russian campaign he served as Senior Ordnance Inspector and was awarded the Tsarist Order of St Stanislaus.

Dr Kenneth Pirie Mackenzie RAMC also found himself in Russia in the summer of 1919 during the last stages of the Dvina Front campaign as the Allied Intervention crumbled under fierce Bolshevik assault. Mackenzie evaded capture and liquidation by the Bolsheviks and was to perform outstanding service again in the 1939-45 war as the senior doctor and surgeon at Rangoon Central Jail, ministering to his fellow prisoners of war. Yet another Grammar medic, Capt William Scott, served as Medical Officer for the Allied Garrison at the northern Russian shipping port of Economia, a suitable posting perhaps for a son of the Granite City.

Archer Irvine-Fortescue RAMC was a Senior Medical Officer with the Dvina Force. In January 1919 in the depths of the Russian winter, he was based at a military hospital at Beresniki in the Archangel district when the Bolsheviks won a decisive victory over the Allies in the battle of Shenkhurst. On 24th January he received a terse message from Allied HQ informing him that the town of Shenkhurst, almost eighty *versts* or fifty miles away, was to be abandoned. The problem was that there were over 100 wounded Allied soldiers in the RAMC hospital there who would have to be removed immediately or face certain massacre by the Bolsheviks.

After five hours hunting down sleighs and drivers, Irvine-Fortescue set out for Shenkhurst with an assistant surgeon, three RAMC support staff and a Manchurian Cossack. It was now very late in the evening and the drivers and ponies he had assembled were work-weary and reluctant to set out on an arduous journey. As the Times Correspondent in Archangel related, 'only by threats and blows could the convoy be moved out of a walk: frequently a revolver had to be thrust under the nose of a driver'. Thanks to Irvine-Fortescue's determination to rescue the men in the soon-to-be-stranded hospital regardless of blizzard and Bolshevik *franc-tireurs*, the convoy arrived at its destination after fifteen hours of 'snow and pine and measly scrub and drivers hovering between truculence and a Service weapon'. There remained the return journey and more tribulations along the snowbound track but all 120 men in the hospital were eventually carried to safety. One report of the evacuation affirmed that Irvine-Fortescue went without sleep from late on the Friday afternoon until his charges reached safety at Kitsa Station three days and nights later. Irvine-Fortescue received the DSO and the Order of St Stanislaus with crossed swords before heading off on a special mission to Persia.

Archer's youngest brother, William Grenville Irvine-Fortesque RE also served in Russia with distinction, gaining a Bar to the Military Cross he had received in Salonika in March 1917. He was part of Syren Force, a unit of 2,500 men sent to the Murmansk Command area to support the White Russians there. William arrived in mid-August 1919, by which time it was clear that the campaign was already lost. The task now was to manage the effective withdrawal of the remaining Allied units in northern Russia. He displayed 'conspicuous leadership in very trying circumstances' under fire at Koikori when he successfully held his section of the line against vastly superior Bolshevik forces.

A little more fortunate perhaps were those FPs who found themselves in warmer climes, venturing into southern Russian territory rather than the cold northern wastes. Typical was Dr John Kesson who ministered to the sick and wounded of the British Army of the Black Sea. This was a force largely composed of units that had been serving in the Balkans, then sent to hold Constantinople after the collapse of Ottoman rule. The Allied mission soon developed wider aims, such as subduing the lingering Turkish resistance in the Black Sea ports and seeing what assistance could be given to the White armies of Generals Wrangel and Denikin in southern Russia. Kesson had already served with the Red Cross in the first two years of the war and then in the RAMC at Salonika and in Italy. He was eventually demobbed and awarded the OBE in 1920, exchanging his participation in the Russian Civil War for a quieter life as a GP in Surrey. As part of the British Black Sea Army another FP, John Nisbet RNR, commanded a fleet of eighteen motor gunboats that policed the strategic waters of the Bosphorus.

The Bolshevik coup in Russia in late 1917 meant that Britain lost its eastern Tsarist ally. It also posed a longer-term threat to British interests in the Near East where first Germany, and later Soviet Russia, would be keen to increase their influence. To counter these threats, General Lionel Dunsterville was charged with putting together a mobile force of 1000 elite troops, drawn from the best men that could be spared from British, Canadian and ANZAC units. This task force, with a support column of forty Ford cars and vans, several armoured cars and two aircraft, set out to cross Mesopotamia and Greater Persia. Its mission was to identify and train pro-British elements and deal with any German or Soviet agitators.

Alexander Sharp was the kind of man that Dunsterville wanted in his unit. Sharp had wireless experience from his time in the Merchant Navy and his spell as a Sergeant in the Wireless Section of the Machine Gun Corps. From April 1918 to April 1919, Sharp was with 'Dunsterforce' in Mesopotamia, Persia, Turkestan and Southern Russia. As events unfolded, the aims of Dunsterforce developed from suppressing pro-German elements to protecting the Baku oilfields from capture by Turkish forces. Dunsterville's objective then changed again to maintaining the British interest in the region amidst a bitter ethnic struggle that ended in a series of dreadful atrocities inflicted upon the civilian population by Bolshevik, Armenian and Azeri forces alike.

Before it extricated itself from the chaos, Dunsterville's force suffered heavy casualties in the battle for Baku in September 1918, losing over 200 men killed or wounded, a fifth of its strength. Alex Sharp survived however and made it to his demob in May 1919. If he ever wondered what he was doing in a battle so far from his childhood home in Allan Street, he might have been cheered to know that he was not the only Grammar FP in that part of the world fighting a conflict that was difficult enough to understand, let alone win. Like Sharp, Capt William Cochrane MC of the Royal Scots was in the middle of an equally complicated ethnic and political mess arising from the power vacuum left by the overthrow of the Russian Empire. His theatre of operations was Batum in the Caucasus where he served until late June 1919, by which time the ink was already drying on the European peace settlement signed at Versailles.

Chapter 13

The War in the Fertile Crescent

The British campaign in Mesopotamia began as an action to secure the Royal Navy's oil supplies. The key port of Basra was soon in British hands with troops of the 6th Poona Division guarding the refinery at Shatt-al-Arab. British control of the Persian gulf was ensured. When Turkey entered the war on the German side however, British involvement in the region succumbed to 'mission creep'. Invading the heart of Mesopotamia, it was now argued, might inspire the Arab population to rebel against their Turkish masters and accelerate the collapse of the Ottoman regime. Planners in London failed of course to take account of the geography and climate of the region which made the logistical problems of invasion almost insurmountable. The scarcity of decent roads meant that most supplies had to be laboriously carried upriver. At times the summer temperatures reached 120°F [48°C]. After a bright start to the campaign, the British were forced to retreat from the ancient Parthian city of Ctesiphon, twenty miles south of Baghdad. The British garrison at Kut-al-Amara, a force of 12,000 men but badly weakened by hunger, dysentery and malaria, surrendered in May 1916 after a five month siege by the Turks. Most of the men taken prisoner at Kut died on the march into captivity in the Ottoman heartlands.

British fortunes in the Middle East only turned in 1917 when the mobile tactics of Sir Edmund Allenby in Palestine forced the Turks onto the back foot. In November that year, Allenby became the first Christian conqueror to enter Jerusalem since the Middle Ages. His victory beneath the hills of Judea at Megiddo [Armageddon], encouraged Turkey to pull out of the war. French, British and Italian troops occupied Constantinople in November 1918 and established the first new administration of the city since the Byzantine capital fell to the Turks in the great siege of 1453. Underpinning Allenby's historic glory however was Britain's massive investment in the railways of Sinai and Palestine in the latter years of the war. The Royal Engineers were much involved in extending, repairing and standardising the old Ottoman lines. Grammarian James Bryce RE served as an officer commanding units of the Egyptian Labour Corps and his efforts on the railways were recognised in 1919 with three mentions in despatches, an OBE and the Egyptian administration's Order of the Nile.

In the Middle Eastern campaigns, the British and Empire forces faced two enemies, the Turk and the hostile environment. A number of FPs succumbed to the heat and disease, especially in the summer months as the Allies struggled and fought along the hot river valleys of the Tigris and Euphrates. Typical of many victims were Lt Lindsay Ogg of the Calcutta Scottish Volunteers who died of enteric fever at Basra in September 1916, and Lt William Milne of the 121st Pioneers, in peacetime a forester from Mintlaw who was in charge of the Eastern Khandesh woodlands near Bombay. Milne succumbed to fever at Baghdad in October 1917. John Badenoch, a teacher, preacher and private in the RAMC, died from heatstroke in the British Hospital in Basra in July that year aged forty. Cholera took many other British servicemen such as Alfred Macrae, a Plocktonian who served as Assistant Commissioner for Police in Mesopotamia and died at Nasireyeh in July 1916. Dysentery was another menace and it accounted for Ian Stephen, 18th Bengal Lancers, who died at Aden in late 1917. Several other FPs died as a result of illnesses contracted on active duty but sometimes only long after the hostilities had ended, such as Robert Cumming RAMC MC who finally died in the spring of 1921 from his wartime 'exposure on the battlefield at Basra'.

Others died more quickly in battle against the Turk such as the Hebridean FP William Macleod of the Seaforth Highlanders who fell in the advance upon Tekrit in November 1916, and Ronald Benton, a junior officer in the 53rd Sikhs who died in June 1916 aged 21. Joseph Stewart left his teaplanting in southern India to serve in the 33rd Indian Cavalry and was killed in action in the Persian Gulf in Feb 1916. John Ellis, elder son of a well-known Aberdeen coal merchant, fell at the battle of Ayun Kara in Palestine in late 1917. Ellis was sheep farming in New Zealand when the war began and immediately enlisted in the NZ Light Horse with the Wellington Mounted Rifles. On 14th November, a day of cavalry gallop, intense machine-gun and rifle fire, and finally combat with the bayonet, the ANZAC troopers took the well-defended Turkish emplacements that blocked the road to the key port of Jaffa. Ellis was a mature soldier and a veteran of Gallipoli who was mourned by his regiment as one of eleven men who died 'in the thick of the fight'. His younger brother James died that same year in France as a Captain in the Gordons.

Many of the Grammar FPs who faced the Ottomans were older men who had already enjoyed successful careers in the Indian Army. One such was Lt Col James Davie, Military Governor of Amara in 1916, who received the DSO for his role in the forlorn defence of Kut. He was forty-five when he was taken into captivity by the Turks. John Gray, a thirty-five year old captain in the 36th Sikhs, was killed in one of the several Allied attempts to relieve the Kut garrison. Lt Col Marcus Hartland-Mahon, an older professional soldier mentioned in despatches in the South African War, commanded the Brigade of Indian Artillery in Mesopotamia. He received the DSO in 1919 for his conspicuous gallantry and ability in command at the battle of Shergat [ancient Assur] in late October 1918, the decisive action on the Tigris that precipitated the armistice with Turkey.

Another senior FP in this theatre of war was Oliver St John Skeen, who had been decorated in South Africa during spells as a staff officer and a field commander in the mounted infantry. Skeen had also served on the campaign that marked the high tide of Britain's imperial ambition, the Tibet campaign of 1903-04, and had taken part in the controversial march on Lhassa. When the war sparked in Europe, Skeen was major of the 62nd Punjabis who were ordered to France in late autumn 1914. When Turkey suddenly joined the war in October, Skeen's regiment remained in their transit position in Egypt.

It is no exaggeration to suggest that Skeen and his men played a crucial role in one of the most significant military actions of the war. An early Ottoman war aim was to capture the Suez Canal, the key artery between Britain and India. Taking the canal would have seriously disrupted British logistics, dealt an immense blow to Allied morale and encouraged dissidents throughout the Empire. On the night of 2rd February 1915, an amphibious Ottoman force launched a surprise assault on the canal zone. Skeen led his men with 'great promptitude and courage', charging the Turks at their most vulnerable as they disembarked from their pontoons. On the 4th, Skeen led a counter-attack on the Turkish positions, bringing effective enfilading fire upon their trenches and causing the surrender of the enemy. The entire Turkish attack group was demoralised by the display of aggression that Skeen and his Punjabis displayed and by 10th February, most of the Turkish units had melted away into the desert.

Skeen's success in these canal actions had a lasting impact on British operations in the area, discouraging any repeated Turkish incursion and winning time for the British to reinforce their hold over Suez and Sinai. Skeen received the DSO for his services at the actions of Tussum and Serapeum. He later served in Aden but was killed in action in the Persian Gulf in 1916.

A Grammar FP also played a key role in another significant action during the British counter-offensive in Mesopotamia in 1917. Hector Macdonald was a Bombing Officer with the Seaforths at the battle of Sanna-i-yat. He went over the top in the initial wave of an assault which captured the first and second Turkish lines. The task now was to block the main Turkish trench with a defensive bulwark made of sandbags, and so create a bridgehead from which the second wave of British troops could eradicate the rest of the Turkish defence. Macdonald quickly realised that most of the bayonet men detailed to protect those making the block had already been killed or wounded. He stood in their place protecting the flank, holding the position but taking wounds from which he died soon after. When writing letters home to grieving families, officers knew to emphasis that the death of a loved one had not been in vain but had been of great value to his comrades and his unit. There was however no need for 'flannel' in the letter which Macdonald's commanding officer sent to his mother. He simply stated the facts. Macdonald's sacrifice was the turning point in an action that 'contributed materially to the great success that day, as a result of which our troops have taken Kut-el-Amara and a considerable distance up the river beyond'.

The life of a soldiering FP in the Middle East was not always dominated by military action. As on the Western Front, the typical experience was often periods spent in rear areas resting, training and re-equipping, punctuated by short, sharp spells of intense danger. After their defeat at Kut in 1916, British forces in Mesopotamia were concentrated in the southern coastal zone where they spent the winter being reinforced and resupplied. There was time now to rebuild morale and relax. John MacNeill of the RAMC wrote home describing a race meeting organised to lift the spirits of the men and dispel something of the monotony of army life:

'Army Service Corps broncos were much in evidence. There were half a dozen 'Duggie Stuart' establishments [a reference to a well-known bookmaker of the day] all of which did a roaring trade owing to the complete absence of favourites. A couple of wet canteens and a big tea-tent added to the gaiety of nations, while a sprinkling of nursing sisters was rapidly absorbed in the general scheme of things. It fears me that these damsels must be getting enlargement of the cerebral contents owing to the fuss made over them, the proportion of eligible males being 300 to 1 or so. Nevertheless, this is a Seventh Heaven compared to the track down from Kut'.

Arguably, other FPs spent their relaxation time more profitably. Captain John Foster of the Indian Army used his spare time to acquire a good knowledge of Arabic. This came in useful in 1919 when he found himself administering a large district in the former Ottoman province of Galilee. Another 'eastern' FP with linguistic interests was John Kelman, a Science master before the war, and an interpreter in French and Hindustani. The latter skill was vital in an army which depended on the services of troops drawn from His Majesty's vast reservoir of colonial subjects.

As the war in the Middle East turned in favour of the Allies, other FPs found themselves serving in the ancient Biblical lands of Sinai and Palestine. Typical of many were the Rev Adam Findlay, chaplain at Gaza attached to the Highland Light Infantry, and Douglas Ritchie, whose 'equestrian' military career began in the Scottish Horse and ended in the Imperial Camel Corps.

At the end of the Mesopotamian campaign, four young men in uniform found themselves together on the banks of the river Tigris. William Tennant, School Dux in 1910 and an officer in the RGA who had served on the North West Frontier and in Persia, Kurdistan, and Armenia, was making his way downriver from Hamadan, the capital of the ancient Medes. Naturally, he bumped into three former Skene Street schoolmates; Alexander Johnstone, Thomas Menzies and James Forbes, all officers in the RAMC. The four young officers looked out across the heart of an ancient land that can lay good claim to being the fount of civilisation. Through the centuries, the same view had been shared by Babylonians, Assyrians, Greeks and Romans. This time, the passing conquerors were Grammarians.

Postscript

Two FPs did their bit for King and Empire in one of the Great War's forgotten campaigns. It was a conflict with modern overtones for the lines of battle were drawn on cultural and religious grounds. Although in terms of geography it was fought on African soil, strategically it was part of the war in the Middle East. Forces of the British Empire and Italy faced a Muslim triple alliance: troops of the Ottoman Empire, of the Sultanate of Darfur in the Sudan, and the conservative Islamic Senussi sect who had their homelands in the deserts of Libya. Stiffened by German military advisers and machine guns brought in by U-boat, this Muslim coalition hoped to oust the British and Italians from their colonial possessions along the northern shore of Africa, Egypt and Libya.

Allied forces faced attack on three sides; on the Alexandrian coastline, in the Western Desert and in the Sudan. The 5,000 tribesmen who emerged from the desert sands in November 1915 made initial gains at Jaafar, Sollum and Sidi Barrani. However British deployment of fast motorised columns supported by the new tool of aerial reconnaissance eventually began to tell against the Senussi who were badly beaten in three engagements the following year. Alexander Hutchieson, a student at Heriot-Watt Technical College and a Gallipoli veteran, served in the Lothians & Border Horse in Egypt in 1916 and saw action against the Senussi. He ended the war in Palestine with the Royal Engineers. Douglas Laing was a signaller at Suvla Bay in Gallipolli who then served in the defence of the Suez Canal. By the autumn of 1916 Laing was part of the Western Desert Force, a mobile offensive unit that travelled quickly across the sands in a mixture of light armoured cars and camels. In late October, the WDF recaptured the oases at Kharga in Southern Libya, forcing the Senussi warriors to disappear back into the desert from whence they came.

Chapter 14
Three Wars in Africa

In 1914 there were two main threats to the British possessions in Africa. The first was the German military presence in the Reich's colonies scattered around the continent. A greater potential danger perhaps came from the Boer population which had caused such trouble for the Empire a decade or so before. Despite these fears, the German colonies in West Africa and South West Africa were subdued relatively quickly. A Boer rebellion in South Africa was also snuffed out in the first months of the war.

However, in East Africa the small German force under the inspirational Paul von Luttow-Vorbeck fought a sustained guerrilla war, making excellent use of the terrain and the belligerent qualities of their tenacious Askari troops. By contrast, the British commanders in the region waged a ponderous campaign. The Allies enjoyed a massive numerical superiority over Luttow-Vorbeck's force of 15,000 men but struggled to cope with the climate, the local diseases and an agile hit-and-run enemy. The Germans in East Africa only surrendered in late November 1918 once the news of the European Armistice had been confirmed. Grammarians made their contribution to these events with more than sixty-five FPs known to have figured in the African campaigns.

In August 1914, German Togoland was defended by less than 700 German reservists and perhaps 1500 indigenous troops. Togoland was also surrounded by the much more populous British Gold Coast to the west and the French colony of Dahomey to the east. It therefore fell quickly to a joint British and French expedition that provided the Allies with their first triumph of the war. FP William Miller played a vital, if not especially glamorous, part in the campaign as Director of Transport for the Gold Coast Regiment at Accra at the beginning of the war. He travelled by motor column with the British force that moved into Togoland, met little resistance and entered the capital town of Lomé on August 12th 1914, little more than a week after Britain went to war.

German Cameroon proved a tougher nut and took the British more than nineteen months to crack. Failure to take the fortress at Mora on the northern frontier between Cameroon and British Nigeria led to a frustrating siege. It was there that Thomas Fraser became the first FP fatality of the war in late August 1914. After losing the coastal towns to Allied naval operations, the German force of around 6,000 men retreated into the interior. Here they enjoyed the advantage that their native troops were operating on home ground. At one point, the Germans even executed a bold counter-attack into Nigeria. The British expedition to Cameroon now faced a long campaign that required taking a series of well-constructed forts one by one. Like Thomas Fraser, Robert Semple OBE was a medical FP who served with the West African Frontier Force. He was present when the last active German troops in Cameroon were finally rounded up in early 1916. Another 'West African FP' was Alexander Findlay, an agricultural chemist with the colonial administration in Nigeria prior to the war. Findlay served as Colour Sergeant of the 3rd Nigerians. Once Cameroon was taken, he spent much of the rest of the war managing plantations in the territory.

The campaign against German South West Africa had more complex roots. The Prime Minister and the Defence Minister of the new Union of South Africa created in 1910 had both been commanders of the Boer rebels a decade previously. When the Great War broke out however, Louis Botha and Jan Smuts declared their support for Britain and confirmed their willingness to send an invasion force into the neighbouring German colony. This decision outraged anti-British elements of the Boer population and inspired a rebellion in October 1914 by several commanders in the Union Defence Force, notably one Colonel Maritz. Charles Cheyne, an FP pharmacist with a UDF Mounted Field Ambulance, now found himself in a difficult position. Cheyne was an Empire loyalist but was serving directly under Maritz, a good commander who enjoyed the support of most of Cheyne's Boer comrades at their remote station on the Bechuanaland border. With some difficulty, Cheyne and several other loyalists had to escape under cover of darkness and make their way towards the nearest loyal police station fifty miles distant.

The 1914 rebellion attracted support from around 12,000 men in the Boer heartlands but it was easily crushed by Botha and Smuts. One of the more stubborn Boer commanders however was General de Wet.

Knowing that the game was up after his defeat at the Battle of Mushroom Valley, de Wet decided to lead his remaining cavalrymen on an eleven hundred kilometre trek across the dry scrub of Bechuanaland to join up with other rebels who had made it to German territory. One of the South African troops that tracked him down across the Kalahari wastes was a remarkable former pupil of Aberdeen Grammar School.

After a spell in the Belgian Congo, Simpson Shepherd returned to South Africa in 1914 to take up an appointment with the City and Suburban Gold Mining Company in Johannesburg. Within weeks, he found himself in uniform and part of General Botha's forces on a mission to pacify the Boer revolt. By November 1914 Shepherd was attached to that newest of military formations, the motorised Machine Gun Section, serving in the Union of South Africa Defence Force detachment that tracked General de Wet and his men as they fled westwards.

Boer cavalry had always banked on their ability to live off a land that they knew far better than the British. They and their horses were tough and accustomed to the harsh local conditions. In late 1914 however, the luck of the Boers ran out. The rains were late and good grass for de Wet's mounts was difficult to find. There was also no escaping the onset of new technology and the way it was changing warfare, even in the vast open spaces of southern Africa. No matter how far they rode into the interior, De Wet and his men could not shake off the relentless horseless carriages. Simpson Shepherd was on one of the dust-raising vehicles that de Wet could see over his shoulder on the horizon behind him. Fully supplied with petrol and rations, the machines just kept plodding across the landscape while de Wet and his dwindling band searched for waterholes or a friendly homestead. When the heat and the dust finally proved too much for the motor-cars, the Union men continued the final leg of the chase on fresh horses and camels borrowed from the Kalahari stations of the South African Police. Pursuers and prey eventually converged on Waterbury, an oasis used by hunters and the only watering hole for many miles.

Shepherd was there on the last day of November 1914 when the exhausted rebel general accepted the inevitable and surrendered, muttering 'It was the motor cars that beat me. They compelled us to maintain a speed that was killing to man and beast'. Shepherd also served under Botha in the successful invasion of South West Africa in 1915 which ended German rule in that part of the continent. Job done in South Africa, he returned to Britain and volunteered for the Royal Engineers. A graduate of the Royal School of Mines with a First Class Diploma and years of practical experience of mining, a commission in one of the RE Tunnelling Sections on the Western Front was inevitable. For the next three years Simpson Shepherd was an underground warrior engaged in the ancient, silent and deadly art of tunnelling deep beneath enemy lines. He was awarded the Military Cross in June 1918.

General Botha's army also included Ian Mackenzie who had gone out to South Africa in 1888. In the South African War, Mackenzie had endured the siege of Ladysmith as a Natal Carabineer and later won the DSO as a captain in the Scottish Horse for his actions at Vlakfontein in 1901. Mackenzie enlisted again in the Great War, serving in the South West African campaign until invalided home to his farm in the Orange Free State. Sadly, after re-enlisting in 1917, he died at Blantyre in Nyasaland in September that year from injuries sustained in an accident.

George Foggo belonged to one of the furthest flung FP families with five FP brothers in South Africa, New South Wales, Victoria, British Columbia and upstate New York. A farmer near Ficksburg in the Orange Free State, George had served and been wounded in the South African War but rallied to the colours once more in October 1914 as a trooper in the South African Mounted Rifles. Like many South African volunteers, he was demobbed early in the war once the situation there had been stabilised. However he later served as a Government Inspector of Shells at the Woolwich Arsenal.

Another FP medic, Finlay Ross, worked through the campaign in German South West Africa, then ran Klerksdorp Hospital in Transvaal until dying of exhaustion and pneumonia in 1917. Charles Anderson, a mining employee of De Beers, served in the Kimberley Regiment appropriately enough. He played a part in crushing the initial pro-German Boer rebellion and then served in the force that took the key German port at Walvis Bay. Control of this harbour, halfway along the coast of Germany's colony, gave Botha the opportunity to build an army of over 32,000 men and carve up the territory in a well-planned operation. Anderson served throughout the German South West African campaign and emerged unscathed, as did George White, once of Seaton Cottage but a fruit farmer on the Cape in

1914. White later went to the Western Front where he served in the Army Service Corps for more than thirty months.

The actions in West and Southern Africa were inconvenient for the Allies but at least these campaigns made no great demand upon their resources. East Africa was very different. There, intelligent German tactics forced the Allies to commit disproportionate amounts of men and money to the region. Approximately 10,000 British and Commonwealth troops died in East Africa, most of them from disease or the effects of the climate. German losses, European and Askari, amounted to less than 1700. The death toll was much higher amongst the native population however. Thousands were impressed as labourers and porters by the European armies in their midst and forced to endure months of under-nutrition and overwork. When the rains failed in 1917, famine and then the global influenza pandemic added to the fatal brew. Conservative estimates suggest that over 100,000 of these unfortunates died as a result of the war in this region.

The conditions in the interior of German East Africa, where much of the fighting took place, were tropical and often dreadful. As one FP dolefully noted in the magazine, heavy rains could suddenly turn the ground underfoot into 'one continuous swamp from start to finish' where troops and bearers had to march 'always ankle deep, sometimes knee deep, in mud and water; men and supplies had to be moved through areas of deep dark woodland, scrub bush and elephant grass up to twenty feet high'. Troops were billeted in bandas, ie huts built to local custom using bamboo and grass bound together with bark strips around a dampened earth floor. Bandas had some advantages as military accommodation; they could be put together quickly on arrival at a new campsite and were cooler than tents made of standard issue army canvas. They were however soon occupied by the local fauna. One FP noted the caterpillars that dropped from the banda roof onto his head, a common hazard in a hut made from fresh vegetation that had still to 'ripen' by cooking in the sun. Rats were constant companions: 'last night two rats or possibly more, were having a good time in my banda after I got to bed. They climbed up the walls of my mosquito net and then proceeded to scuttle about on the sheet forming the roof of it'.

FPs were soon and painfully acquainted with many of the more exotic creatures to be found on the Dark Continent:

'there is a small animal in this delightful country called a chigger. He belongs to the flea fraternity and his special home is the human toe, just at the junction of nail and skin. You get a feeling, half tickling, half pain, in some toe and when you look there is a white blister with a black spot in the centre. If you are wise, you take your toe and its guest, not to a doctor, but to your own African boy. They are experts at getting the intruders out. If you do it yourself you will almost certainly burst it and scatter the eggs. I've seen some taken out the size of a small split pea. Since coming here I've had five in my toes, and as my boots have the holes left by ancient nails, I rather suspect members of the chigger clan are harbouring in these caves waiting for my feet.

Oh, it's a fascinating country this for the entomologist, and the beasts in question are not at all shy. Just as W was going to put his helmet on, an enormous tarantula dropped out. Yesterday I watched an encounter between some chickens and a scorpion, a big brute, six inches long and all black. I'm reading HG Well's War of the Worlds and I'm tempted to wonder if his Martian creations are the after-effects of a flying visit to German East Africa. Sometimes I hate the tropics with a bitter hatred'.

The scarcity of food and supplies was another issue that troops had to face in this faraway corner of the war. Items could be ordered easily enough from the port of Zanzibar but there was little guarantee that anything useful would reach men in forward positions in the interior. In the drier months, supplies were taken inland by trolleys on narrow tracks but these only went so far inland and once the rains came, the trolleys and their tracks would often subside into the soaking wet black cotton-soil. It took an estimated fifty tons of supplies to feed the labourers needed to push, carry and drag one ton of supplies to the uniformed men at the Front. One FP in particular had to deal with the logistical problems posed by the difficult campaign geography. Lt Col John de Castilla DSO was an engineer and veteran of the South African War who donned uniform again in 1916 as Major in charge of Lines of Communication in the Nyasa-Rhodesian Field Force. He ended the war as the Inspector responsible for Lines of Communication in German East Africa.

Despite the best efforts of men on the ground, supplies that did reach the Front were often packed in ways that made sense in a London warehouse but offered little resistance to the powerful insect life of Africa. Troops were often thrown back on what they could source locally. Egg-laying fowl were particularly useful as long as the local help wasn't too ambitious:

'my boy generally fries my eggs, however this morning I found a thing on the plate looking like a lady's crocodile-hide bag, rather over-boiled. This proved to be an omelette. It was not so resistant as it looked, though for a time each mouthful leapt obstinately from one jaw to the other; the bacon however was as usual impregnable, in the present delicate state of my jaws anyway, and I thought of sending it to the Ammunition Column'.

Inevitably, numerous FPs figured among the casualties of this faraway campaign, victims of the climate and conditions rather than of any human foe. They included Wilfred Wilson whose engineering career began with the Great North of Scotland Railway Company at Kittybrewster. After attending the Royal School of Mines, Wilson worked in Siberia, South Africa, and was prospecting in the Belgian Congo in the immediate pre-war years. Like Simpson Shepherd, he quickly received a commission in the Royal Engineers but died of influenza at Dar-es-Salaam in December 1918 just as he was on the point of embarking for home.

Other casualties of the African conditions included Hugh Bisset, once of Burnside House and a cavalryman in the South African Horse, and George Littlejohn of the South African Rifles. Both died from malaria contracted in German East Africa although Littlejohn lasted long enough to be invalided back to Pretoria where he died in April 1917. George Bell of the South African Scottish also fell seriously ill but recovered to fight another day on the Western Front. Capt Robert Easton RAMC worked on hospital ships in the Mediterranean from 1914 to 1916 but was invalided home in early 1918 after two tours of duty in East Africa.

Climate, environment and logistics all conspired to make the East African campaign a difficult one for the imperial troops stationed there. And there was still a war to fight against an enemy who was often perilously close by: 'the German camp is only about two miles away and there are occasional bouts of firing between us daily'. Even here in the far-off African bush however, the new technologies of war were beginning to make an impact:

'as we neared Rumbo, we sat watching one of our aeroplanes from Kilwa flying over and then dropping a few bombs on the German camp. A few dull explosions and it flew back again to breakfast at base, 26 miles off. They say the German blacks are horribly scared by the 'tin bird' dropping bombs on them; they scuttle right and left into the bush whenever they sight it coming. Things seem to be going well here, this place was taken only a few days ago. There are three or four sharply rising hills round the ridge we are on, something like Dufftown but unless your imagination is vivid, the resemblance doesn't hold in other respects eg you don't generally hear machine guns popping near Dufftown or see aeroplanes floating up towards Ben Rinnes'.

More than a year after the Armistice, Theodore Watt received a letter from Corporal George White ASC, home from France and restored to his life as a fruit farmer at Orchard Siding in the Cape Province. White's letter describes just how isolated some servicemen had been during periods of the war in Africa. 'Many thanks' wrote White 'for sending me the school magazines in 1914-15, though they never reached me then. I was on the warpath in German South West Africa, which explains matters. We were continually on the move'.

Chapter 15

Other Far Flung Fields

The vast majority of Great War Grammarians did their service on the Western Front fighting in the familiar regiments and corps of the British army. However, the diaspora of talented Scots throughout the Empire meant that some Grammar FPs found themselves fighting in places far from home in units with exotic names such as the Ferozepore Brigade, the Nagpore Mounted Infantry, Wilde's Rifles and the 34th Prince Albert Victor's Own Poona Horse.

Capt John Gray was a career soldier in the Indian Army who served with the 36th and 47th Sikhs. In August 1914 he and his men found themselves in Tientsin in north eastern China, part of a symbolic force of 1500 men sent to bolster the small British garrison there and show solidarity with Britain's Japanese ally. Britain's military presence in this distant spot was a response to the presence of the German East Asia naval squadron at nearby Tsingtao. This force, the Reich's only 'blue-water' squadron capable of acting independently from home base in Germany, was a threat to British and Japanese interests in the region. Gray acted as Transport Officer for the quickly assembled Tsingtao Expeditionary Force, liaising with the Japanese Command.

The Tsingtao expedition met with a number of initial difficulties, not least poor weather and flooding that hampered Allied operations, but the school magazine assured its readers that Gray and his men gave 'a splendid account of themselves'. Gray, it seems, had the gift of command; he was 'an extraordinary favourite with his Sikhs and had a wonderful power over them'. Once the Japanese were able to bring their superiority in numbers to bear, Tsingtao fell quickly and the German cruisers fled across the Pacific to meet their end at the Battle of the Falklands in the South Atlantic. After Tsingtao, Grey was back in Peshawar in 1915 for a spell of action on the Indian frontier, talking part in 'considerable fighting with the frontier tribes who were very troublesome in this part of India'. The

following year, Gray transferred to Mesopotamia where he met his de: 'amid more rain and mud' in a failed attempt to relieve the besieg garrison at Kut.

John Angus, originally of Strichen, also saw action against tl Germans in northern China. A merchant navy skipper before the war, l witnessed the Japanese bombardment of Tsingtao in his role as command of the Admiralty supply transports in the area. Like Gray, Angus late transferred to the Mesopotamian campaign where he served as an inlan water transport officer in the Royal Engineers, organising the river ship used to move men and supplies up and down the Tigris and Euphrates.

Visitors to the Western Front today are often intrigued by the more than forty Chinese cemeteries scattered across the region. These are the last resting places of members of the Chinese Labour Corps, a force of almost 140,000 labourers recruited in Allied territories in Asia such as Hong Kong and shipped to the killing fields of Europe. These men undertook many of the laborious but essential tasks needed to keep the British war machine running smoothly; unloading ships, carrying supplies, digging support trenches, and filling sandbags. After the Armistice, they were involved in the unpleasant but necessary jobs of recovering the remains of the dead, clearing the fields of unexploded shells, and filling in the redundant trench network. Estimates of this unit's total casualties vary but a figure of 10,000 men is probable, many of whom died in the flu pandemic of 1918. Capt Robert Gibson commanded companies of Chinese labourers near Boulogne and Calais in 1917-18. In all probability, Gibson had good skills in the Chinese language. Originally an engineer on the King's Cross-Waverley line, he worked for the Chinese Imperial Railways on their stretch from Peking to Mukden in Manchuria from 1899 to 1916. George Combe certainly understood Chinese, entering the British Consular Service in China as an interpreter in 1901 and rising to the rank of consul at Chefoo in the north east of the country by 1914. Three years later he was back in Europe commanding the 138th Chinese Labour Company.

Only slightly closer to home were those FPs stationed in South East Asia and Burma. Thomas Hector was a surveyor in Shrewsbury, having originally trained at the Philorth Estate office near Fraserburgh. On mobilization, Hector joined the King's Own Shropshire Light Infantry who

were sent to Rangoon in Burma in December 1914 to restore order after disturbances there.

Hector next found himself in Singapore, again dealing with insurrection. On Feb 15th 1915, Muslim troops of the Indian Army seized a consignment of ammunition, took control of the local barracks killing the British officers in command there, then released and armed over two hundred Germans, the crew of the German cruiser *Emden*. In two days of anti-British rioting, forty eight officers and civilians lost their lives. These well-trained and well-armed mutineers were only overcome by a coalition of Allied naval personnel, the Malay Volunteer Rifles, some of the Shropshires and 'all available men'. In his later missive to the editor of the school magazine, Hector indicated that these were the same rebels that had 'foully shot' Dr Angus Legge in the first weeks of the war. In due course, thirty-six mutineers were executed. The other court-martialled troops were 'allowed' to serve in labour battalions in the East African campaign where they would inevitably face dreadful conditions and suffer heavy losses.

Hector also helped suppress a rebellion in May 1915 as part of the Field Expedition to the province of Kelantan in the north east of the Malayan peninsula. This disturbance was led by a Muslim notable, known by the nickname of To'Janggut or Old Long Beard. As ever in history, some commentators have portrayed this character as a heroic freedom-fighter while others have only seen a troublesome bandit. The cause of the rising may have been a desire to depose the local pro-British Sultan or merely anger at heavy increases in the local taxes levied by an unpopular administrator. What is not in dispute is that To'Janggut stabbed and murdered a police sergeant and then marched on the nearest local town with over 2,000 of his followers armed with guns, spears and machetes.

A force of 1,500 men which included Thomas Hector was duly sent up to the province from Singapore by the British authorities and To'Janggut quickly met an end. His death shocked the native population of the province who believed he was invincible; local legend held that his skin could not be pierced by British bullets. Unfortunately for Old Long Beard, the sepoy who despatched him used a bayonet for the job. Like many of his contemporaries, Hector had initially been 'disgusted with disappointment' at being sent on policing duties in the East, rather than getting a chance to take part in the Big Show on the Western Front. He eventually got his wish,

leading a detachment of the Royal Fusiliers on a raid on the Kemmel Sector south of Ypres in July 1918 for which he won the Military Cross.

At times of crisis such as these, British subjects resident in agitated colonies usually found themselves called to volunteer in the task of helping deal with these imperial stresses. Typical of many FPs in this situation was Arthur Stephenson, a water engineer for the Federated Malay States Administration who joined the Malay Volunteer Rifles at the time of the difficulties there and later transferred to the Gordons once the colony was calm. John Stewart, another Strichen loon to attend the Grammar, did his bit in Burma. Stewart passed the entrance exam for the Indian Civil Service in 1904 and was stationed in Burma for a decade before the war began. Attached to the Burmese Archaeological Department, he explored the temple ruins in the vicinity of Pegu, the ancient capital of the kingdom of the Mon people. Once the hostilities began however, Stewart commanded in the Mandalay Sappers and Miners and saw distinguished service in Mesopotamia and then in Baluchistan in 1919. Stewart was awarded the Military Cross in 1917 and went on to a professorship in Burmese Studies at the University of London after the war.

The most distant of these 'far flung FPs' was without doubt Major Charles Dawson, once of Lonmay but by 1914 the Government Medical Officer on Savage Island in the South Pacific, 1500 miles north east of New Zealand. In late August 1914 a task force of New Zealand troops landed on German Samoa. It met with no resistance from the German administration there and occupied the colony until 1920 when Samoa became a formal trust territory of New Zealand. Major Dawson served as Principal Medical Officer with the Samoan Expeditionary Force in 1916 and was still living in the capital of Apia two years after the Armistice.

In India, the British had been playing 'the Great Game' against Tsarist Russia on the North-West Frontier for over half a century. In 1914 they faced interference from a new trouble-maker on this long-sensitive flank of Empire. The Tsar was now Britain's ally but the Kaiser hoped to stir things up in Central Asia and force London to divert more resources to the protection of the Raj. Disturbances in Persia were the preliminary move in a German attempt to form a bridgehead from which to send troops into Afghanistan and influence the Amir into joining an anti-British alliance. One prominent German agitator in the region was the legendary diplomat

Wilhelm Wassmuss who 'went native' and became known as the Lawrence of Persia. In reality, most frontier tribes needed little persuasion from Berlin to take up arms against the hated British. As a result, imperial forces were required to strenuously police the Persian-Afghan frontier and maintain the East Persian Cordon.

One FP casualty in this field of action was William Chalmers of the 19th Punjabis. In late 1915 Chalmer's regiment was moved from its main base at Quetta to undertake patrols on the dangerous Baluchistan frontier. Writing home to his brother in the Irish Fusiliers, he remarked that 'things are not so quiet as they were a little tine ago...the Germans have started on the tribes around here'. Chalmers and his men ran into a band of hostile Baluchi tribesmen near Seistan on 13th April 1916 where he was killed in action aged 26.

In all, more than a dozen FPs served on volatile stretches of the Indo-Afghan border between 1915 and 1919, taking part in campaigns once vital to the Empire but now largely forgotten. William Melvin, an Indian Army engineer, helped construct the Mohmand Blockade in 1916-17. This series of fortified blockhouses and deep field-lines of barbed wire was designed to keep the highland Pashtun clans out of the richer, settled lands around Peshawar. Thomas Milne took part in the 1917 expedition against the Mahsuds, one of many British military operations that failed to subdue this fiercely independent people.

In early 1918 Marri chiefs from Baluchistan visited the British base at Quetta to witness a visit by the Viceroy. The chiefs sensed that the British had been weakened by four years of manpower losses. They resolved to attack Fort Gumbaz on the edge of their territory. Waves of Marri tribesmen duly launched themselves against the eighty strong garrison there. Hopelessly outnumbered, the British contingent abandoned most of the fort and holed up in two redoubts that could give each other supporting fire. The defence of Fort Gumbaz had something of Rorke's Drift about it. The Marri swordsmen fought no less bravely than the Zulu. Against modern rifles, they enjoyed the same level of success.

Although the fort was held, this affront to imperial pride could not go unpunished and a disciplinary expedition was organised. A well-equipped force easily dispersed several large congregations of Marri warriors who were belligerent but carried primitive arms. Villages were razed, crops burned and hostages taken. The region was soon subdued and the tribal chiefs made the required display of renewed obedience to the Political Officers of the British Raj. Two FPs, John Drummond and Herbert Dunn, took part in this demonstration of imperial might. Dunn, an officer in the Army Vet Corps, was in command of the expedition transport. He probably witnessed the comic events when forty weary infantrymen, sick of marching in the hard Baluchi terrain, claimed expertise as horsemen in order to hitch a lift on the expedition's mules. The animals were duly fitted with saddles and rope stirrups. The scheme worked well until the mules unanimously changed gear from walking to trotting and the landscape was filled with abandoned troopers and disappearing riderless animals.

Few British servicemen travelled as widely in the upper Indian region as William Robert Tennant, originally of the RGA but later attached to the Indian Mountain Artillery. Tennant spent most of the Great War at Lahore, Amritsar, Kasur and Ferozepore, then found himself helping to police the perennial troublespot of Waziristan where the tribes never accepted the British claim to rule over them. In the final months of the war, Tennant saw further spells of duty in Persia, Kurdistan and Armenia before entering the Indian Civil Service after his demob in 1919. Another FP with plans to soldier on in India was Lt Arthur Henderson. At the end of the European war in which he had been badly wounded twice, Henderson transferred from the Gordons to the Royal Gurkha Rifles. It was alongside those most tenacious of imperial troops that he was killed in action near Dakka on the Afghan-Waziri border. Lt Col John Simpson was also no stranger to the North-West Frontier. As a young officer he had seen action against the frontier tribes in 1897 and again in 1904. After tours of duty in Mesopotamia, Macedonia and Southern Russia, his war finally finished back with the Waziristan Field Force in 1920.

One distinguished FP did manage to bring about a temporary cessation of hostilities in this troublesome region. Andrew Skeen was the brother of Oliver who had died in the Persian Gulf in 1916. In late 1919 he was Deputy Chief of General Staff in India and in charge of the operations to pacify Waziristan. With the Great War over, British commanders in India not only had the manpower to deal with insurgents but access to the new weapons that had been developed on the Western Front. A Reuters report of 19th November 1919 described a meeting between Major-General Skeen and 'one truculent chief who spoke boldly and almost insolently'. Skeen decided that a demonstration of British might was required and ordered his aircraft to put on a display of their bombing capability the following morning. The chief, who had previously dismissed the bombing threat, was now seen wringing his hands as the sound of explosions rolled over the Wazir hills. Theodore Watt noted that 'the submission of the Waziri chiefs was announced shortly afterwards'.

Other FPs served on fronts closer to home but which again have largely been forgotten by the general reader. Nevertheless, the service rendered by Douglas Christian Watson RE was truly memorable, even by the standards of the Great War in which exceptional acts were frequent occurrences. A surveyor and engineer, Watson served in France before joining the British Mission to the Royal Serbian Army in 1915. He was therefore one of the few FPs to fight in what might be called 'the core conflict' of the First World War - the war between Serbia and Austro-Hungary that resulted from the assassination at Sarajevo in June 1914.

On 12th August 1914, three massive Austrian armies invaded Serbia but were eventually repulsed by the Serbs who were skilfully led by General Putnik. However, when Turkey and Bulgaria entered the war on the side of the Central Powers, the fate of the weakened Serbs was sealed. They now faced invasion by German, Austrian and Bulgarian troops under the able Field Marshal von Mackensen. The help that was eventually sent from Britain and France was too little, too late; two divisions arrived but made little progress beyond their base at Salonika in north-eastern Greece. In a swift campaign in late autumn 1915, the Central Powers shattered Serbian resistance and Serbia itself ceased to exist.

The remnants of the Serbian army now embarked upon an epic retreat, marching through the difficult terrain of Montenegro and Albania. Their hope was to reach the Adriatic port of Durazzo where Allied fleets could transport them to safety. The column of Putnik's remnants also included many tens of thousands of Serbian civilians who had chosen to flee their homeland, a wise decision as the atrocities inflicted by the Austrian army upon those left behind were amongst the worst of the twentieth century. However, the route to safety was across a rough highland landscape where roads were poor and in places non-existent. Winter set in earlier than usual. Rations on the long cold trek dwindled quickly. Hunger and exhaustion took their inevitable toll. Albanian bandits also harried the refugees, picking off stragglers. Captain Douglas Watson was one of a small group of Allied troops who accompanied this tragic exodus across the unforgiving geography of the Western Balkans.

A fellow officer recorded Watson's efforts to help the Serbs reach safety thus:

'it was largely due to his personal efforts on the River Mati in December that the route to Durazzo was rendered practicable and the Serbian Army, then utterly worn out, was induced to undertake the final march to safety. It was thanks largely to his untiring efforts that the entire army got away. Without those efforts many hundreds more must have died, and possibly many thousands would have been captured. He continued his invaluable work in Albania until February, and then commenced at once almost equally important and valuable work in Corfu'.

A medic with the British Mission to Serbia also noted that Watson 'did much to save the Serbian Army; he was instrumental in passing more than 40,000 Serbs over three rivers, thereby both saving their lives and doing great work in the Allied cause'. A sizeable, and still useful, force of men had been saved. The Serbs were shipped to Salonika where they regrouped and eventually took their place in the Allied defensive line across the southern Balkans that became known as the Macedonian Front. Watson however had exhausted himself and he died in Athens of paratyphoid fever in June 1916 aged 32.

Altogether, more than sixty Grammarians served in the Balkans campaign, mostly at Salonika or on the Macedonian line. Lt-Colonel Maurice Williamson RAMC won the British and Greek Military Crosses whilst stationed in Salonika and Sofia and was twice mentioned in despatches. Another FP medic to distinguish himself in this sector was Capt James Davidson RAMC who served as Medical Officer at the British Hospital in Belgrade, a busy place on the very front line of the Austro-Serbian struggle. As the war unfolded, Davidson found himself working in Malta, Cairo and Rouen but the Serbian government-in-exile remembered their earlier debt to him and awarded him the Order of St Sava in late 1917.

In that year, a number of FPs found themselves in north eastern Italy in the struggle between Italy and Austria. Repeated Italian attacks along the Isonzo river had failed to break through. The war degenerated into a murderous stalemate fought in Alpine passes where the 'trenches' were dug from ice and rock rather than mud. By 1917 many Italian units were demoralised by the excessive discipline of their commanders, by heavy casualties that seemed increasingly pointless, and by the news that experienced German divisions were now moving to the Alpine front. When the Italians fell back at Caporetto in late 1917, British troops were hurriedly moved to the sector, taking part in a campaign fought at times within sight of the Gulf of Venice. They included one of the most remarkable of the 'Schoolhill' FPs who had started his education at the Grammar in 1855. This was Sir Alexander Ogston KCVO and Surgeon in Scotland to Victoria, Edward VII and George V, a medical pioneer acclaimed throughout Europe and the scientist who coined the term staphylococcus.

Sir Alexander was seventy when the Great War began. His interest in military surgery had already taken him to the Egyptian War in 1884 and South Africa in 1899. In both of these conflicts he was decorated for his surgical contribution and his personal bravery. His experience of battle medicine led him to found the Volunteer Medical Staff Corps, one of the units that eventually morphed into the RAMC. Before the Great War, numerous Scottish field medical units enjoyed Sir Alexander's hospitality at summer camps on his estate at Glendavan on Upper Deeside where they honed the skills they would later need in wartime. Having retired from his post of Regius Professor of Surgery at Aberdeen in 1909, 'AO' was free to volunteer his skills where needed and he spent the first winter of the war operating at a military hospital in London.

By April 1915, Sir Alexander was in Salonika before proceeding to Belgrade where he took charge of the hospital supporting the British Naval Force on the Danube, an impressive sounding unit that consisted of a forty-five foot picket and a platoon of Royal Marines. In 1916 he was serving as Colonel of the British Red Cross Ambulance in Italy, working in the ruined city of Gorizia, newly captured by the Italians in a grimly pyrrhic victory. He continued to work on near Gorizia, supporting the Second Italian Army Group until late 1917 when he was made a Cavaliere of the Order of the Crown of Italy.

A Scot who had travelled widely in Europe and been impressed by German medical advances, Ogston was openly critical of complacent medical practices in the British Army and in turn was regarded as an outsider by the London Establishment. On more than one occasion he had to rely on his connections with the Royal Family to get the backing he needed for his plans. Nevertheless, his pre-war efforts played an important part in stimulating the medical preparations necessary for a prolonged continental war. A man in his seventies, his wartime contribution as a surgeon in the field was probably unique. Ogston was however not the only older 'maverick' Grammarian to serve on the Italian Front. Thomas Wardrop, a retired bank manager from Sydney, also got involved in this cold Alpine war despite being well past the normal military age. In 1915 Wardop was in France driving motor ambulances for the French Army. The following year he performed the same duty with the Italians. In addition to Sir Alexander Ogston, two other FPs were decorated by King Victor Emmanuel III; Herbert Bower of the 4th Gordons was made a Cavaliere of the Crown of Italy and Maurice Johanneson RGA MC received the Silver Medal for Valour.

Perhaps the most isolated FP posting during the war was served by Captain, later Major, Arthur Shepherd RAMC, who spent 1916 on the remote penal colony on the Andaman Islands in the north-eastern Indian Ocean. The Andamans were the British equivalent of the French Devil's Island. A penal settlement from 1789, and much enlarged after the great mutiny of 1857, Port Blair on the largest island in the archipelago was the site of the notorious Cellular Gaol. This circular, seven-spoked penitentiary of 693 cells was designed so that communication between inmates was impossible. It was used for especially dangerous criminals and political prisoners. Despite being surrounded by desperate men of all types, and having two servants who were themselves convicts, Shepherd reported that his five month sojourn there had been uneventful. However, he assured the Grammar editor that he was also now 'an expert revolver shot'.

As this book demonstrates, Grammar FPs, often boys barely out of the classroom, undertook an impressive array of wartime duties in lands far distant from Scotland. Lieutenant George Howie of the Army Vet Corps was given a particularly challenging task when serving in India in 1917. It was a mission requiring all the energy and ingenuity for which Morland Simpson's Grammar School had hopefully prepared him. The School Pupil Roll describes his orders in a brief, laconic entry: 'sent to China for mules'.

Chapter 16

New Ways of Waging War

Three iconic weapons dominate our visual memory of the war on the Western Front: gas, machine guns and tanks. Grammar FPs used these weapons and in some cases they made a contribution to their development. To the men in France and Flanders, these weapons were daily reminders that they were waging a war that was increasingly technical. Their survival, and victory if it was still possible, also increasingly depended on new systems of signalling and reconnaissance.

The School Records name twenty FPs who suffered in varying degrees from gas attack. Almost all of the Grammar's gas victims suffered in late 1917 or 1918. By this stage in the war, the German chemical weapons of choice were mustard gas and phosgene. Troops exposed to mustard gas suffered internal and external blistering and temporary blindness was common. Phosgene was more insidious. The initial inhalation often went unnoticed by the victim and the impact of the gas often only became apparent 36 to 48 hours later. By then it had caused irreparable damage to the lungs, and death was much more likely.

Of the Grammar's gas victims, only two are specifically recorded as dying as a result of being gassed. Capt James Mackie RFA was badly gassed in September 1918 and died at Queen Mary's Nursing Home in Edinburgh in August 1919. George Scott, our midshipman eye-witness at the Battle of Coronel in 1914, transferred to the RFA in 1915 and was gassed in 1917. He died in Edinburgh in April 1918. Two other gas victims, Charles Anderson and John Lindsay RAMC were invalided home and took no further part in the hostilities. One Gordon Highlander, George Taggart, was discharged as medically unfit in June 1918, eight months after his exposure to chemical warfare. Bar one, all of these FP casualties were gassed on the Western Front. The exception was William Gillanders who served in the London Battalion of the Royal Defence Corps. This unit was largely composed of older or wounded men and was charged with defending the capital's strategic points such as docks and railway yards. Gillanders had the bad fortune to be gassed when a Zeppelin dropped its canisters on the Isle of Sheppey in the Thames estuary.

Some FPs seem to have possessed a remarkable resilience to 'the Hun stuff'. Several medal citations mention men carrying on regardless of the poisonous fumes swirling around; Major Charles Reid DSO remained in command of his battalion throughout a heavy bombardment of gas shells despite being affected himself. Clifford Chance 'cleared all the wounded, re-established the chain of evacuation and repeatedly led his squads through heavy fire and gas shelling, and by his magnificent example maintained the morale of tired, shaken stretcher-bearers'. Harry Middleton RAMC, though suffering from the effects of gas, 'remained at duty, dressing the wounded for four days until ordered to hospital'.

The use of gas in war was illegal under the terms of the Hague Agreements of 1899 and 1907 so its use was therefore a war crime. However, once the Germans crossed the ethical line by shelling Allied lines at Ypres with chlorine bombs in April 1915, the Allies could now deploy their own chemical weapons whilst retaining the moral heights. One of Haig's first tasks on becoming Commander-in-Chief in December 1915 was to expand the Special Companies to a strength of over 5,500 men with an ability to attack the enemy using gas canisters and gas shells fired from mortars. With exquisite British hypocrisy, the troops that were organised into the 'Special Companies' of the Royal Engineers were not at first permitted to use the word gas when describing their new weapon; it was to be referred to simply as 'the accessory'.

The work of the RE's Special Brigade was top secret but eight FPs are known to have served in its ranks. Little about their activities was mentioned in the wartime issues of the School magazine but the obituary of George Dawson in autumn 1916 confirmed that these 'special soldiers' were up to something very 'hush-huh'. Dawson was a Mathematics and Science Master at the Grammar School in 1914. He enlisted in the Royal Scots but in August 1915 responded to 'a request from HQ for men with a knowledge of chemistry to hand in their names' and was quickly transferred to the SB. Dawson died on 28th June 1916 near Serre on the Somme. He and a colleague were working in the firing line, engaged in preparations for an assault planned against this heavily fortified German position in three days time. Both men were killed by a shell that burst near them.

Of the other Pioneer-Chemists, Hubert Stewart served in A Company which specialised in the wind-driven delivery of gas, while Richard Girdwood belonged to a unit trained to fire gas-filled shells by mortar. John Grant of the 6th Gordons joined the Special Brigade in August 1915 and also spent time in France in its Gas Section. Harry Shand was trained to use the Livens Projector, a cumbersome, experimental flamethrower operated by a team of eight engineers. Sitting in a shallow tunnel that jutted out into No Mans Land, a long, heavy tube directed a stream of burning compressed gas at the enemy. Four Livens projectors were used at the Somme, with mixed results.

A number of FPs underwent anti-gas training. This consisted of learning how to detect and identify incoming chemicals, protect oneself and comrades from the effects of gas, operate the growing array of alarm devices such as the Strombus Horn, and construct a gas-proof dug-out. William M Anderson served as Chief NCO Instructor at the Anti-Gas School at Otley near Leeds. James Milne was in charge of the anti-gas training for units in the Machine Gun Corps during the last year of the war. One eminent FP worked to combat the gas peril at a more strategic level. This was James Philip, Professor of Chemistry at Imperial College, who served as a member of the War Office's Chemical Warfare Committee. Philip worked on methods of protecting troops from the effects of exposure to gas including improved alarms, masks and clothing materials, and barrier pastes and lotions. He was made a Fellow of the Royal Society in 1921.

The increasing technicality of war after 1914 meant that a new training infrastructure had to be established. Typical of the new training centres was the Machine Gun Corps School at Grantham in Lincolnshire. In the early months of the war, the BEF organised its own training in the skills of machine-gunnery at Wisque near St Omer. However, the experience gained in the first year of the war taught the Army that specialised units with tactical training were needed to maximise the weapon's potential. Accordingly, the Machine Gun Corps was formed in October 1915.

Several FPs served at the MGC School at Grantham. Ian Clarke of the 4th Gordons transferred to the MGC in 1916 and served as an instructor until returning to France in Feb 1918. Now acting Major, Clarke received a third wounding in July but survived to be demobbed in September 1919. One of the four FP Spark brothers from the Durris manse, Archibald Douglas Spark MC, followed a similar route. Spark served as Machine Gun Officer for 1/7th Battalion Gordons. After being wounded in July 1917, he passed the staff course for Grantham and joined his fellow FPs there as an Instructor, before also rising to the rank of acting Major. Another acting Major in the MGC was James Cruden, a professional soldier who had enjoyed spells in the Scottish Rifles and Black Watch before the war. Transferred from the Gordons to the MGC in 1916, he was later awarded the Belgian *Croix de Guerre*. Other FPs known to have been students at Grantham included Alexander Buthlay of the London Regiment, Sgt Alexander Williamson of the Gordons who was commissioned on passing the Grantham course and John Williamson of Torphins, who was serving as a 2nd Lieutenant in the MGC in March 1916 but was killed in action eighteen months later.

In all, more than forty FPs served either in the machine gun companies embedded in the first regiments to fight in France and Flanders, or in the Corps itself. The men selected for these duties had to have exceptional resolve and steadfastness. On both sides, offensive planning emphasised the need to liquidate machine gun units as a matter of priority. Machine gun units were often placed in forward, dominating positions in the tactical landscape. This made them obvious targets for snipers and mortar bombers which helps explain the MGC nickname of 'The Suicide Club'. The Corps suffered over 62,000 casualties of whom 12,500 were killed.

The Grammar contribution to this appalling loss included William Henderson, an outstanding cadet on the Lewis Machine Gun course who was appointed Machine Gun Officer in his company. He was shot through the head by a German officer while leading his platoon into an enemy trench in April 1917. Lt Iain MacLennan of the Royal Scots came third out of 300 cadets in his passing-out exams at machine-gunnery school in 1916. He received his first commission in March 1915 whilst only seventeen and still a pupil at the School. He was killed in May 1917. These FPs were amongst Aberdeen's contribution to the soldiers honoured in George Coppard's magnificent memoir *With a Machine Gun to Cambrai*. Coppard captured the grim, determined spirit of the Corps in one sentence; 'The

Machine Gun Corps was not a famous regiment with glamour and whatnot, but a great fighting Corps, born for war only and not for parades'.

FPs were also no stranger to the third iconic weapon of the Great War; the landship or tank. The first tank units operated under the aegis of the MGC, and the independent Tank Corps only came into being in July 1917. Capt Finlay Finlayson served first in the Gordons and then the MGC before being transferred to landship training. Captain Harry Coutts MC took an identical route to the tanks. Capt Robert Ledingham spent much of the war in the Royal Artillery but was transferred to the Tank Corps Command Depot in Yorkshire after a spell recuperating from wounds. Donald Campbell went straight into the Corps in April 1918, but he was barely eighteen years old and spent his time in uniform training at Wareham and Winchester. George Michie was promoted to the position of Tank Gunnery Instructor within two months of his transfer to the Corps in January 1917. He then enjoyed three other promoted posts before the end of the year; Officer in Charge of the Corp's Gunnery School, Adjutant to the Corp's Driving School, and Camp Commandant of the Corp's Firing School, not the expected career of an ordained Church of Scotland minister.

Finlay Finlayson, and another Tank Corps FP George Stephen, were both attached to the Christchurch Experimental Bridging Centre near Bournemouth. The early tanks struggled to cross wide trenches until a system was developed for dropping a fascine, a chain-bound bundle of brushwood, into the trench ahead. This fascine could only be used once, so the Christchurch technicians were hard at work developing a reusable steel platform for trench crossing known as the Inglis Bridge, when the Armistice was announced.

The citation for Harry Coutts' Military Cross in 1917 describes the limitations of the early tanks and the expectations of multi-tasking placed upon the men that crewed and officered them. Coutts led his tank to its objective 'in spite of considerable difficulties, and drove the enemy out, making good the position by getting out his men, with their guns, into the shell-holes nearby. He then went back himself to bring forward some infantry who took over the position, he and his crew remaining with them till dark, assisting in the consolidation. By his courage and determination, this strong point which had previously resisted all efforts at capture, was taken with practically no loss'.

Curiously, the trench mortar has largely slipped out of our public historical memory. Soldiers on both sides of the 1914-18 struggle certainly appreciated its usefulness. German mortars, or *minenwerfers*, were well engineered pieces capable of delivering a 210lb shell onto a target over 1000 yards away. It was probably the product of a minenwerfer, described by Watt as an 'aerial torpedo' that ended the life of Lt John MacPherson of the 6th Gordons in March 1918. MacPherson was struck directly by the projectile and died 'after two months of great suffering'.

At the start of the war, British troops were equipped with obsolete, unreliable mortars. The War Office in London saw little need to develop a more effective mortar and preferred instead to use up its existing stock of mortar ammunition which in some cases dated back to the Victorian age. The eventual adoption of the Stokes mortar in 1915 took the personal intervention of Lloyd George, then Minister of Munitions. The 3.2 inch Stokes was light, and thanks to its high trajectory it could be fired at the enemy by men sheltering in their own trench. Experienced troops could fire twenty bombs per minute onto enemy lines over 800 yards away. Most soldiers could learn to use the Stokes mortar without extensive training, unlike later heavier pieces that needed crews to operate effectively.

James Thomson of the 4th Gordons was seconded to the 154th Trench Mortar Battery in 1916. He described his experiences in a letter home to one of his masters at the School:

'I have only been away from the Battalion on this new job for a month, but I have 'strafed' the Boche quite a lot already. In the morning we all synchronise our watches and register our respective targets. The time creeps on and we have a last look at our mortars and ammunition. Five minutes - four minutes - 'Is your gun all ready, Corporal?' - 'OK sir' - one minute - 'Number 1 gun fire'. At first you can pick out the different guns. The sharp shriek of the field guns, the hoarse cough of the 'hows', the hollow wail of the mortars and the sharp staccato rat-a-tat of the machine guns. You take a look over the parapet. Suddenly there is a swish and a red rocket leaves the Boche trench. Then another. Then suddenly there is quiet once more and only a few star-shells break the sulphurous haze over No Mans Land.

For all this whirlwind of shrieking projectiles, you see something like this in the next communiqué: 'There were reciprocal artillery duels in the sector north of _____ last night. Considerable damage was done to the enemy front line system.' Oh well, c'est la guerre, but I shouldn't mind being back in your class'.

Some of the new military training units set up in the Great War were a result of the unfolding conflict in the skies. George Thomson served at the RFC Aerial Gunnery School at Hythe in Kent established in 1916. The school's main aim was to improve air-to-air and air-to-ground gunnery and it developed the combined gun-camera which helped the RFC better analyse its battle performance. Another FP sent back to the aviation classroom was Reynold Collier Brown, an air mechanic with 8 Squadron until he was commissioned and promoted to the rank of Instructor at 6 School of Aeronautics, Bristol in 1918. 6 School was a training centre for pilots who had mastered the preliminaries and its curriculum encompassed the nitty-gritty of flying at the front; combat, aerial photography, wireless cooperation with artillery and infantry units, and navigation in the disfigured landscape of the Western Front.

Aerial photo reconnaissance had become a key discipline of war. The RFC, whilst publicly affecting little serious interest in the new science, photographed the entire German trench system in preparation for the Battle of Neuve Chapelle in March 1915. Several FPs served in its photographic sections of the RFC such as Robert Brown, a photographic artist in Saltcoats in peace-time and then photographic mechanic with 4 and 5 Squadrons of the RFC. Victor Gurner performed a similar role at 3rd Army Headquarters, also helping to prepare strategic maps from the photographic data. Different technical skills were employed by James Ball who served in the RAF Drawing Section in 1918 and by David Duff who worked in the Meteorological Section of the Royal Engineers.

Two letters that appeared in the February 1915 magazine response, provided evidence that the enemy was also taking aerial reconnaissance very seriously and improving its air to ground communication. In the first, an FP with the Royal Scots expressed his frustration at having to 'hang about under cover until evening to avoid being spotted by German aeroplanes and finding ourselves being shelled'. In the second, an engineer on duty in France described enemy aircraft at work reconnoitering the trenches below: 'two or more German aeroplanes have flown over here and were only slightly fired at by our guns. They seemed to take a good survey of our positions. However our aeroplanes do exactly the same to them and our big guns shift positions frequently to prevent being shelled'. Anti-aircraft artillery assumed a new importance and many of the almost two hundred FPs who served in the Royal Artillery and its associated units will have undergone anti-aircraft training. One FP with a particular interest in anti-aircraft gunnery was the much travelled William Hunter, once of Lodz, who was attached in 1917 as an Intelligence Officer to the Staff for Anti-Aircraft and then later to the Anti-Aircraft Section at GHQ.

Most FP gunners underwent technical instruction within their regiment but several Grammar FPs found themselves in specialist artillery schools. These included Alexander Halley, a Gordon Highlander who gained a commission in the RFA and studied at the Siege Artillery Formation Centre near Market Drayton in Shropshire. By the end of the war, Halley was an Instructor at the RFA's main artillery school at Chapperton Down on Salisbury Plain. Chapperton was largely concerned with conventional bombardment as practised on the Western Front but other RFA students there such as William Salmond learned the different skills needed by anti-aircraft gunners. By contrast, Major Harry Simpson trained men in the use of much smaller weapons in his role as Officer Commanding at the Officers' School of Revolver Practice. The skills he passed on were vital to the young army officers he instructed. In the close combat needed to win contested trenches, they had to be confident in their ability to use their handguns in a controlled and concentrated manner.

The Royal Engineers had long placed a premium upon rigorous technical training, as the foundation of their college as far back as 1812 indicates. Robert Asher was only one of several FPs who were educated by the RE at their academic centre at Chatham. After spells in France, he lectured at the Reserve Centre at Newark-on-Trent where trainee sappers were drilled in the arts of trench engineering. Douglas McMillan, a railway surveyor in Canada before the war, served as an instructor in road and railway making, and explosives, at the Pioneer School at Reading. Major George Nicol DSO began the war in the 4th Gordons but from April 1915 onwards he was underground with the Royal Engineers, first with the 174th Tunnelling Company and then in command of the 178th. Tunnellers worked under intense pressure, having to dig their passageways silently to avoid enemy detection and risk the sudden breach of their galleries by enemy sappers bent on brutal combat with sharpened tools and anything else to hand.

Sound also mattered to Minto Gillanders, Principal Master of Science at Elgin Academy before enlisting in the Royal Horse Artillery. He was quickly put on the Special List and from 1916 to 1918 he served in, then commanded, Sound Ranging section 'R' of the Royal Engineers. At the start of the war, the British used unreliable visual methods to get the bearing and range of enemy artillery batteries. From late 1916 onwards, low-frequency microphones allowed engineers to separate the sound made by the firing of the shell from its later sonic journey through the air. Men like Gillanders who were good at sums quickly made the necessary calculations from the data. By early 1917, sound ranging sections were accurately pinpointing the enemy artillery to within 25 metres. Captain Gillanders was awarded the MC for his efforts in 1919. Another FP 'Sound Ranger' was John Riddell who served as a 'computor' with the 'JJ' Sound Ranging section until wounded in 1918.

In the first wartime school magazine, fourteen signallers were listed by Theodore Watt. These included Herbert Macbeth RNR who spent the first two years of the war as Chief Signalling Officer at the Cromarty naval base. William Benton RE was attached to the RND in France as Brigade Signal Officer from 1915 to 1919. Sydney Ogilvie's war resulted in a posting that must have appealed to any Grammarian with a taste for the classical Mediterranean. Chief Petty Wireless Officer Ogilvie RNR was posted to HMS *Heroic*, a sloop of the West Irish Coast Patrol. In 1915 the *Heroic* sailed from the chilly coasts of Ireland to the Aegean and Ogilvie was based at Mytilene on Lesbos until 1917. He saw out the war a little further north at Mudros where the Armistice between the Turks and the Allies was signed in October 1918.

Many Great War FPs were wireless operators on ships of the merchant navy. Others worked at cable stations. David Wright was a Post Office telegraphist before the war but from 1915 to 1917 he was stationed at the Governnment's cable relay station at Peterhead where messages to and from Britain's Russian ally came and went. Robert McCallum RNVR trained at the Royal Navy's Signalling School in the grounds of the relocated Crystal Palace at Sydenham. After completing his training at the renamed HMS *Palace*, McCallum returned northwards to the military telegraph station at Stoneywood. One of his predecessors there was Alexander Aitken, a member of D Company of 4th Gordons while still at the School. Barely seventeen, Aitken had a keen interest in signalling and passed the required course at Fort George in July 1914. Too young to go to the Front, he was posted to Stoneywood until he was old enough to enter the fray. He died of wounds in a French hospital in May in 1917.

Of the many Army signallers in the FP records, mention must be made of David Anderson of North Loirston, signaller in the Canadian Mounted Rifles, who died at Passchendaele in October 1917 while trying to repair telegraph wires damaged in a bombardment. William Bruce, Signalling Officer RE, also died near Ypres in April 1918 after two years at the Front. Charles Giles had tried his hand at banking, accounting and fruit growing in Canada before the war. His first posting back in Europe was as a Signaller at the HQ of the Canadian 2nd Contingent. He was awarded the Military Medal in 1917 but was killed in action exactly one month before the Armistice on 11th October 1918.

A useful contribution to the war effort was made by James Macbeth who worked on the Marconi International Code which made it easier for telegraphists to correspond in different languages. The work provided a quick guide to military information in nine languages including Russian and Japanese. Theodore Watt described the code as a marvel of 'ingenious compilation', a judgment he was well qualified to deliver.

The growing dependence of the Air Arm upon wireless can be seen from a few simple statistics. In the Battle of Loos in 1915 the British used 60 ground wireless stations to receive information from reconnaissance planes overhead. Nine months later at the Somme, there were 600 such stations. By the end of 1916, over 2,200 personnel were engaged in RFC wireless communications along the Western Front. The official report on the battle of Vimy Ridge in 1917 commended the effectiveness of Allied air to ground communications. Information relayed from RFC air patrols to ground artillery resulted in the destruction of 256 hostile batteries with 86 enemy gun pits totally destroyed and another 240 damaged. Numerous FPs performed radio duties for the RFC and RAF including David Harvey, a science undergraduate at Glasgow, George Laing a Marconi Telegraphist First Class, and Alexander Smith, wireless operator at RAF HQ in France in the final months of the war.

Another FP airman also provided aerial intelligence but did so from a balloon rather than a plane. William Matthews joined the RFC Balloon Section in late 1915. The first British balloon unit had proved its worth in May that year at Aubers Ridge near Arras, providing crucial information on German troop movements. British observation balloons typically contained 30,000 cubic feet of hydrogen in the form of illumination gas. Two to three miles behind the Front at an altitude of approximately 3500 feet, they were safe from enemy guns and still able to command a clear view of the surrounding landscape. Matthews survived his two year stint in 'the Balloons' and was demobbed in 1919.

The internal combustion engine earned its spurs in the very first days of the war, helping to save Paris and capture the Boer rebel General de Wet. Over sixty FPs served in the Army Service Corps, many in its Motor Transport Section. Arthur Scott spent the last eight months of the war with the 1038th Motor Lorry Company as part of Allenby's Desert Mounted Corps in Palestine, Syria and Turkey. Alexander Mitchell served with the ASC [MT] Salonika in 1917 and then with the Royal Serbian Army on the Macedonian Front. His war only finally ended in August 1919 when he was invalided out of the Batum escapade.

The Great War is rightly remembered as a grim conflict decided by industrial resources and evermore deadly technical innovations. But just occasionally, the war was fought the way that some had expected back in the summer of 1914. Alexander Gold served with the Royal Scots in Palestine where the British found the space and the dry ground suitable for finally bringing cavalry into play. Gold was at Gaza in April 1917 and witnessed one of the last cavalry charges in British military history: 'Early in March we arrived before Gaza, the great Turkish stronghold. We advanced time and again in the face of terrible fire, across the waving cornfields. Our cavalry, a glorious sight to see, thundered across the plains to the Turkish flanks'. Alas, the cavalry charges were in vain for the Turkish positions were strongly defended, and the defeated British horse warrior rode off into History.

Chapter 17

Interns & Prisoners

When the war began, a number of civilian Grammarians had the bad luck to suddenly find themselves behind enemy lines. Henry Watt, Lecturer in Psychology at Glasgow University, was interned in the early days of the war and remained as a guest of the Kaiser for ten months. Alfred Quin, a student of the German language, was also caught out by events, ending up at the Engländerlager at Ruhleben-Spandau outside Berlin but nevertheless managing to send a greetings card to the school magazine to mark Christmas 1914. At Ruhleben, Quin may have run into George Wyllie of 212 Westburn Road, a fellow FP who had travelled to the old university town of Erfurt in the summer of 1914 and spent the entire duration of the war as an internee as a result.

Ruhleben was a 'special' camp for civilian internees and perhaps its proximity to the International Red Cross office in Berlin ensured that conditions at Ruhleben were relatively humane. The five thousand or so mostly British inmates enjoyed a number of privileges and largely avoided the harsher discipline on offer to many military prisoners-of-war. Some of the responsibility for running the camp was devolved to the inmates who policed themselves to some extent and ran their own library, postal service and a small tobacco shop. Sport played a part in relieving the tedium and there was ample space for rugby, football and cricket at Ruhleben for the camp was located on a former racetrack complex.

Despite these attractions, Ruhleben was not for Thomas Mackay of 51 Cotton Street, an FP with experience in the herring export trade and one of several Britons marooned in Königsberg on the German Baltic coast. He was determined to avoid internment. Unable to contact the British Consul in Danzig and desperate to return home, Mackay and three other Britons decided to pass themselves off as Prussian officers called to their regimental colours. This was an inspired but risky stratagem. In order to avoid being questioned by inquisitive hoteliers and curious railway stationmasters, they played the role of swaggering Junkers, cuffing and bullying all and sundry until they made their way to the German-Danish border. As enemy aliens, crossing the border in wartime without papers was an action that risked summary execution if caught. Fortunately, a Norwegian skipper agreed to smuggle them past the German sea patrols to Copenhagen. Mackay made his way to Bergen where the British Consul there arranged his passage to Newcastle. Mackay immediately joined the Gordon Highlanders but died in September 1917 of wounds sustained in France in 1915.

Notes about uniformed FPs captured on service soon became a regular item in the pages of the school magazine. Some notes were heartening, such as that regarding William Donald of the Toronto Regiment, at first reported as missing in action but known by June 1915 to be a POW at Giessen near Frankfurt. Information about captured FPs often made its way back to Aberdeen thanks to the work of International Red Cross staff visiting the camps. Their communications brought news and relief to the worried families of missing and captured servicemen throughout Britain, and so it seemed in the case of Private Andrew Smith of Altdouray, Ballater. He was reported missing in action in October 1914 and his family initially presumed that he had died in the great charge of the London Scottish at the battle of Messines. The following year however, wonderful news trickled back to Aberdeen via the Red Cross in Geneva that Andrew had indeed been wounded in the chest but had been nursed back to good health at the Lazarett in Schönbeck in northern Germany and then sent to a standard prisoner camp at Döberitz in Brandenburg near Berlin. A second, heart-breaking, message arrived in 1916. It explained that the German authorities had mistakenly confused the long-dead Smith with a surviving Irish soldier of the same name. Other families suffered the agony of a long wait without news. Often it was a 'returned' prisoner of war arriving back in Aberdeen who extinguished a family's hopes by passing on bits of gleaned news, as happened in the case of Sgt Alexander McKenzie of the 11th Gordon Highlanders whose death on March 22nd 1918 was only confirmed by word of mouth many months later.

Messages home from POWs were invariably plucky and positive, designed to reassure worried families that their loved ones were safe. A typical postcard from Sgt Harry Lamb of the Highland Light Infantry sent to his home in Broomhill Road explained the circumstance of his capture but put a final positive spin on his predicament: 'by the fortunes of war, I am now a prisoner. We were cut off and were without food and water for eight days, and combined with these discomforts I was also wounded. I have two shrapnel wounds in back and left shoulder fractured, but I am getting on as well as can be expected'.

One of the most colourful of Great War FPs, Norman Oliphant Macaulay Foggo, ended up enjoying 'the hospitality of the Hun' after a short but spectacular contribution to the war effort. On leaving the Grammar in 1910, Foggo departed Caledonia's shores and entered the fruit ranching business in British Columbia. After learning to fly in Toronto and gaining more flying hours in Texas, Foggo completed his aerial combat training back in Scotland at Montrose Air Station. Before leaving for the Front, Foggo flew north one day to circle the School before heading over to Bridge of Don to perform a similar salute above his old family home at Braehead. Foggo's war was spectacular but short; its zenith and nadir were both encompassed in one day, 8th August 1918. He shot down three German planes in the morning, and bravely returned to the air for a second round of combat 'after lunch'. Sadly he was brought down behind enemy lines, wounded and taken prisoner but he survived the war going on to study engineering at the University of British Columbia back in Vancouver.

The most senior FP to fall into enemy hands was Lt.Col James Davie DSO who was captured by the Turks after the siege of Kut-al-Amara but survived his captivity and continued his successful military career in India after the war. Another FP in Turkish captivity was Captain [later Major Sir] John Frederick Ferguson of the Durham Light Infantry who was wounded and captured in Palestine in April 1918. He survived to enjoy two highly successful careers in the interwar Army and the Metropolitan Police.

As a medic rather than a combatant, Capt Alexander Rose of the RAMC enjoyed a relatively privileged status as a prisoner of war. Captured in October 1914, he was repatriated after eight months in German captivity. On his return to the front, Rose was promoted to Lt-Colonel and received the DSO in 1917. Two other RAMC prisoners, James McConnachie MC and John McKenzie MC, were captured in the rapid German advance of spring 1918 but both had been repatriated to Britain by early November as the war ground to a conclusion. When it became clear to both sides in 1915

111

that the war was not going to be settled quickly, high level negotiations led to arrangements whereby seriously wounded prisoners were sometimes given priority for release into relatively relaxed internment in the neutral states of Switzerland and the Netherlands. Later in the war, this clemency was sometimes extended to other categories of prisoner such as elderly men. This probably explains the release from Ruhleben of the sixty-six year old civilian William Buyers of the SS Yarrowdale.

The Ludendorff or Spring Offensive of 1918 was the last great gamble by the German High Command. Having reached a peace settlement with the new Bolshevik government in Russia, Berlin now had the chance to transfer most of its troops to the West for the first time since 1914. In this final *Kaiserschlacht* or Battle for the Emperor, the Germans hoped to snatch victory before the manpower and industrial potential of the United States could be deployed. The offensive began in the early hours of March 21st with an artillery bombardment of over 1.1 million shells followed by a carefully co-ordinated infantry rush that claimed 20,000 British lives and 35,000 wounded. It was the darkest day of the war for the British Army since the debacle on the Somme in July 1916. By early May however, the Germans had begun to run out of steam, and found themselves stretched out along a thin line that was difficult to supply and defend. Nevertheless this final German assault made gains that looked impressive on the map and it had resulted in large numbers of Allied prisoners.

The school magazine of June 1918 recorded this black episode in the war when outright German victory in the war suddenly seemed possible. Watt listed the names of fifteen young FPs who had been captured in the desperate days of March and April. In fact, more than twenty FPs were taken prisoner during the Offensive and its immediate aftermath, twelve of them in the first onslaught of 21st and 22nd March when the Allied lines were under most pressure.

Theodore Watt was always keen to include news of prisoners in the School magazine whenever possible, knowing that FP servicemen around the Empire appreciated news of their missing comrades. Inevitably, not all Grammar prisoners emerged unscathed from the conflict and notes in the school magazine often reported the death in captivity of captured FPs. The fate of Gordon Munro RAMC was typical; wounded and captured near

Courtrai in Belgium in early 1915 and reported as having 'died in the hands of the enemy'. It transpired that he died in a German military hospital in October of that year. Another FP, John McBain of the Royal Field Artillery, 'last seen running a telephone wire over to newly captured trenches', was severely wounded on the first day of the Somme and died in a German military hospital at Vrancourt eight days later. One of the sadder items in the magazine reported the death of Lt John Chalmers, a member of the school's Gordon Highlander Territorial Company since August 1914, who served in France for almost all of the war. Chalmers was taken prisoner on the 21st March 1918 during 'the last throw of the Kaiser's dice'. He died of appendicitis at the POW camp at Mainz in Hessen on 20th November 1918, nine days after the Armistice.

The annals of the FP club say relatively little about the treatment that Grammar prisoners of war received at German hands. Throughout the 1914-18 war there was little central coordination of POW camps by the government in Berlin and so local conditions varied considerably. The general tone of each camp largely depended on the attitude of the individual commandant and his staff. Instances of harsh treatment stemmed from the frustration of camp officials, often older or incompetent officers relegated to police duties. In the first weeks of the war, British prisoners of war certainly did experience hostility from camp guards and from local populations. This initial outburst of xenophobic anger towards French and British military prisoners died out quickly however once the German populace realised that the war was going to take some time and that many of their own boys were going to spend many months behind Allied wire.

In fact, after the war settled down in early 1915, POW letters and diaries record numerous instances of kindness by German civilians and camp guards. The School records also suggest that FP prisoners generally had access to adequate levels of medical care. More than a dozen FPs are known to have been wounded when they were captured, and most of these received sufficient medical attention from the foe to recover and see out the war. Typical of these men was Arthur Gill, of Duthie Terrace and the Highland Light Infantry, who was wounded when captured in August 1917 but well enough to set out for Western Australia and take up farming there two years later. Thirty-three FPs are known to have spent time in German prisoner of war camps and of these only the three mentioned earlier,

Chalmers, McBain and Munro, perished. Significantly, of these three, two died in the care of German military hospitals while Chalmers died of appendicitis, a condition that exacted high levels of mortality well into the twentieth century.

Inevitably, daily conditions for prisoners in the camps varied from decent to harsh. By 1915 however most commandants had improved the kitchen and sanitary arrangements in their camps and many had organised work routines in the locality for their charges. This was technically an illegal practice under the regulations governing the treatment of POWs but most bored prisoners went along with it in return for small privileges, as did German prisoners in Britain when they were invited to carry out forced labour. In well-run camps there were plenty of tasks to keep bored soldiers busy. Harry Lamb MM served as librarian at the Dülmen camp near the Dutch border from 1916 to 1918. Robert Abbey of the Canadian Mounted Rifles was captured at Zillebeke on the outskirts of Ypres in June 1916 and also ended up at Dülmen, before moving on to the Gardelegen and Zerbst camps. Abbey used his period of captivity to get involved in the British Prisoners' Aid Society and the Canadian Red Cross. At the end of the war he worked with the Repatriation Commission of the British Consulate in Rotterdam.

As far as the chaos of war allowed, conditions for British prisoners were generally reasonable and were sometimes particularly so for more senior British officers who sometimes enjoyed separate accommodation in larger requisitioned houses and public properties, rather than in the wooden barracks where the other ranks were billeted. The greatest dangers facing Grammar POWs in the Kaiser's Germany were frustration born of tedium, diseases such as dysentery and by 1918, the shortage of food of any quality as the Allied naval blockade increasingly struck home upon the Reich.

The inevitable difficulties that prisoners faced in communicating with their families back home added to the misery many felt at their enforced captivity. Camp commandants knew that restricting access to postal services was always an effective tool in calming any recalcitrance in the ranks. Lack of news led to anxiety back home and must have done so in the case of the family of Lt Gavin Allardyce MA WS MC. Allardyce had been out in France for most of the war but was reported missing in late October 1918. His family must have feared the worst. In fact he had 'only' been wounded and captured by German forces on the 20th of that month. The news of his survival suddenly reached Aberdeen in late November. His captors had kindly sent him on a four and a half day tour across Germany by ambulance train via Hanover and Berlin. The voyage finally terminated on the Reich's eastern march at the picturesque city of Marienburg, the historic capital of the medieval crusading Teutonic Knights. The only British officer on the train, Allardyce reported that he had been treated 'quite well' and was recovering from his wounds in the hospital at Marienburg when the Armistice was signed. Germany was by then convulsed by an abortive Communist revolution. Probably for his own safety, he was transferred to an officers' lager at Graudenz. There of course he bumped into a fellow FP and fellow officer in the Gordons, Norman Robson, who had been taken prisoner in the Ludendorff offensive earlier in the year. The hostilities finally over, Allardyce sailed from Danzig to Leith, arriving back in Scotland safe and sound on 1st December.

Sometimes the FP boot was on the other foot. Several FPs were involved in the management of internees and the ever increasing numbers of enemy prisoners in camps in Britain and across the Empire. Three of these FPs were medics. Capt Dr John Brown RAMC served in France from 1914 until he was wounded in June 1917. Once back on his feet, he served as Medical Officer for the 6,000 inmates at the POW camp at Brocton on Cannock Chase in Staffordshire. Brown evidently did his duty by the prisoners for a camp inspection in 1918 recorded that the prisoners' health was excellent. Unfortunately over 175 of the Brocton captives were to succumb to the mis-named 'Spanish' flu before the end of the year.

Capt Andrew Niven helped deal with the mopping-up of the war in the Middle East when he served as Senior Medical Officer at the POW Camp at Maadi, then ten miles outside Cairo on the right bank of the Nile. In 1917 Maadi held 5,500 prisoners and received a highly positive commendation from International Red Cross inspectors. By the time Niven arrived in 1919 however, the Ottoman Army had collapsed, the number of inmates at Maadi had soared and the camp population was in the grip of an outbreak of pellagra, a hideous condition which reduced its victims to walking skeletons.

A third FP medic to deal with captives was Capt James Pirie of the Australian Army Medical Corps who acted as Senior Medical Officer at the

Concentration Camp for German and Austro-Hungarian aliens at Holsworthy on the outskirts of Sydney from 1914 to 1920. Five thousand enemy aliens were held at Holsworthy. Some were merchant marine crewmen who had the bad luck to be in Australian ports when the war broke out, while others worked for German companies trading 'down under'. However, over seven hundred of the internees were naturalised British subjects or native-born Australians of German descent. Many were Serbs or Croats who were nominally subjects of the Austrian Emperor but had fled Austrian oppression to try their luck in the new, free land of Australia. Conditions in the overcrowded camp were poor and insanitary. The discipline imposed by the commander was harsh but ineffective. Many of the guards were corrupt and failed to crack down on a criminal gang within the camp that intimidated and brutalized the other inmates. Riots and beatings were common; suicides and violent deaths not uncommon. One imagines that Dr Pirie had a busy time of it in his six years there.

Chapter 18

Practitioners of the Dark Arts

During the Great War, a number of Grammar FPs did their bit for the Empire by operating in the fields of propaganda and espionage. Two in particular, George Mair and Ernest Ewart, proved to be fine exponents of the dark arts of propaganda, both making an immense contribution to the Allied war effort although they operated in very different circles.

George Mair was an exceptionally able scholar who took his first degree at Aberdeen before his eighteenth birthday and his second at Christ Church before his twenty-first. Both degrees were First Class Honours awards. After Oxford and a spell at the Sorbonne, he enjoyed a highly successful career as a journalist on the editorial staff of the *Manchester Guardian* between 1909 and 1914. He was at various times the *Guardian's* leader-writer, political correspondent and theatre critic. When war broke out, Mair was the Assistant Editor of the *Daily Chronicle*. He volunteered for military service but finding himself deemed unfit, he resigned from his newspaper post to devote himself to government work. We can safely assume that he was quietly headhunted. After spells in the Home Office and the News Department of the Foreign Office, by 1918 Mair was Head of the Department of Information. Much of his work was highly confidential and initially funded from the Secret Service budget, but one of his 'above board' tasks consisted of reviewing the attitude of the foreign press to developments in the war and briefing senior Whitehall figures accordingly. In this role, it is almost certain that Mair worked within, or alongside, Military Intelligence Section 7 [MI7] who were responsible for collating a daily review of the foreign press for perusal by the very top levels of the British government.

Mair had excellent French, a skill that marked him out for important roles liaising with Britain's main ally in the long war against the Boche. He can be glimpsed conducting a party of senior French officials 'through the arsenals and manufacturing centres of this country' in the summer of 1915, a time when politicians in London and Paris were coming under public pressure for their failure to provide adequate supplies of war material to the men in the trenches. He later served as Director of the Press Section of the British Delegation at the Paris Peace Conference in 1919 from which emerged the ultimate peace settlement with Germany and its allies. As the unwieldy set of treaties neared completion, Mair was charged with producing a précis of the complex settlement that would make sense to the man on the Clapham omnibus. After thirty-six hours in a locked room, Mair emerged with a lucid account of the treaty decisions that won him the praise of the Prime Minister Lloyd George and Lord Balfour. His précis was released to the press and became the basis for explaining and selling the Peace Settlement to the general public.

For his work during the war and at Paris, Mair was made a Companion of the Order of St Michael and St George [CMG]. President Clemenceau also made him a Chevalier of the *Légion d'honneur*. While in France, President Woodrow Wilson invited him to a private meeting at which the President gifted Mair a gold cigarette case in appreciation of his contribution to the Allied victory. Mair also had the honour of personally conducting the Prince of Wales around Paris during his 1919 sojourn in the city. In 1920, Mair was appointed Assistant Director in the League of Nations Secretariat in Geneva and then headed up the League of Nations Office in London. It was a sign of his many contacts at the highest levels of government, and their confidence in him, that he was trusted to help oversee this keystone of post-war British foreign policy.

Mair was however much more than an effective bureaucrat in wartime Whitehall. Thanks to his father who had been a Fleet Surgeon, Mair had an excellent grasp of naval matters and strategy. He was also fascinated by flight. He had first been intrigued by a travelling group of French pioneers aviators that he met in Blackpool in 1909. That same year, he accepted the invitation of the showman and aerial adventurer Colonel William 'Buffalo Bill' Cody to 'go up', becoming the first British journalist to fly in a plane and then describe the experience to the reading public. As one of the sharpest wits to inhabit London's dinner clubs, Mair was also on friendly terms with many of the prominent men of letters of the day including George Bernard Shaw, JM Barrie, HG Wells and WB Yeats. He returned to journalism shortly before his untimely death at the age of 38. The Grammar magazine devoted six full pages to his obituary and tributes, one of which hinted at the 'many dangers in his obscure work' that he had undertaken at times during the war.

There was nothing obscure about the contribution made by the school's other notable propagandist. Ernest Ewart was a best selling author who wrote many articles and books about the war under the pen-name of Boyd Cable. Ewart served in the Lovat Scouts during the South African War but after a spell with *The Times*, he spent the immediate pre-war years travelling in the East. He first appears in the FP war record in the Royal Field Artillery in September 1914 and by November he was in action in France. Transferring to the RFC, he served in the air arm to June 1919 when he was demobbed with the rank of Lieutenant-Colonel. Ewart had a successful career as a professional soldier and airman but his distinctive contribution to the war effort was as a prolific author of powerful pieces designed to convey a sense of what was happening on the Western Front to the British public. Books such as *Between the Lines*, *Action Front* and *Grapes of Wrath* offered gritty, realistic accounts of modern conflict. They dispelled any lingering romantic preconceptions about the nature of war that the public might have retained from the tales of derring-do in distant colonial wars that were popular in the previous century.

In a series of visionary articles in the popular *Cornhill Magazine* entitled *Airmen o' War*, Ewart educated his readers back in Blighty about the way in which airpower was transforming the modern battlefield. The British public was becoming familiar with tales of duels in the air between dashing 'aces'. Ewart however was more interested in explaining the fundamental ways in which aircraft had changed the strategy of warfare forever, hoping 'not only to chronicle some of the wonderful work done in the air but also to show the connexion between it and that of the armies on the ground, the assistance rendered in so many ways by the air arm, and its value in a battle and in a campaign'.

Books by Ernest Ewart and Boyd Cable were held in the school library and caught the imagination of the wartime pupil cohort. Ewart's graphic descriptions of the conflict were in stark contrast to the sometimes anodyne reporting of the war in newspapers. The desire for his books was such that it sparked a revival of interest in the library, not always the busiest location of a Skene Street lunchtime. 'Demand is outstripping supply' noted one amazed prefect librarian. Ewart's contribution to public morale during the war was recognised in 1919 when he was awarded the OBE for his services to the Propaganda Branch of the Ministry of Munitions.

Ewart's popular output was of its moment and is almost entirely forgotten today by all except historians. He does however have a major claim to having popularised one of the enduring phrases of the Great War. Kaiser Wilhelm II may [or may not] have dismissed the British Expeditionary Force of August 1914 under Sir John French as a contemptible little army. However it was Ewart who ensured that the phrase 'The Old Contemptibles' entered everyday language and was not allowed to fade away. Ewart picked up on this piece of soldier slang and used it as the title of a series of articles in the *Cornhill Magazine*. These articles eventually became a book that retold the startling heroics of the BEF from Mons to Marne as it crucially delayed the German advance on Paris, ensuring that the war would not be over by Christmas.

Ewart himself later recounted in 1919 how he had first heard the term:

'It was in 1915, in the days before service chevrons and wound stripes gave any indication of a man's service. I heard several men of the new Army talking amongst themselves rather contemptuously of some of the 'new hands' then coming along, referring to Neuve Chapelle and other actions they had been in, doing their best to impress the fact on all around that they were veterans and 'old-timers'. Another man outside the group had been listening and saying nothing until one man, evidently taking him for a Johnny raw, asked him how long he had been out. The position was made clear in a sentence, and without any mention of dates and actions and so on, 'I was one o' French's bloomin' old original contemptibles'.

As Theodore Watt noted, 'it struck Boyd Cable as typical of the British soldier to accept the Kaiser's jeer at our little army and twist it into a crown of glory'.

Ewart was keenly aware of how quickly the Great War had become a struggle that would be decided, not by valour on the field but by logistics and technological innovation. In his own field of aviation, he had seen ever faster and more powerful planes become derided museum-pieces within a few short months. He also appreciated that these new technological weapons also demanded men with the skills to make best use of them.

When drawing up characters for his novels, he had only to look at his fellow Grammarians for suitable examples of the new kind of soldier.

One such modern warrior was James Thomson, another able Grammarian with a brace of First Class degrees from Aberdeen and Cambridge, who pitched up in Flanders with the King's Own Yorkshire Light Infantry in 1915, and again at the Somme the following year. Fortunately the Army noticed his technical abilities and language skills and seconded him to Intelligence. Thomson then undertook special training in the analysis of aerial reconnaissance photographs. Intelligence briefings from Thomson and his ilk began to inform the decisions of field commanders, allowing them to target their resources more effectively. Attached to Corps Squadron RAF in the latter months of the war, men like Thomson were at the very heart of the communications revolution that powered Britain's Fourth Army to victory in the West in the summer and autumn of 1918.

Communications of a different sort were the forte of William Hunter, our escapee from Lodz. Hunter's time spent working and travelling in various parts of Germany and Poland before the war meant that he had picked up linguistic skills that were vital in wartime and yet possessed by relatively few British servicemen. Hunter not only knew the enemy tongue well but could understand some of the colloquial forms of German used by troops from different parts of the Reich. By mid 1916 he was employed at the War Office trawling though the letters, diaries and notes picked up by Allied troops on the battlefield after actions, or 'acquired' by the Directorate of Military Intelligence Section 6. Amidst much everyday dross, linguists such as Hunter found nuggets of valuable information that were fed into the decision-making process at Staff GHQ in France.

Expertise in languages has always provided a fast track into Intelligence work and so it proved for several Great War Grammarians. Mention has already been made of Clement Cobban whose fluency in Russian eased his rapid elevation to Staff Officer in the War Office. Herbert J M Milne's contribution to the war effort also relied on his linguistic ability. Before the war Milne studied at Cambridge and then worked in the Manuscripts Department of the British Museum. In 1916 he was attached to the War Office Military Intelligence Department, working in the section dedicated to reviewing developments in the foreign press. In this role, he almost certainly ran across his fellow FP George Mair. In 1919 Milne returned to his papyri and scrolls in order to pursue a productive career as a scholar of Egyptian fragments and Biblical Codices.

Before the war, Howard Gray enjoyed a successful career in journalism culminated in a staff post on *The Observer* and the position of leader-writer on the influential *Pall Mall Gazette*. By 1917 the British public was very war-weary. The Cabinet was unsettled by the spring revolution in Russia and by the news that a meeting of socialists in Leeds had called for a Workers' and Soldier's Council on the Petrograd model. Lloyd George decided to put British propaganda under political control for the first time in the war, establishing the National War Aims Committee. Gray was called up to serve as a staff writer for the NWAC, charged with freshening up British propaganda and reminding the public at large why they were waging this dispiriting, never-ending war. The NWAC was arguably one of the most important keys to maintaining British morale and national cohesion in the long haul towards victory and peace.

All field officers perform some intelligence work when monitoring enemy deployments and collating evidence found on the battlefield after combat or retrieved from the corpses of the enemy dead. Some officers however are required to perform dangerous intelligence missions of a more intensive nature and that was the nature of the task with which the admirably Cromwellian sounding Oliver Ironside was charged. After transferring to the Indian Army at Peshawar, Capt Ironside was asked to undertake secret work in Afghanistan. For eight months he was based at Landi Kobal, producing a report the situation across the Frontier that was 'much appreciated by the high authorities' on his return to British India. Sadly this able officer died in military hospital in Bombay in 1919 aged 22. Other FPs sent on similar missions included William Leslie, who was both a barrister at the Middle Temple and a medical practitioner in London. Although well past the age for military service, he made himself useful undertaking 'special service work' of an undisclosed nature for the War Office in France and Belgium.

In the June 1918 magazine, Theodore Watt noted that the FP Peter Chalmers Mitchell had been awarded the OBE in the previous year. Mitchell was a biologist by trade, secretary of the London Zoological Society and *de facto* the man in charge of London Zoo. Later in life, Mitchell would be feted for his humane attitude to the public display of animals and his revolutionary open wild animal park at Whipsnade. Alluding to Chalmer's background in zoology, Watt remarked that 'no indication is given officially as to the particular services that Mitchell has rendered. Perhaps his special knowledge of camouflage in animals has been turned to account in these days'.

This thin attempt at humour stands out in vivid contrast to the hundreds of well researched items in the thirteen editions of the magazine that Watt produced during the Great War period. As a well-kent figure in the city, Watt could not have strolled far down Union Street without meeting the friends and family of men posted on duty, all eager to pass on their news to him. He would have known a great deal, and suspected more, about some Grammarians that could not be recorded on his filing cards. Occasionally Watt had in fact informed his readers that there was more that he could tell about an individual's war service but the Censor would not let him. Peter Mitchell was such a case.

The Roll of Pupils that Watt published in 1923 shed some light on the mystery. In 1916 the civilian Mitchell had been made an Honorary Captain attached to Imperial General Staff and engaged on special duties for Military Intelligence. He made many missions to France and to Holland between 1916 to 1918, a period when Holland was a neutral state and a curious place for an alien zoologist to fetch up in wartime. Mitchell in fact worked throughout 1917 and 1918 for MI7 which specialised in propaganda and censorship. He was also the brains behind MI7's greatest weapon, *Le Courrier de l'Air*, a propaganda news-sheet dropped from the skies behind German lines.

Mitchell understood that the best way to demoralise the enemy was to avoid the sensational, inflammatory style of propaganda used earlier in the war. *Le Courrier de l'Air* did its job by simply providing accurate, factual information on the progress of the war, with an understandable emphasis upon items detailing the Royal Navy's successes against the U-boat and the arrival of American supplies on this side of the Atlantic. It was certainly effective. Seventy-eight editions of *Le Courrier* were produced between April 1917 and August 1918. Each edition's print run of 5,000 copies fell upon enemy-held French and Belgian territory, and latterly within the German Reich itself. Its impact on German morale was significant and the German government understood its power. The news-sheet infuriated Generals Hindenburg and Ludendorff, the real leaders of Germany by this stage in the war, who are said to have called the copies floating earthwards 'poisoned arrows from the air'. German civilians found in possession of *Le Courrier* were liable to a year's imprisonment and a fine of 10,000 marks. In December 1917, two RFC airmen carrying a consignment of *Le Courrier* were forced to land behind German lines. They were denied their rights as prisoners of war and were treated instead as spies; both were sentenced to ten year's penal servitude.

To avoid other RFC aircrews having to run this risk, Mitchell devised an alternative method of delivering *Le Courrier* using hydrogen balloons with a length of slow-burning fuse that released bundles of the newsheet at intervals. This was so successful that Mitchell's unit was soon dropping a wide variety of demoralising material such as photo postcards from German prisoners of wars happy with their treatment in Britain, humorous cartoons by artists attached to MI7 such as Bruce Bairnsfather and Frank Reynolds, and invitations to German troops to surrender. By the end of the war, Mitchell's unit MI7(b)(4) had despatched over 32,000 of these aerial propaganda balloons. These carried a total of almost 26 million items towards the enemy lines and beyond.

Mitchell also compiled a sharp analysis of the strengths and weaknesses of Allied and German propaganda which informed British Intelligence thinking for decades to come. Mitchell received the military CBE in 1918 and was knighted in 1929. At the beginning of the Second World War, British Intelligence revived Mitchell's unit and its new commander Lt Col Professor de Beer remarked that he just 'took up the work where Mitchell left off'.

Postscript

Two FP engineers worked on one of Britain's best kept secrets, the 'Mystery Port' at Richborough in Kent. It was clear by early 1915 that the antiquated harbours on the south coast of England were struggling to cope with the immense amount of material and large numbers of men crossing the Channel to and from the Front. To reduce the delays, a much larger, purpose-built harbour was needed. In 1916, this was built at Richborough in a relatively isolated part of Kent near the Isle of Thanet, some distance away from the larger towns in the area and most prying eyes.

From the outset, Richborough was built on a scale to meet the demands of modern industrial war. The 2000 acre site could handle traffic of over 20,000 tons per week more quickly and efficiently than any other port in the land. Its special feature was its revolutionary 'roll on roll off' facilities which allowed railway freight carriages bearing tanks and lorries to be shunted directly onto the decks of adapted freighters.

Robert Holmes had extensive experience as a civil engineer, working on harbour and railway projects in West Africa and Mexico. In 1916 he was a Major in the Inland Waterways and Docks section of the Royal Engineers, involved in the planning and construction of Richborough and especially the integration of its mechanical and dock facilities. After the war, now Colonel Holmes OBE, he oversaw the reorganisation of railways in the Allied Mandates of Syria and Palestine. Alexander M Robertson's background was also in railway and harbour engineering. After a spell in the employ of the Caledonian Railway in Glasgow, he was involved in expanding and modernising the Royal Albert Dock in North Woolwich to meet the pressures of war in 1915-16. He was mobilised to the same section of the Royal Engineers as Robert Holmes in 1917 and probably worked with him in his time at Richborough.

Keeping Richborough secret was one of the great British successes of the war. Proof of this was the fact that while German aerial bombing continued to target all the main ports in southern and eastern England, this vast facility on the tip of eastern Kent went unscathed and in fact quite unnoticed by the enemy. It had of course not featured on any of the maps of England bought up in large quantity by visiting German scholars and tourists in the years immediately preceeding the war.

Chapter 19

The Munitions Men

In 1914, Britain's munitions industry was not geared up for a prolonged war, and especially one in which field artillery was to play such a dominating role. The Shells Crisis of May 1915, when the British assault at Aubers Ridge allegedly petered out for lack of ammunition, highlighted the need for a more co-ordinated approach to military supply. This debacle led to the creation of the Ministry of Munitions under the energetic leadership of David Lloyd George. The new Ministry's powers included the ability to prevent workers from leaving the industry, in a sense conscripting the workforce. It could also direct the efforts of companies in cognate industries such as railway manufacturing towards the production of weapons.

Around sixty FPs were involved in the munitions industry in different capacities but two 'back room boys' in particular made a major contribution to Britain's struggle to develop the right weapons in adequate numbers. After the Grammar and Edinburgh University, Francis Ogilvie [later Sir Francis] became a Science master at Robert Gordon's College then enjoyed successful spells as Principal of Heriot-Watt College and Director of the Edinburgh Museum of Science and Arts. Recognised as the foremost science educator of his day, he was appointed Director of the Science Museum in Kensington in 1911.

It was clear from the outset of the war that technological innovation was the key to victory against Germany, whose powerful surge in maths, physics and chemistry in previous decades gave them a distinct advantage over the British. Ogilvie understood this and his proven administrative skills and real understanding of science meant that he was destined to hold important posts in government. From 1915 to 1917 he served as Assistant Director of the Trench Warfare Research Department and then as Assistant Controller of the Chemical Warfare Department. In these posts, Ogilvie had an opportunity to influence the direction of the war effort by organising technical information about weapons and their deployment in a format that could be passed on to politicians and the top brass. An honorary Major during the war, Ogilvie was knighted for his services in 1920.

The Grammar School can lay claim to producing another significant technocrat in the shape of Alfred Esslemont. His youth was spent studying developments in electrical engineering in Europe and the USA. Posts with several power companies in northern England gave him administrative and technical skills that fitted him for vital war work after 1914. Esslemont joined the Ministry of Munitions and by 1917 he was Director of its Optical Munitions and Glassware Division, 'responsible for the supply to the Forces of all instruments aiding human vision'.

Civilian readers of the school magazine in Aberdeen, skimming its pages before sending it off to a son or nephew on some distant Front, may have imagined that Esslemont had something to do with the production of naval telescopes. And he did. However, the technology used in the Great War, especially in its latter stages, had raced far ahead of the public's understanding. Electrical and electronic instruments now played a vital role in military communications and in the detection of the enemy. Many of the 'new weapons' depended upon instrumentation that needed specialised glass parts. In particular, the vital work being done by aerial photographic reconnaissance necessitated new higher standards of optical glass production in the factories now under Esslemont's directorate.

A second key post as Controller of Potash Production, essential for the manufacture of explosives, only underlined Esslemont's pivotal role in the British munitions industry. Under Esslemont's direction, a serious deficit in the production of scientific instruments for military use was transformed into an abundance. He was lauded profusely in the Commons for his exertions and made a Commander of the British Empire, the first Grammar FP to receive this newly created honour. Further responsibilities and honours would surely have come to Esslemont but for his untimely death in September 1918 aged forty-one.

Ogilvie, Esslemont and a third FP, James Pirie, all had a hand in the development of the Stokes mortar, one of the key weapons of the war. Once he had finally secured a green light for his weapon from a dithering Whitehall, Sir Wilfrid Stokes approached James Pirie, managing director of an industrial contractor in London, for help in manufacturing the gun. Both

Ogilvie and Esslemont were involved in the design process, as was Pirie's wife: 'for the making of the bubble which formed the spirit level in the clinomoter the service of Mrs Pirie had to be requisitioned, and in doing this important piece of work she latterly became very expert, and eventually worked direct for Woolwich Arsenal'. According to one apochryphal tale, Mrs Pirie's expertise allegedly stemmed from observations that she had made while using and cleaning kitchen utensils.

Other FPs performed less spectacular but no less important roles in the field of munitions. Sir George Stegman Gibb served on the Government's Committee for Production from 1915 to 1918 and was its chairman in the last year of the war. Inflation, rising commodity prices, a shortage of skilled labour and a 'vigorous' trades union movement all threatened British industrial war production. As a result, the Committee on Production was set up in 1915 to intervene in difficult local wage disputes. It was soon recognised as the national arbitration tribunal for wage and condition settlements in industries such as the foundry trades, chemicals and ship-building. Fifty trades unions signed up to accept its recommendations on rates of pay. The Committee's reputation for evenhandedness, helped limit the threat of industrial action during the war. At the local level, similar issues will have loomed large in the work of Robert Cook, managing director and chairman of the foundrymen Barry, Henry & Cook in West North Street. During the war Cook served as vice-chairman of the Aberdeen Munitions Committee which co-ordinated local industries that contributed to the war economy.

Several FPs held senior administrative posts within the Munitions Ministry itself, principally the Honorary Secretary & Treasurer of the FP Club James Milne, a chartered accountant and tax expert. Milne played an important role advising the government in the politically sensitive area of war-profiteering as an official in the Limitation of Profits division of the Munitions Ministry. There was public repugnance during the war at the idea of private companies making excessive profits from arms manufacturing, and the government was keen to get value for its money. Milne's acknowledged expertise on issues such as the Excess Profits Levy was invaluable in this complex and sensitive area. He later rendered advice to the government in his equally important role in charge of the Machine Tool Contract Directorate. These areas of endeavour may seem very dry when contrasted with the deeds of uniformed men. However by 1916 Britain was in a long war of attrition in which small resource efficiencies and cost savings mattered. Milne's work helped the government get more from the British industrial complex at a critical point in the war.

Chemistry also mattered in World War one. The Defence of the Realm Act passed on 8th August 1914 gave the Government powers to requisition industrial buildings and scientific facilities of national importance and the Rainham Chemical Works in east London was taken under Government control the very next day. It was the only source of military grade TNT in Britain at that early stage of the war. Within a year however TNT was being produced at a new purpose-built factory at Oldbury in the West Midlands. George Newlands, assistant in Geology at Aberdeen University in 1914, contributed to the war effort at this new HM Explosives Factory, first as a process chemist there and then as plant superintendent.

In the early 1870s Alfred Nobel built his first major dynamite plant at Ardeer near Stevenson on the Ayrshire coast, a site chosen for its relative isolation and its access to the sea via the Garnock and Irvine rivers. Ardeer was the largest dynamite factory in the world at the start of the Great War. Amongst its 13,000 strong workforce were at least two Grammar FPs. David Sharp, a lecturer at the Royal Technical College in Glasgow, worked as a chemist at Ardeer from August 1915 onwards. George Horatius McKenzie also worked there towards the end of the war, first as a chemist then as assistant superintendent in its Propulsive Department.

FPs also helped produce other chemicals used in the manufacture of explosives. John Brebner, a chemistry graduate of Glasgow Technical College, supervised the production of sulphuric acid in his role as general manager at Cunninghams Ltd in Leith. George Fraser served as a Pioneer Chemist in the RE Special Brigade until wounded in 1916. His war service continued however as Works Chemist at HM Factory Greetland near Halifax. Greetland was the main source of Lyddite or picric acid, a somewhat unstable high explosive substance which was distilled, dried and packed there before being sent to the shell-filling factories.

Chillwell near Nottingham was one of the twelve National Filling Factories organised by the government to supplement the production of the Woolwich Arsenal. Between 1914 and 1918 it finished over 19 million shells.

Harald Merrylees ran his own engineering company in Liverpool until 1916 when it was commandeered by the government. Merrylees was then required to help manage the Filled Shell Store at Chillwell, the largest ammunition stockpile in Europe. Alexander Smith also worked as manager of a National Filling Factory, no doubt thanks to his pre-war experience as the owner of a brass foundry in Birmingham.

In addition to these senior management posts, FPs also carried out a wide variety of roles in the munitions industry in research and design but also as hands-on makers, fillers and finishers of weapons; some almost certainly worked at the National Shell Factory in Aberdeen, formerly McKinnon's Iron Workshop in Spring Garden. Some spent the entire war employed in the munitions industry. William Barnett, an electrical apprentice with Miller Brothers, makers of optical and scientific instruments in George Street, stayed with the firm throughout the war. Another FP engineer, Alexander Reid, worked in the Munitions Ministry's Small Arms and Machine Gun department. The chemist Charles Cheyne, last seen escaping after dark from his rebellious Boer comrades in Bechuanaland, came to London once the war in South Africa was over and did munitions work at Woolwich until the Armistice.

The quality of munitions was a hot political issue in the first half of the war. Soldiers at the Front were rumoured to be angry at the high failure rate of shells; too many were duds unlike the better engineered products whizzing over from the German lines. Irish, socialist and even suffragette saboteurs were blamed for the inconsistency of product from Britain's munition factories. The Northcliffe press used information leaked from the Front to embarrass politicians and generals who were deemed to have failed the boys 'over there'. Inspection was tightened up and FPs were part of that process. Frederick Ewart, brother of the popular novelist Boyd Cable and a former gunner, was of one of numerous FPs who served in the Munitions Ministry's Inspection Department. The most senior inspectorial FP was probably Harry Wilson who had been an HM Inspector of Factories since 1892. During the war he sat on the government's Armaments Committee for Glasgow and West of Scotland and received the OBE in 1918.

Aberdeen's shipyards were busy places throughout the Great War and especially so after 1916 when German U-boats came perilously close to cutting Britain's supply lines. A huge effort was needed from Britain's shipyards to replace the terrible wastage in merchant and naval shipping. Unsurprisingly then, Walter Jameson found himself being asked by the government's Shipping Controller to resign his commission in the Royal Defence Corps and concentrate on his day job as Director of the John Duthie Torry Shipbuilding Company. Another FP engaged in war-time shipbuilding was Alexander McRae who served his engineering apprenticeship with Hall Russell's. By 1914 he was a naval architect with Swan Hunter in Newcastle. During the later war years he held senior positions at their Neptune Works and was awarded the MBE in 1918.

Several FPs contributed to the development of new naval weapons. The engineer William Anderson returned from the USA in 1915 to work at the Royal Naval Torpedo Factory near Gourock. Benjamin Disraeli Milne was more concerned with stopping torpedoes getting through to their target. Before the war, the Admiralty had experimented with various anti-submarine devices. One of these was the paravane, a winged bomb trailed alongside or behind a ship and charged with enough explosive to destroy a hostile submarine if contact was made. Milne worked on paravanes and 'other devices for the destruction of submarines' as did James R Milne, lecturer in Natural Philosophy at Edinburgh before the war. A physicist in the Royal Navy's Anti-Submarine Division, Milne later worked in the Admiralty's research station at Wemyss Bay on the Clyde.

FPs overseas were also heavily involved in making munitions. Alexander Taylor's career in commercial law prospered when he left Aberdeen for Canada and by 1917 he was on the board of several major corporations there. Writing to Watt, Taylor described the impact that the war had had upon the various companies controlled by Taylor's employer, the Lake Superior Corporation: 'One of those companies is the Algoma Steel Corporation, the largest steel company in Canada. It has for some time been turning out huge shell orders for the British Government. We are having an extremely busy time, but the cause is well worth it'. Another Canadian 'munitions FP' was Ernest Young who moved to Vancouver in 1911 to manage the North Shore Iron Works there which became a major source of Allied material in subsequent years.

Several FPs had a hand in the production of munitions on the southern side of the 49th Parallel. Alister Mackinnon began his engineering career at the Loco Works in Inverurie but in due course progressed to the slightly more exotic location of Buenos Aires. In 1915 he was a munitions inspector in Sheffield where the government had three National Projectile Factories. The following year he joined the British War Mission to the USA inspecting the quality of the output from American munitions factories that was destined for use by British armed forces. The school magazine recorded that McKinnon was travelling up to 3000 miles each week[!] between America's centres of heavy industry such as Cleveland and Chicago. He was awarded the MBE in 1918 and three years later was working somewhere pleasant again, this time as a civil engineer in Paris.

John Ogg CA worked as financial controller for the Aetna Explosives Company of New York, formed in 1914 to meet the expected rise in demand for explosives from combatant nations. It quickly amassed lucrative contracts worth over $30 million to supply France and Russia with TNT, picric acid and the fulminate of mercury used in detonating fuses. John's brother William, also an FP and CA, sought his fortune in the US as well. By the time America joined the war in 1917, William was Controller of several metals and transport companies vital to the US war machine. By 1918 he was President of the American Zinc, Lead and Smelting Company.

Far from the skyscrapers of Manhattan, two more Grammarians did their duty ensuring that the best quality arms and munitions were available to British troops. Lt Col James Black acted as chemical examiner for the government in the Punjab, testing the munitions supplies destined for army use. Capt Angus Urquhart RGA was stationed at the Dum Dum Arsenal near Calcutta where the soft-pointed expanding bullet of the same name was trialled in 1896. Between 1914 and 1920 Urquhart served at six ammunition centres in British India and was Major Superintendent of the main cordite factory on the sub-continent.

Timber was a key military commodity and its supply quickly came under the auspices of the Munitions Ministry. FPs again played an important role in this aspect of the war effort. Robert Troup had worked in the Indian Forest Service since 1897, latterly as director of the Burma Forest School and the Indian Forest Research Institute. In the last two years of the war he served as Military Controller of Indian Timber. Nearer home, several FPs were involved in the ruthless harvesting of Scotland's forests that virtually denuded the country and necessitated the formation of the Forestry

Commission in 1919. Ormonde Kilgour was typical of this group. Discharged from the Gordons in 1915, he completed his diploma in Agriculture at Aberdeen the following year. He worked as a Surveying Officer for the Timber Board throughout the latter years of the war. George Paterson MC, also invalided out of the Gordons, was attached to the Forestry Directorate in France, serving in Bordeaux and Paris until 1919.

The FPs named in this chapter are only a selection of those who worked to build up the supplies to the imperial war machine. In contrast, Henry Reid helped tidy things up once the show was over. Once it was clear that the new German Government would in fact accept the Peace Settlement handed to them, the British Civil Service began the laborious process of negotiating contract cancellations and reducing the immense piles of war material sitting in warehouses throughout Britain and the Empire. Major Reid, a surveyor and contractor before the war, was attached to the Government Disposals Board and played his part in the process of selling off surplus war supplies. By the end of 1919, the government had recouped £141 million from disposal sales but that was a mere four per cent or so of the estimated £3,450 million that Britain had spent in the long struggle.

Chapter 20

Medics at War

Grammar FPs made an immense contribution to the medical side of the war effort. During the war, over two hundred and eighty Grammarians served in the Royal Army Medical Corps, of whom around 235 were qualified physicians. Fourteen FPs served in the Indian Medical Service while another twenty were attached to the medical services of the Royal and Merchant Navies. Sixteen Grammarians served in the medical services of the armed forces of Australia, New Zealand, South Africa and Canada. Two FP medics were in the US Army Medical Corps, while one Dr Cornelius Suvoong, served as medical officer in charge of the Chinese Republic's main arsenal at Hanyan [now Wuhan in Central China]. Suvoong was promoted to the rank of Mandarin due to his efficiency in the post. To this body of men should be added several FP dental surgeons in uniform, a number of medics attached to British expeditionary forces in the 'lesser' colonies' and over thirty civilian medics who are recorded as having made a significant contribution to the military's medical arrangements during the war. Grammar medics served in every major theatre of the war around the globe; while most performed their work in the casualty clearing stations, field ambulances and hospitals of the Western Front, many others were active in the very different conditions of the Middle East, East Africa and the Balkans, often holding senior rank and winning high honours.

Grammar medics not only shared the dangers of the front-line with the men they tended but they took their share of casualties. Capt Arthur Kellas, a field ambulance commander and brother of the famous mountaineer, was killed at Gallipoli in 1915. Capt Joseph Milne DSO, Medical Officer with the King's Liverpool Regiment, was killed near Ypres in February 1917. Milne was well over military age when he left his practice in the east end of Aberdeen to join the Highland Casualty Clearing Station in 1915. A colleague in the RAMC noted that while 'trench work does not agree with most men on the verge of fifty, Joseph seemed to thrive on it'. A volunteer for the bloody mess of front-line medicine, Milne 'repeatedly tended the wounded under heavy shell fire, utterly regardless of his personal safety. No man ever earned the DSO more worthily'. Other fatalities included Alastair Peter MC, Medical Officer with the Seaforths, who died of wounds sustained under fire in France in 1917 and Lt James Rae RAMC who drowned that year when the troopship HMS *Arcadian* was torpedoed off the Greek Coast with the loss of 277 lives.

Numerous medics also died later from exhaustion or illness contracted on duty. Capt Clement Macleod MC served with several front-line medical units in France from the early days of the war until invalided home in March 1919. He never recovered from 'the results of his long and arduous period of active service' and died at his Murtle home in 1920. When the war broke out, Duncan Burgess, a medical professor of international note, was appointed Officer in Charge of the large military hospital in Sheffield. The strain of the work proved too much for a man at the end of his career and Lt Col Burgess died in 1917 aged 66. Another elderly Grammar medic in uniform was James Beattie of Cocklarachy near Huntly. As a young medical student, Beattie had journeyed several times to the Arctic aboard whaling ships. Entering the RAMC in 1915 when already in his sixties, he served at Gallipoli and survived the sinking by torpedo of the hospital ship *Asturias* in 1917. He died a year later on board HMHS *Aberdonian* at Southampton from a combination of exhaustion and pneumonia. Capt William Millar, a veteran of the Balkan campaign, died at Dieppe of exhaustion and pneumonia in October 1918. Dr Clifford Bell RAMC began his war service in the X-Ray department of the 1st Scottish General Hospital in Aberdeen in 1915 and died in that institution in February 1919 aged 48.

In all, a total of eighteen Grammar medics died as a result of the war, either killed in action or dying later from wounds or from their exertions during the war. A number of FP medics were also taken prisoner including Major James McConnachie MC, Capt John McKenzie MC, Capt John Elder and Capt Alexander Simpson: all captured by the Germans during their great push in Spring 1918.

The enormous effort and sacrifices made by this group of men did not go unrecognized. Grammar medics were awarded a total of eighty six decorations; thirty-one awards of the Military Cross, four with Bar;

seventeen awards of the DSO, two with Bar; eighteen awards of the newly-created honours of the military OBE, MBE and CBE while eight received decorations from the governments of Greece, Serbia, Belgium and France. In addition, of the nine Grammar FPs admitted to the chivalric orders for their service at a senior level in the war, six were medics.

The citations for many of these awards describe men working selflessly under immense pressure at the front-line, disregarding the dangers around them in order to concentrate upon the endless task of trying to save the lives of damaged comrades - and sometimes those of the foe. Dr Murdo Macrae was awarded the Military Cross in 1917. The *London Gazette* described how, lacking stretcher-bearers, Macrae went out into no-man's-land and 'carried in seven or eight wounded men who otherwise would have died in the snow'. Dr Anthony McCreadie won his MC 'for conspicuous gallantry and devotion to duty under heavy shell fire and in most trying circumstances'. McCreadie worked alone for thirty-six hours in an exposed position, carrying in the wounded when necessary. For many front-line medics, this was all in a day's work; McCreadie had already displayed similar acts of heroism on numerous occasions before he was himself wounded and gassed. Dr Archibald Anderson won his MC by leading his stretcher-bearers under heavy shell fire to collect twenty-five wounded men who were lying within fifty yards of the German lines. Dr James McConnachie displayed a similar disregard for his personal safety. In charge of a front-line collecting post for the wounded, he ignored sustained heavy shelling and several counter-attacks by German troops.

Other citations for FP medics describe their refusal to abandon the wounded despite their proximity to the front line; Hugh Davidson DSO and Bar only left his advanced dressing station when ordered to do so. Kenneth Mackenzie DSO was honoured for staying in contact with retreating infantrymen, and searching the battlefield for wounded men in the face of heavy fire. Major Herbert Milne MC and Bar remained at his dressing station for three days under continuous shelling. When the post was hit by a shell killing three men, Milne patched up fourteen wounded around him and led them to safety just before the post took another direct hit.

Several eminent Grammarian medics held important posts during the war. In June 1915 the school magazine noted that Sir William Watson Cheyne Bart CB and Honorary Surgeon-in-Ordinary to King George had been engaged as a senior consultant to the Admiralty. A year later Sir William was admitted to the Most Distinguished Order of St Michael and St George Cheyne [KCMG] in the New Year's Honours List. He served as Consulting Surgeon at HQ Royal Naval Hospital at Chatham, undertook tours of duty in Malta and Gallipoli in 1915 and ended the war with the final rank of Surgeon Rear-Admiral. Elected MP for the universities of Edinburgh and St Andrews in 1917, Watson Cheyne was a member of a special parliamentary committee sent to France that autumn to investigate the state of the Army Medical Services there.

Other medical FPs held high rank in the Royal Navy such as Sir James Smith MVO CB Deputy Surgeon-General RN who commanded the naval hospital on Malta and was promoted to the rank of Surgeon Rear-Admiral in 1916. He was also admitted to the rank of Officer in the French *Légion d'honneur* in 1918. Lt Col John Binnie, of Kansas City Missouri but once of Fonthill Road, rose to Consulting Surgeon of the US Army Medical Corps in France, winning a personal citation from General Pershing for his endeavours. Lt Col Farquhar McLennan DSO, whose family hailed from Achnashellach, was appointed DADG of the Army Medical Service at the War Office in late 1915 but he managed to escape his desk in Whitehall serving as officer commanding of various field ambulances and hospitals in the last year of the war. McLennan was only one of several FPs who performed senior administrative roles on the medical side of the war effort such as Colonel Charles Profeit DSO CMG and Companion of the Order of the Star of India who organised military medical capabilities on the Western Front and for the police operations on the North-West Frontier in 1919-20.

The most controversial medical Grammarian of the Great War was arguably Sir [Robert] John Collie CMG whose professional expertise was of great interest to the government and the public in wartime. Collie first came to public attention in the pre-war years for his work in exposing cases where workers feigned injury in order to take advantage of the new legislation on workmen's compensation. As Medical Examiner for several public bodies such as the London County Council, the hardworking Collie did his best to ensure that public money was only disbursed to the genuinely deserving. His views and his methods were publicised in two books *Fraud and its detection in Accident Insurances Cases* (1912) and *Malingering and Feigned*

Sicknesses (1913). His efforts to protect the public purse brought a knighthood in 1912 but also an unhelpful reputation in the yellow press as 'the relentless foe of the fraudster'.

During the war, the concept of 'shell-shock' had begun to evolve as a way of explaining the behaviour of men who had broken down on active service. Collie was sceptical of this condition which he felt could easily be feigned or exaggerated, 'either consciously or unconsciously'. The Army was quick to enlist Collie as a temporary colonel in its medical services and use his skills in detecting malingerers. By 1917 Sir John was both Director of Neurasthenic Institutions and President of the Special Medical Board on Nuerasthenic and Shell Shock Cases. In 1918 he also headed up the board of the Pensions Ministry responsible for assessing which injured servicemen were genuinely worthy of a service pension and which should receive the government's preferred, cheaper option of a one-off cash gratuity.

Collie's critics portrayed him as an unthinking man who simply dismissed the shell-shocked victims of industrial warfare as 'inadequates'. He was however known to be an intelligent, listening physician who worked exceptionally hard to support and rehabilitate those who he felt were genuinely war-damaged. He founded one of the first homes for servicemen suffering from 'nerves', and a pioneering psychotherapeutic clinic at Lancaster Gate in London at the end of the war. Collie was clearly a complex man, caught between his professional obligations and the prevailing public attitudes of his time which generally viewed the new ideas about battle trauma with suspicion. When reviewing Collie's publications, Theodore Watt took a positive view and well captured a man trying to bring all his abilities to bear on the difficult job at hand: 'Sir John Collie is certainly the greatest medical detective of our day. He reveals himself in this work, especially in the chapter devoted to malingering in the Army, as a doctor of broad human sympathy, with imagination and a rare power of observing important details. He is never harsh, for the malingerer who has his close attention, has also in a manner his appreciation. Knowing the difficulties of the game, he is able to assess the merit of a good performance. Detection is the more valuable when it is hardly won'. Sir John was made a Companion of St Michael and St George in 1918.

Other medical FPs worked in the fields of psychology and neurology without attracting as much attention as Collie. Major Frank

Collie RAMC, partner in a prominent London medical practice, served as an adviser to the Psychological Board from 1916 to 1919. Thomas Lumsden was Medical Officer in charge of the Electrical Department of the Special Surgical Hospital in North London in the latter stages of the war. Dr Harold Finlayson, a medical officer in the Royal Navy and the RAMC, latterly served as a member of the Special Neurological Board of the Ministry of Pensions. He was one of numerous FP medics whose skills in assessing the physical and mental damage that servicemen had incurred were required by government ministries after the war. Typical of this group was Murdo Macrae MC, originally of Shieldaig but a government medical officer in New Zealand in 1914. Macrae was attached to the Argylls and the Northumberland Fusiliers from 1915 to 1918 but transferred to the Ministry of Pensions as the war came to a conclusion.

Not all Grammarians in the military medical service were qualified physicians. Sixty-five FPs from non-medical walks of life are known to have served in the RAMC and other medical support units. A small number helped in the Royal Navy's Auxiliary Sick Berth Reserve. Four of these were aboard the hospital ships and two were appointed on entry as Surgeon Sub-Lieutenants. Most however entered the RAMC as privates, performing a wide variety of support roles such as motor ambulance drivers, stretcher-bearers, wound-dressers, water orderlies and assistants in military operating theatres and dental surgeries. Around half of the group were stationed at hospitals at home, several serving at 1st Scottish Medical Hospital in Aberdeen. Of the remainder, the largest group of twenty did all or most of their service on the Western Front. Thirteen were posted to the Balkans or the Middle East. Three saw service in southern Russia and Persia.

For some of these non-commissioned FPs, the RAMC was their first experience of military life. After a year or so in its ranks, several transferred to combatant roles in other units. William Joss was invalided out of his Field Ambulance Unit in January 1916 but returned to the fray as an officer in the Northumberland Fusiliers with whom he won the MC and Bar. Before the war, James Mathewson Milne was a schoolmaster with a doctorate in literature from Rennes University. After an initial spell as a private in the Lowland Field Ambulance in 1915, he ended the war as a captain in charge of Anti-Gas Training in the Machine Gun Corps Training Brigade. Several RAMC medical attendants such as Private George Kelly and John Elmslie, a Royal Navy Sick Berth Attendant, undertook medical degrees after being demobbed. William Joss was severely wounded in 1918 but graduated MB ChB in 1923. The experience of war led the Rev Alexander Catto and Rev George Wright in a different direction. They both did spells as privates in the RAMC but then transferred to the Army Chaplains Department. William Todd, an FP in the Australian Infantry Dental Service, never reached the war. In November 1918, his troopship had just reached the Panama Canal when news of the Armistice was quickly followed by fresh orders to return back home to Sydney.

Like their qualified officers, medical orderlies shared the dangers and rigours that faced their combatant comrades. Charles Cable Cromar Bruce was a corporal in the Canadian Army Medical Corps who served in France from May 1916. He was killed at Vimy Ridge in May 1918. Several others were severely wounded and some invalided home, notably Thomas Wardop, the sixty-seven year old retired bank manager who wore himself out serving as an ambulance driver in the French and Italian armies.

Several Grammar medics wrote about their experiences in the school magazine. These pieces sometimes contained information and insights that the Army Censor might have preferred left unexpressed. Captain George Shand was mobilised on August 5th 1914, the day after war was declared, and spent the first months of the war tending to the wounded of the original BEF, the Old Contemptibles, throughout their retreat from Mons. He remained at the Front until 1917 when he was invalided out. He then served as a bacteriologist at the Royal Army Military College at Millbank in central London, involved in research into Trench Fever.

The magazine edition for February 1915 contained Captain Shand's description of the conditions that medics faced in those first frantic weeks of the war the previous autumn:

'I was posted to No. 6 Clearing Hospital. We had rather a rough time at the beginning. We were at St Quentin and Aulnoy getting the Mons and Le Cateau wounded. We just managed to clear from St Quentin in time with nearly 500 wounded but minus all our kit and equipment. Then we were on the Aisne, near Soissons for some three weeks. We had four days marching to get there - four days I shan't forget in a hurry. Some mornings we started at 3am and we never stopped before 9 at night. Added to that was wet weather and the fact that we hadn't had an opportunity of being refitted with horses, blankets or

waterproof sheets and consequently had it a little harder than we otherwise might.

From the Aisne we migrated to Bethune. There we had a huge school, and in a fortnight we passed through over 4,000 wounded. Many a night we got in 200 at a time. Our receiving room or surgery was a dining hall almost as big as the Grammar Hall. You can imagine what it looked like full of wounded with only six medical officers to tackle them. It takes a little doing to find beds for 600 wounded when you only have 200 stretchers and mattresses. In November the Germans shelled us out of the place, and we had to do a hurried move'.

As the war settled down into trench stalemate, systems for processing the wounded were established behind the lines. Although these were hastily improvised, medical facilities at the Front could be better than those that some troops were accustomed to back home. Soldiers at the Front also soon came to realise that a trip to the army doctor had its perks, as this FP reported in 1916:

'Well, I have had my first experience of a hospital. The motor ambulance trundled me back the six miles from our base to the field ambulance. The man in charge was Colonel Robertson, sometime doctor in Albyn Place. I had tea with the doctors and was then sent to bed. The ward was nice, airy and clean and the fresh air was delightful after the stuffy dug-outs. That morning the Major came to see us and said we had to go back another stage. We were sent to a hospice which I take to be a poorhouse, and are domiciled in a wooden hut in the front garden. There are 14 beds - with sheets! We have indeed got to the back of the Front. The doctor said that I had probably trench fever, but to stay up for lunch and go to bed after. There are nurses - also evidence of returning civilisation. One is going around dispensing sweets now - rather a pretty one too! Have seen nothing for ages but these terrible old French women'.

In contrast to this jolly trip, descriptions of army medical treatment by those on the receiving end could be graphic. In June 1916 Theodore Watt printed an anonymous letter from an FP wounded earlier in the war. The letter was written with his left hand for reasons that were described in a blunt, matter-of-fact manner. It gives one wounded man's view of what befell him. It also describes the process of medical care that many thousands of Great War troops experienced:

'Up we got. I wasn't a minute out when thud came a bullet on my right elbow and down I flopped, too late of course. It was a smack of a different kidney but it was bearable. There was a flash on my right, and then something hit me with what I can only describe, in the language of the Halfpenny Horrible, as a sickening thud. I felt as if my arm was blown into fragments and for a while I really thought it was blown off below the elbow, for my sleeve was torn off and the sight underneath was not encouraging.

I can't say I took it in a Spartan manner. I roared at full concert pitch and then fell to cursing the Germans and the War and everything connected with it. I think it was instinctively to prevent my mind dwelling on the horror at my side, for I never for an instant lost consciousness. I soon gave up making a row and started to try and claw myself into the ground with my left hand. The ground was soft, so I succeeded in scratching a little hollow for my head and I lay there. The cannonade was frightful; shrapnel came screaming overhead, generally bursting a little behind me, and time and time again I was struck with earth and stones kicked up. From the left the machine gun played intermittently and in front I could see the flash of musketry fire when I ventured to raise my head. Everywhere the air was alive with bullets singing past. Once I tried to shift my pack from my back - a too prominent object in the landscape - and at once a dozen bullets struck the earth within a radius of five feet of me, so I lay still. Except for some dead or wounded near me there was not a soul to be seen in any direction. By this time I was certain that my chance of escaping was absolutely nil, and having accepted this fact I got quite calm and indifferent.

The blood was coming from my arm in little spouts, so I knew a small artery must be cut, and I remembered how Petronius in Quo Vadis slit one of his and awaited the end, and I wondered whether mine would be that way or via another piece of shrapnel. I thought the odds were very much in favour of the shrapnel. Then the fusillade increased in violence and the shells burst nearer me. I knew it was all up and I turned my face upwards because I didn't want to get hit on the back, and I lay there watching the shells burst as if it had been an exhibition of fireworks. Well, as you know, none of them did burst over me or I wouldn't be telling the tale.

About two hours after, the firing lulled a little and moved away to the left. One or two of the heaps near me started to crawl away out of sight without getting hit, so I made up my mind to have a shot at it too. I managed with some trouble to rid myself of my equipment and left with scarcely a pang all the beautiful socks and shirts and tobacco that I had been carrying about. Some khaki-clad figures had stolen up and lined a hedge on my right, so *off I stumbled in their direction, tenderly carrying my arm, which I was pleased to find still attached to me. Two of them helped me over to the first field-dressing station, and there they bound me up, put me on a stretcher, and carried me a mile or so to a cottage, where by good luck a motor car was just about to move off. I was planked into it and off we went. After 40 minutes drive, we landed at a hospital in a small town, and my arm, which was still leaking considerably, was again dressed by a young RAMC officer. Then a dozen or so of us were put in a motor ambulance crouched up in a sitting position, and we drove off. We had the most miserable journey I've ever had - bumping over the abominable roads. It came to an end at last and we were stuck in the waiting room of the hospital. The wards were just about full up, so finally they put me in the officers' ward. They cut my clothes off me and took them away to be destroyed, for they were all sodden with blood, leaving me without a possession except the things I had in my pockets. It was nice though to get into a clean bed, and after getting my arm dressed and an injection of morphia I slept like a top.*

Next day, Sunday, I smelt chloroform for the first time and I came out of it quite nicely, without ever feeling sick. They cleaned up the wound and put in some stitches. On Wednesday the word came that we were all to be cleared out and sent back to England. So we got taken down to the hospital train and reached Boulogne about 6.30pm only to find that there were two other trains full of wounded waiting for the boat, so they shunted us down here to be the Duchess's guests. By 8 o'clock most of us were safely within these gorgeous halls [the Duchess of Westminster's War Hospital at Le Touquet] and getting into the most inviting-looking snowy-sheeted beds, and a little later we were eating hot soup from Her Grace's own hand. We seem to have come into a very Paradise and are lucky indeed to be here in what is probably the best hospital in France.

This has grown into something more like the manuscript of a novel than a letter and it's Sunday evening by now - my second day's hard writing. I believe I'm beginning to 'form a hand' in this beastly left-handed writing and if only I could hold the paper firm I could do better. I hope I haven't been too realistic in my description of unpleasant things, but as it all ends happily (at least I hope so) perhaps you won't mind'.

Chapter 21

Volunteers and Padres

In 1914, the YMCA mobilised almost as quickly as some of the combatant armies. Over 200 YMCA centres across Britain's transport network sprung up within ten days of Britain's declaration of war, ready to offer refreshment and reading materials to any troops passing through. These first centres were often little more than makeshift stalls providing a mug of tea or hot chocolate to men en route to training bases and the southern ports. By November however, the 'YM' network had spread across the Channel and its distinctive red triangle sign would soon became a common sight in French and Flemish towns.

As in Britain, the YMCA initially concentrated its resources at ports such as Boulogne and strategic railway junctions such as Abbeville. The military authorities appreciated the value of the work done by voluntary organisations in lifting the spirits of the men, so when the YMCA wanted to extend its support work nearer to the Front in 1915, permission was readily granted from on high. The YMCA built a series of recreation huts equipped with cooking facilities, reading and games areas, and large enough to host touring entertainment companies and cinema shows. Closer still to the firing line, smaller refuges were often created close to the Casualty Clearing Stations where men returning from action could find respite while waiting for the dressing staff to attend to lesser wounds.

The YMCA operation in France and Flanders was impressive. At any point after 1915, almost 1800 YMCA volunteer workers were on duty somewhere along the Western Front. Although many were women, workers closer to the Front were often men either too old for military service or deemed unfit for military service but still eager to 'do their bit'. Equally impressive was the huge response to the call for volunteers from a whole range of local and national charity organisations and churches. The Army, usually but not always, provided its men with their three basic needs of food, clothing and shelter. It also knew how to keep them occupied with work and sport, but it generally left the task of relieving the tedium of the men's spare time to the voluntary organisations.

As the war proceeded, the improvised efforts of the first nine months of the war were replaced by more co-ordinated and systematic approaches to providing entertainment and support for servicemen. The bureaucratisation of even this element of the war effort can be detected in the school magazine notes concerning volunteer FPs in the latter part of the war. These record the administrative work of FPs such as Sir John Duthie of Cairnbulg who served as Senior Assistant Director-General of Voluntary War Organisations for which he was made a Knight Commander of the British Empire KBE in June 1918. Nevertheless, there was always room in the British war effort for initiatives by the talented and energetic individual: in 1915 Dr John Cowan, a GP working in Worcestershire, founded the Malvern Royal Naval Convalescent Hospital which continued to operate through to the end of the war funded wholly by voluntary contributions.

Twenty-four FPs are known to have served with the YMCA. Of these, seventeen were ministers with charges back in the British Isles. Fourteen were ministers in the Presbyterian United Free Church, with one Baptist pastor, a Congregationalist and Thomas Clugston Stuart, a minister of the Irish Presbyterian Church in Coleraine. Most of these men did relatively shorts spells at the Front of six or less months but some were in it for the longer haul. One early FP volunteer was Peter Diack who worked for the YMCA at Rouen and then in Egypt in the first two years of the war. As the number of trainees and wounded built up in commandeered accommodation throughout Scotland, Diack returned home to help run YMCA facilities in Aberdeen and Edinburgh. The Congregationalist Reverend Joseph Carnegie first volunteered at a convalescent hospital near his church in Leicester, then did an eighteen month long stint at Dieppe. He travelled into Germany with the occupying British Army over the Rhine in April 1919 and stayed there until the end of that year. Kenneth McLennan's work for the YMCA took him from his UFC charge in Fortrose to France and then the Black Sea via Salonika where he served until March 1920.

The Reverend James Webster of Marnoch was an old 'China hand'. Originally a chemist, he had gone to east in 1882 as an ordained missionary of the United Presbyterian Church of Scotland. Webster played an important role in organising relief for Chinese refugees

145

in the Russo-Japanese war of 1904-05. In the Great War, he worked in France from 1917 to 1920 organising the support provided by the YMCA for the Chinese Labour Corps. He was awarded the Order of Wen Hu - the Striped Tiger -by the Republic of China.

Of the lay YMCA volunteers, some like Charles Buchan did their bit prior to enlisting in the Forces. Buchan did a year with the YMCA before joining the Gordons in February 1916. James Stuart, an older man with an long career in the British administration of Fiji, spent much of 1918 back in Europe where he did a four-month tour of duty with the YMCA at their hut at Taranto in southern Italy. Fresh lecturers were always in demand in the volunteer huts to help bored soldiers while away the dull evenings at rear bases. The troops probably listened very attentively to Alexander Findlay, a chemistry professor at Aberdeen. During the war he carried out 'chemical investigations' for the Government, something that was sure to be of vital interest to trench-dwellers who lived in fear of the gas cloud.

A series of lighter evenings was provided by volunteers such as Alfred Milne, Head of Music at Dundee High School, who supervised musical activities in YMCA huts and centres, and by Robert MacLennan, a well known playwright who led the Scottish Firing Line Concert Party that toured the huts on the Western Front over Christmas 1916.

Around twenty-five FP volunteers made a contribution to the work of the Red Cross. Most worked on the medical side of the organisation's work, serving as wound dressers at Red Cross medical stations; Gordon Key, a medical student, did a spell at the Rouen casualty centre throughout the first nine months of the war. Others, like James Jamieson were dressers on hospital ships. Jamieson served for a while on the luxurious steam yacht *Liberty* which had originally been built in Leith for the American publisher John Pulitzer. Others were ambulance drivers on the Western Front, notably the Rev Patrick Gordon, minister at Glenbervie, who did a three year stint with the Red Cross and was awarded the French *Croix de Guerre*.

Many of the Red Cross FPs were medics either awaiting call-up to the RAMC or too old to join its ranks. William Leslie MC served as a surgeon with the Russian Red Cross in 1914 before spending the rest of the war on the Western Front in the RAMC. He eventually returned to Russia in 1918 as part of the Allied Expedition. Other medics such as Alexander Reid, a surgeon in Inverness, were older civilians who did their bit in Red

Cross hospitals back in Blighty. As with most other aspects of the war, Grammarians ended up running things. Several FPs held senior positions in the Red Cross and were honoured for their work notably John Riddell MA MB CM LL.D MVO. Riddell was the surgeon in charge of the naval wards at Aberdeen Royal Infirmary and also the Red Cross Commissioner for North East Scotland. He was awarded the CBE in 1917.

FP clergymen were also keen to do their bit and there were two volunteers for the Army Chaplains Department in the very first Muster Roll of volunteers compiled by Theodore Watt in October 1914. In addition to the reverend FPs helping as volunteers, another forty-eight served as military padres, some in the Army Chaplains Department attached to specific military units, some as Royal Naval Chaplains working aboard ship or at HM dockyards and RN hospitals. Of these forty-eight FPs, twenty were Church of Scotland ministers, seventeen belonged to the United Free Church, six were Episcopalian, two Church of England and two Roman Catholic. The last in this group, Eugene de Faye, was a pastor in the Reformed Church of France and a professor at the Sorbonne who served with the 32nd French Army Corps from 1915 to 1917.

Over at the Front, the main Christian denominations ran hut systems similar to the YM network. The Church of Scotland ran more than twenty-five centres manned by around 350 volunteers. The FPs George Knight in 1917 and Andrew Angus in 1918 both worked in the Scottish Churches' Huts. The Rev George Wright, who ended the war as Chalpain to GHQ France, also worked in the huts before joining the RAMC as a private. The Salvation Army, practical as ever, not only ran its own huts but contributed over thirty Salvation Army Motor Ambulances and a pool of trained drivers and crew.

The service and bravery of FP chaplains at the Front was recognised and two were awarded the Military Cross. Father Joseph McHardy MC, a student at the Scots College in Valladolid and then a professor at Blairs, was wounded alongside the Tyneside Scottish in 1917. The Rev Professor David Nichol MC served as a chaplain in France, Belgium, Salonika, Egypt and Palestine from 1915 to 1918. John Macrae was awarded the Belgian *Croix de Guerre* for his service from 1915-1917. James Soutter, a Stockholm Olympian in 1912 and minister at the Scots Kirk in Nairobi, served as the Senior Presbyterian Chaplain with the East

African Expeditionary Force from 1914 to 1916. He was mentioned in dispatches by General Smuts. Another FP divine who was mentioned was the Rev Robert Burnett, attached to the Argylls in Egypt and Syria. The Rev Alexander Spence paid a heavy price for his involvement in the war effort. Spence served at the Scottish Churches' Hut at Trouville during the war and then ministered to the Army of Occupation in Western Germany in 1919. He died of pneumonia at Cologne Military Hospital later that year.

Several FP chaplains were attached to the RAMC, often serving as ambulance men or stretcher-bearers. One such was David Rees, a United Free Church minister in Ayrshire who resigned his charge and enlisted as a private in early 1915. He served with Field Ambulances for the next four years, except for a spell when he was invalided home from Salonika in 1916. William Harper was a Church Army chaplain at the Somme before working for the RAMC at various home camps in 1918. David Munro's war service began as a private in the Gordons but ended in France with the Home Counties Field Ambulance in April 1919. Three reverend FPs served on hospital ships; Father Joseph McHardy MC did tours of duty on HMHS *Glenart Castle* to Canada and in the Mediterranean; Father Joseph McClement also served on hospital ships throughout the war; Charles Cowan ministered on the hospital carrier *Carisbrooke Castle* but was at Jutland on the dreadnought HMS *Canada*.

Others found alternative ways of doing 'something useful'; the Rev Alexander McBain spent the first thirteen months of the war guarding German prisoners in Ireland. Donald McDonald of the Free Presbyterian Church in Portree and John Cameron of the UF Church in Hopeman both used their fluency in Gaelic to minister to Highland sailors and dock staff at Portsmouth, Devenport and Chatham. Some FP men of the cloth felt the need to assume a more active role in the conflict: the Rev Cecil Simpson answered the nation's call, resigning his charge in Elgin and meeting his death as a lieutenant in the Seaforths in the spring of 1917. The Rev Colin Kerr left his parish of Kettins in Forfarshire to become a gunner in the RGA. He later served in the Special Brigade of the Royal Engineers but returned to his original calling in June 1917 when he was appointed as an Army Chaplain. Alexander Monro was minister in Ancrum, Roxburghshire before the war. He served in the Gordons in France in 1915 till invalided home. After a spell as a captain in the West Riding Regiment, in 1918 he was transferred to the Ministry of Health with responsibility for the arrangements for the repatriation of British refugees and British civilian prisoners of war. He received the OBE in 1920.

Some servicemen may have derided the chaplains as 'holy Willies', but most troops, coming from a society that was deeply imbued with Christian values, welcomed their presence. One anonymous FP stressed how much he enjoyed attending the chaplain's services for 'after being kept safe for 18 days, a couple of church services is a very small thanks-offering'. The FP also noted the practical support that chaplains provided: 'The padre has started running a canteen in the trenches, where men can buy tinned fruit, biscuits, chocolate etc'. A willingness to share the discomforts and dangers faced by the men usually won over any deriders. One particular Highland padre certainly passed muster due to his willingness to spend time 'in the support line with us, in order that he might see how it was working. He is an old sport, our padre; many of them would not live in the trenches. I showed him over the place and took him round the saps and the firing line'.

Chapter 22

Running the Imperial War Machine

Running the nation, the Empire and the war effort was an immense task and one in which many Grammar FPS were involved, sometimes at the very highest levels. Sir James Scorgie Meston LL.D, CSI, KCSI and later Baron Meston of Agra and Dunnottar studied at King's College Aberdeen and Balliol College Oxford after leaving the Grammar in 1880. He then enjoyed a stellar career in the Indian Civil Service in which he held many high posts on the legislative and financial side of British administration in India. In March 1917 he was one of the small number of imperial representatives invited to join with British government ministers in the first meetings of the Imperial War Cabinet, a ground-breaking moment in the evolution of the Empire's colonies into Commonwealth Dominions.

In his time in Whitehall, Meston may have met up with a fellow Grammarian, the Rt Hon. Robert Munro KC, MP for Roxburgh and Selkirk and Secretary of State for Scotland. Another knighted FP and an expert on international law, Sir John Macdonell KCB, was appointed in late 1918 to chair the government committee charged with investigating enemy breaches of the international agreements on conduct in wartime. Also in late 1918, Sir George Stegman Gibb resigned from the chairmanship of the Government's Committee on Production to concentrate on his work as chairman of the National Road Board and devote more time to his support for the League of Nations Society. In addition, one of the school's most prestigious FPs, the colonial administrator Sir William MacGregor GCMG CB, was sworn in as a member of the Privy Council in 1915.

Numerous Grammarians served in the British Foreign Office during the war. John Locke Irvine was stationed at the British Legation in Copenhagen from 1916 to 1919. Arthur Chalmers plied his trade as a diplomat in the Far East, fulfilling spells as Consul General in Yokohama and Seoul and was made CMG in 1917. William Peters, a Carnegie Fellow resident in Moscow when the war began, initially worked for the Russian government department concerned with restricting supplies to the enemy. After the Soviet coup in late 1917, he worked for the British Foreign Service in the realm of Commercial Diplomatic relations and remained in the new Soviet Union until the early 1920s. Arthur Brown and John Craig also did their bit in the field of economic espionage. Brown, an advocate in Edinburgh, spent most of the period 1915-1918 with the War Trade Intelligence Department in Whitehall. Craig, whose professional experience was in ship-broking, spent three years in the Hague, working to maintain the restriction of supplies to hostile states.

War or no war, Britain's overseas possessions still had to be governed and FPs did their bit at every level of the imperial civil service, especially on the Indian sub-continent. Claud Barron CIE, CSI and CVO held numerous senior posts in the government of India such as chief secretary to the Punjab Government and Commisioner of Delhi, and also found time and energy to command the 5th Punjab Light Horse. His brother William finished the war as Senior Government Inspector of Railways based at Lucknow. [A third brother Robert served with distinction in the Indian Medical service and was awarded the DSO.] William Trail MC was a professional soldier in India before the war and then served in France from 1914 to 1916 with the Lahore Division of the Indian Expeditionary Force. He was invalided back to India in November 1916 where he was appointed to the office of Assistant Military Secretary to the Commander-in-Chief in India. George Pittendrigh, Professor of English Literature at Madras Christian College sat as the university member on the Madras Legislative Council throughout the war period and was awarded the Kaisar-i-Hind Medal 1st Class in 1919. Policing the Empire occupied the energies of numerous FPs such as Major Frederick Gerrard CIE Deputy Commissioner of Police and Chief Censor at Basra, and George Carroll, District Superintendent in Seoni in the Central Provinces Police and recipient of the King's Police Medal for a special act of gallantry in 1920.

By 1916 it was clear that Britain was committed to a total war and that an increasing number of areas of national life would have to be controlled and regulated by the State. This led to a proliferation of Committees, Boards and Ministries with specific administrative responsibilities, and Grammarians sat on many of these new governmental bodies. The impact of the U-boat on Britain's supply lines led to food rationing and the creation of a new Ministry of Food in 1916. Given the importance of keeping the sea lanes open and the merchant fleet at maximum capacity, London took an ever-increasing interest in the merchant navy, so posts for FPs emerged in the new Ministry of Shipping. Some of those who filled them included James Lawie who transferred from the Admiralty's Transport Dept, and Laurence Smith, invalided out of Belgium in 1916, but able to use his long pre-war experience of merchant shipping throughout the rest of the war in the Naval Transport Dept in Hull. In the difficult months of late 1916 and early 1917 when the U-boats seemed to be winning the war, almost every commodity became an essential war supply and its import, production and distribution was a matter of government concern. Textiles such as cotton were now important war materials and therefore appropriate control boards were established in Whitehall. Hubert Henderson served as the Secretary to the British Cotton Control Board from 1917 to 1919 with a spell in America as Secretary to the British Cotton Mission to the USA in 1918. Henderson was awarded the MBE in January 1919 before proceeding to a career lecturing in economics and journalism.

As the State took ever more control of the nation's resources, there was a need to extend the existing systems of land requisition and compensation. Enter James Augustus Souttar, a much-travelled architect with a successful practice in London, who served as a Supervising Valuer in the National Lands Directorate from 1917 to 1920. The war-time State also continued to push itself into aspects of personal life once thought sacrosanct, such as the private financial life of British subjects. There were vigorous national campaigns to encourage investment in war bonds. Alexander T Cruickshank, advocate in Aberdeen and one of the masterminds behind the Rubislaw project, was awarded the OBE in 1918 for his efforts as chairman of the Aberdeen Central War Savings Committee. Charles Michie, a businessman in Calcutta who had returned to Aberdeen, gave his time and energy to the care and condition of the burgeoning numbers of disabled that had resulted from the war. He served as secretary of the North of Scotland Disablement Committee and as regional representative to the Ministry of Pensions. He was awarded the MBE in the 1918 Honours List and a CBE in 1920.

The supply of manpower remained the Government's keenest concern and ensuring that the military's needs were met remains the best example of an area of the British war effort that developed from a local, voluntary activity into co-ordinated state action. Once the initial spasm of war-fever had subsided, the fact that Britain was now committed to a long war in Europe gradually became clear. Recruiting new men into the armed forces became a task of national necessity and one that several FPs performed energetically. At the start of the war, responsibility for local recruitment was often down to local committees staffed by vigorous individuals such as Professor John Duff, a classicist at the University of Durham. Caught up in the patriotic fervour of the moment, Duff played his part by helping to recruit men for the Tyneside Scottish Brigade in 1914 and 1915. In this first period of voluntary enlistment, another successful FP recruiter was Sgt Kenneth McIver of Aultbea, a schoolmaster who joined the Seaforths in October 1914. Prior to leaving for the Front, McIver used his time in the reserve battalion to recruit over 1100 Highlandmen to the colours. Promoted to a captaincy in the Cameronians, he served in France from November 1917 until his death in March 1918.

Another Highland FP and prodigious recruiter was John Morrison, originally from Bernera, Lochmaddy but by 1914 minister of the United Free Church at Alvie by Kincraig in Strathspey. Like several other FP preachers who heard the call to arms, John resigned from the cloth and put on the kilt becoming a private, and then an officer, in the Cameron Highlanders. His first two years in uniform were spent as a recruiter throughout Inverness-shire and the Western Isles, a role for which his noted skill as a preacher and his fluency in Gaelic doubly equipped him. He died at St Quentin in Sept 1918. James Crombie RFA was an Assistant Recruiting Officer in Aberdeen in the first months of the war before transferring to France where he won the MC in 1917. John MacHattie, who worked in the architectural department of the London County Council before the war, was also a piper. This fitted him well for his role as a recruiter for the London Scottish in the first two years of the war. However, his stirring tunes of glory were no longer needed at home once compulsory conscription was introduced, and he transferred to France and Germany where he was demobbed as Pipe Major in March 1919.

A retired clergyman, George Walker also did his bit to encourage the nation's youth to enlist by publishing *For the Great Cause; Some Bits of Spiritual Munitions Work*, a book of patriotic sermons setting out the justness of Britain's involvement in the conflict. Certainly the most exotic FP recruiter was Kenneth Allardyce, formerly of Queen's Terrace but latterly resident in Nabavatu, Fiji. By 1916, Allardyce had risen in the Fijian Civil Service to be Secretary for Native Affairs, at which point he raised a contingent of native volunteers who served as the Fijian Labour Corps under his command in France and Italy during the last two years of the war.

After the introduction of conscription in 1916, recruitment became a matter for government but FPs continued to play a role in the new compulsory system. The Ministry of National Service was created by Order-in-Council on the 23rd October 1917, a point in the war when the disaster at Passchendaele was exacerbating the drain on manpower. The Ministry had powers with respect to conscription as well as decisions relating to 'reserved' staffing in strategic industries. Its conscription powers extended over claims for exemption from military service and claims for discharge from men already in the ranks.

Numerous FPs worked for the ministry. Of these David Stewart was probably the most senior. Stewart was the managing director of the Aberdeen Comb Works but also Lt Col of the 4th territorial battalion of the Gordon Highlanders in 1914. He was gazetted to the Reserve as an Honorary Colonel early in the war and spent the remainder of the conflict engaged in recruiting duties, latterly as a National Service Representative. John Lillie, an advocate at the Scottish Bar in Edinburgh before the war, did similar recruiting work in Ayrshire after his discharge from the Lothians and Border Horse through illness. Alexander Smith of the Territorial Force Reserve was a busy recruiter both in the days of enlistment and after conscription was introduced. Drumming up new men for the ranks was a task often entrusted to the returning wounded. Typical of these was George McConnachie, a lieutenant in the Scottish Rifles in France in 1915-16, who, was employed as a recruiting officer in the Aberdeen district by the Ministry of National Service after being wounded in 1916.

Military Tribunals heard claims and appeals for exemption from compulsory military service. The most frequent reasons underpinning claims for exemption included medical unsuitability, the need to look after dependents, or the need to maintain a useful business. There were also the well-known claims made on grounds of conscience. Although too old for active service, Lauchlan McKinnon, advocate in the family firm of the same name, was Commander of the Aberdeen Volunteer Training Corps. He later became Honorary Colonel of the City of Aberdeen Volunteer Regiment and Chairman of the City of Aberdeen Military Tribunal. As such, he will have heard local cases involving exemption claims. William Cameron, partner in the law firm Esslemont & Cameron, was also a lieutenant in the Territorial Reserve in August 1916. From that point onwards, he was engaged in the administrative side of recruitment in the three NE counties and in Shetland. Cameron fulfilled the role of Italian Consul in Aberdeen and was responsible for mobilizing Italian manpower of military age in the North of Scotland. In this role, he organised the safe transfer to Italy of 'many hundreds' of refugees of Italian origin or descent who had landed up in northern Scotland after fleeing 'invaded and disturbed territory' in Europe. He was awarded a knighthood in the Order of the Crown of Italy in 1919.

In 1916 one Grammar FP helped make an unusual contribution to the war effort by taking the public's attention away from the bad news coming in from several Fronts and reminding them of the 'British values' that the war was being fought to defend. Before the war, Robert Selbie Clark was a Carnegie research zoologist undertaking fishery investigations at the British Marine Biology Station in Plymouth. In late 1914 he sailed on the Endurance as a scientific member of Shackleton's Imperial Trans-Antarctic Expedition. In May 1916 Shackleton reported from Port Stanley in the Falklands that the Endurance had been destroyed by the pressure of ice more than six months before. He had been forced to leave twenty-two of his men on the inhospitable rocks of Elephant Island in the South Shetlands while he and a smaller group set out in a small boat in search of rescue.

Clark was one of those left behind with dwindling supplies, desperately hoping that Shackleton and his five companions could successfully make the 800 mile voyage to the nearest human settlement. On their uninhabitable home, fuel for staying warm in the cold, wet climate was scarce and the tents, clothing and bedding used by the 'Elephant Islanders' were therefore damp almost all of the time. Their diet, largely consisting of seal and penguin meat, soon lost its appeal. Some in the group were suffering badly from frost-bite; others were deeply discouraged as their hopes of rescue evaporated. Clark, a reserved hardworking man, was thought dour by some on the expedition. However, he made a major contribution to the morale of his stranded companions. From a recipe of sugar, ginger, water and methylated spirits, he conjured up an alcoholic drink that has gone down in history as 'Gut Rot 1916'. Miraculously, all twenty-two men survived the four long months that elapsed before Shackleton returned to Elephant Island in a rescue vessel.

When the story broke, the nation's attention was briefly turned from the war to this tale of determined heroics that belonged to an earlier age of endeavour before the beastly war. No sooner was he back in Blighty however but Clark, quickly married and wearing his Polar Medal with clasp, was gazetted into the RNVR. He spent the last two years of the war minesweeping in the Humber and Tyne sectors of the North Sea and organising the safe deployment of the North Shields Area fishing fleet.

Chapter 23
The Impact on the School

In 1914, sharing the Skene Street buildings with the Central School had pushed the Grammar day forward by an hour. If an 8.00am start seemed uncivilised to some pupils, there was worse to come with the introduction of Daylight Saving Time throughout Britain in 1916. One outraged pupil levelled both barrels at the legislators who had interfered with the Grammar clock by yet another hour:

> *'A year and a half ago, most of us waxed wroth at the idea of commencing work at 8am. Now, due to an altogether infamous Act of Parliament, we start at the grisly hour of seven. It was a matter of small importance to the Members of Parliament who passed the Act, that the clock should be put forward an hour. It is at 3pm that they begin the intensely arduous duty of drowsily listening to some futile debate. But we, we now begin work before the world is properly awake; we are toiling while the morning dew is yet on the ground; cock-crow merely signifies that we have completed a substantial portion of our daily labour. To employ a somewhat colloquial phrase, it's really a bit thick'.*

As the war unfolded, there were other strangers in the School who were even more exotic than the scholars from the Central. A party of ten Serbian boys, refugees from the battle-torn Balkans, became honorary Grammarians towards the end of 1916. The boys received much of their education in their own language under the tutelage of a Professor Georgevitch. In other ways however, they quickly settled into the life of the School, rapidly picking up English thanks in part to their regular attendance at the revived Debating Society. The magazine's pupil editor in 1917 noted how easily once-alien names such as Boris, Luka and Dragoslav now fell on the ear. That Easter the Serbian contingent enjoyed a pleasant holiday 'on the spacious desmesne of Dunecht' courtesy of Lady Cowdray. Their finest hour came in the schools sports that summer when one of the Serbs, Shukovitch by name, won first prize in the weights with a fine put that excited the spectators at the new games field. The Serbians also led the School tug-of-war team that easily routed a fairly strong pack of FPs. There was genuine regret when the popular 'Serbian colony' left Aberdeen in the late spring of 1919 and returned to the Balkans, at that moment under reconstruction on the map-tables of Versailles.

The use of the Whitehall Place field for drilling had forced the School's sporting life into abeyance in autumn 1914. However the following summer saw return to sporting 'business as usual' with the Cricket XI taking on teams from Robert Gordon's and the Royal Asylum. The school tennis club sparked back into life under the secretaryship of Eric Linklater. The annual Athletic Sports were also revived that September and plans were made for the coming [rugby] football season. That autumn, the School XV played twice against the officers and men of the 3rd and 4th Gordon Highlanders, losing 14-3 and 21-5. In both matches the School played well but eventually succumbed to heavier opponents. Nevertheless these contests were excellent training for the only match that mattered, with the School crushing Robert Gordon's College 18-3 soon after.

The School XV's best wartime result against a Service side came in December 1916 in a match with the officers of the 3rd Gordons. Though the Highlanders were 'a heavy lot', in a game played on a very boggy pitch the School emerged with a creditable 0-0 draw. A combined team of FP and School footballers also scraped a 3-0 win against Gordons Officers a year later but by that stage in the war, regimental rugby teams had inevitably been weakened by events elsewhere. Throughout the war years, Grammar enjoyed a clear superiority over Robert Gordon's College, posting a succession of impressive results such as the 27-0 win in the first 'local derby' played on the New Field in October 1916. The first cricket match there against RGC also finished with the right result, the School winning easily by 44 runs.

In magazine editions in the later stages of the war, Theodore Watt allowed longer, more detailed descriptions of the goings-on at the not-yet baptised Rubislaw, knowing that many FPs on active duty enjoyed reading the sporting news from home. These articles also reflected the great pride that the school community felt in fulfilling its pledge to fund its share of this huge project. By the summer of 1916, the recreation round had been enclosed with stone walls to the east, north and south and a wooden fence to the west. Levelling and laying out the field had been problematic as the remains of the old Victorian Bleachfield buildings had to be blasted. The burn running beneath the field had to be made safe and a subterranean network of pipes laid down, although a little more attention might have been paid to drainage here and there. Most of the ground had been sown by spring 1916 and rolling the new turf that formed the cricket square was soon well underway in preparation for the summer. Three tennis courts were ready for service and the School Tennis Club was already making good use of them on finer evenings. In June 1916 the pupil editor reported that 'the Bleachfield playing-ground will undoubtedly be ready for games next season unless some errant Zeppelin loses a casual bomb in its direction'.

During 1915 the cultural life of the Grammar had also gradually revived. The talented Eric Linklater, later a prolific and popular author, helped resuscitate the School's oldest club, the Literary and Debating Society. The syllabus for 1915 initially made little mention of the war; topics included *Is the present cinema-craze detrimental to public welfare?* and *The historical topography of Aberdeen*. However, later open sessions showed that Grammarians did have a strong interest in matters military: questions discussed included *Do we owe more to the Navy or Army? Is the Battleship or the Submarine the greater Naval Force? What of the Balkans and Gallipoli? Has the War improved the people?*. Positive debates in 1918 on female suffrage and the equal mental capacities of the sexes reflected the changing perceptions of female ability encouraged by the experience of total war.

The Library was now enjoying an unusual surge in popularity thanks to its stock of war tales by writers such as the FP Boyd Cable, Ian Hay, author of one of the most popular books of the period *The First Hundred Thousand*, and Herman Cyril McNeile whose short stories from the Front were published under the name of Sapper. The Judicial Night, a popular comic event in the pre-war school in which pupils acted out a preposterous court case, was given a wartime twist. Judicial Night became Military Tribunal Night in which six implausible candidates pleaded for exemption in front of a Conscription Board who appeared to be 'preoccupied' ie sozzled. New exhibits for the School Museum arrived from FPs in uniform such as a French history book found at Festubert with shrapnel embedded in it, and fragments of a Zeppelin downed in Yorkshire.

Empire Day provided an opportunity for pupils to demonstrate their patriotic feelings and it was celebrated with gusto. In 1915 the school 'bellowed out *Rule Britannia* and *The Marseillaise* to honour our brave ally'. The belated but still welcome entry of the USA into the war was marked by a rendition of the *Battle Hymn of the Republic*. On Empire Day 1918 the School saluted the Canadian contribution by singing *The Maple Leaf For Ever*. Empire Day however was not just an exercise in musical jingoism. Speakers also had a chance to stoke up the patriotic fervour of the school body and urge them to do their bit for the war effort.

The School responded. Collecting became an everyday fact of Grammar life throughout the Great War. Weekly collections for war funds took place from the outset of the war and the pupil editor of the School Notes encouraged his fellows to contribute as much as possible: 'we cannot all be at Bedford [the Gordon Highlander's training camp] but we can all do something even here'. Pupils on holiday in the country returned bearing 'rural gifts' that could be preserved and sold for the comfort of soldiers. Sixty-nine lbs of produce were handed over one day in autumn 1915 by one band of scholars. Another collection for the Aberdeen mine-sweepers at the Dardanelles sent out packages of tobacco and cigarettes, 'delights as yet unknown to us except by repute'.

The visit of a tank to the school premises in early 1918 prompted great excitement and 'an excess of patriotic enthusiasm' amongst younger pupils. It also elicited the grand sum of £206 from the members of the school's War Savings Association. The inexhaustible Scouts were also inescapable, collecting for the Red Cross at every Grammar gathering in the school calendar such as the Swimming Gala and the Sports. A collection for Serbian POWs drew out another £11 from pupil and staff pockets. The school gymnastic squad demonstrated its skills on the parallel bars at the Music Hall to raise funds for the Red Cross. At the 1916 Empire Day celebrations, the boys in the school hall were exhorted to collect sphagnum moss which was badly needed for dressing wounds. Fifteen hundred spectators turned up for a Red Cross cricket match between Grammar FPs and Aberdeenshire at Rubislaw in August 1917. The Gordon Highlanders Band and the Oakwood Pipe Band played selections during the match, hopefully at a decent distance from the wicket square, while afternoon tea was served to the wounded soldiers watching the match in the enclosure. Despite the musical distractions, Grammar won comfortably by 41 runs.

There were also the collections for School projects. At the start of the war, the FP Club had decided that 'no special effort' would be made during the hostilities to raise funds for the new recreation ground. Nevertheless the fund stood at over £1185 in February 1915, allowing the Club to pay over its promised £1000 to the School Board. The Club now moved ahead with its secondary aim of raising another £1500 in order to put the new field 'on a really sound footing'. Contributions slowed however and this 'field fund' was eventually absorbed into the more ambitious project to build a Memorial Pavilion to honour those lost in the war. Though there is little evidence of war-weariness in the editions of the magazines that spanned the hostilities, the School Notes pupil editor did hint at donor-fatigue in a comic reference to the 'terrifying collection plates' that encouraged pupils to 'exit the Hall smartly' on Empire Day 1918.

Grammarians did more than just hand over their pocket-money. They gave up their time and energy for the war effort. By October 1914, thirty-three Grammar Scouts were already engaged in 'responsible work with the Coastguard', and at military points and hospitals throughout the Aberdeen area. Twenty-seven Grammar Scouts received the War Service Badge for their assistance to the local naval and military authorities in early 1915. Many of these pupils were supervised by William Douglas Simpson, the Rector's younger son and later a pioneering historian of Scotland. After being discharged as medically unfit from the Gordons, Simpson busied himself organising the Sea Scouts in the Admiralty Coastwatching Service, first for Aberdeenshire and then throughout Scotland. Other pupils served in the YMCA, acted as orderlies in the Fire Stations and helped to release manpower by assisting with council duties such as lamp-lighting. In their spare time, many boys at the Grammar also made items such as splints and book troughs for donation to the local military hospitals. By 1917 over three-quarters of the boys in the School aged over fourteen could say they had done their bit.

Britain's chronic timber shortage offered Grammarians another way to contribute to the struggle for survival. Vast amounts of timber were needed in the mines and in the trenches. It was also needed for the burgeoning network of military roads and railways on the Western Front.

German control of the Baltic cut Britain off from its traditional sources of timber in Scandinavia and Russia. By late 1916 the shortage was critical. Britain was thrown back on its own timber reserves and Scotland in particular was to be denuded in the last two years of the war.

In the summer of 1917, squads of Grammarians spent their holidays at Cawdor and Fochabers hard at work in the forests, sleeping in caravans, cooking for themselves and putting in long hours felling timber. A large number of pupils volunteered again for forestry work the following summer, working across northern Scotland from Bonar Bridge to Daviot, 'some felling, some loading, some snedding and a fortunate few given charge of horses'. The work was relentless but it brought tangible and intangible benefits to the boys involved as one magazine correspondent indicated: 'How welcome was the gaffer's whistle at 5 o'clock. How eagerly we threw aside axes and saws and rushed home to an enormous tea, but still how willingly we returned next day to the resin and the hard work. Were we not proud on our first pay-day, when most of us for the first time handled money earned by our own labour?'

Food shortages and rationing meant that enthusiastic youth was also needed on the farms. In August 1918, over a hundred older pupils responded to the call for help with the harvest, the School Board wisely granting them an extra month of leave from Skene Street. The boys were stationed in two camps, one at Turriff and one at Echt, from where they went off to local farms as required. It was by all accounts an enjoyable tour of duty; 'Who will ever forget the happy days spent in the field reaping, stooking, forking, herding and raking? Not the least part of the day's enjoyment was when lowsing was over. When the never-to-be-forgotten holiday came to an end, the harvesters returned to School, tanned by the sun and the open-air, and strengthened by the healthy work and the splendid food the farmers supplied. If the call came again, it would find us more than willing to go'. One senior pupil was later honest enough to note that he cherished the memory of not one, but two red-letter days from the month of November 1918. The first was the 11th when the Rector announced to the School that the war was at an end. The second was the 28th when the harvesters received their hard-earned fees in cheque form.

The glow of bucolic good health didn't last. The School was affected by the first wave of the influenza pandemic that found many victims amongst the weakened populations of warring Europe and accounted for an estimated 250,000 in Britain. The happy harvesters had only been back at their desks for a fortnight when the illness struck and the School was closed for three weeks.

Many of the masters at the Grammar were older, married men so the call to arms had only had a limited impact on the staffroom. Of the younger men, some were quickly in khaki, the first being Mr Dawson who was training in Kitchener's Army in Edinburgh by October 1914. Another early recruit was the School's gymnastic instructor Mr Summers who was also Colour Sergeant of the 6th (Territorial) Battalion of the Gordon Highlanders. By that time, the popular Classics master Mr Knox had also taken his place in the ranks as a Second Lieutenant in the 3/4th Gordons; he was to be invalided home from the Front in the summer of 1916. The music teacher, was also unavailable to play the piano at the school's Christmas sing-song in 1915. He was now on duty elsewhere as Lt Hyslop. The magazines mention one other unnamed staff member leaving for the War. He received the best wishes of the pupil editor of the school section in February 1916: 'Another master has left us to strafe Prussians. We hope he is most successful. While he was here he had much popularity and well developed biceps. These gifts ought to tell a lot in his new profession'. Sadly, the death of one former Grammar teacher, Lt John King, was announced in late 1916.

In the bitterly cold winter of 1917-18, Grammar pupils still found time to lampoon the eternal unprepared-ness of the town council: 'This winter the sledging was excellent. Those who were enjoying it heartily commended the war economy policy followed by the Town authorities in not putting salt or sand on the roads'. And any fears the reader may have had concerning enemy espionage in the heart of Aberdeen were dispelled by the announcement that 'the prominent member of the Modern School who tried to blow himself up during the holidays is not a German spy. He is a scientist.'

Chapter 24

Colonial Connections

Much of the manpower that allowed Britain to keep fighting on multiple fronts throughout the long and wasteful war came from its Empire. Many Grammar FPs who had gone out to the colonies in the years before the war now returned home to get involved in 'the Big Show' back in Europe. The largest contingent of these 'colonial' FPs came from Canada. Approximately eighty Grammarians are known to have served in Canadian military units although several others returned to the old country and fought in British regiments. A number of Canadian FPs distinguished themselves in action such as Capt Charles Walker DCM and Sergeant Charles Giles MM who were both decorated in 1917. This group of FPs also included the one Great War Grammarian to win the Victoria Cross.

A letter from an eminent FP in Canada indicated the extent of the war fever that had taken hold in Britain's largest Dominion. Alexander Gordon taught at McGill University in Montreal during most of the war. In May 1917 he wrote that patriotic feeling in Canada continued to strengthen there. Despite 'a deep undertone of sadness', the Canadian commitment to the imperial war cause was undiminished: 'McGill is now almost as depleted as the home Universities and the men left are all in khaki serving the Empire in some capacity or other. The campus is given over entirely to drill. In addition to drafts for the Princess Patricia's and other less famous battalions, we have sent to France a completely equipped hospital, and a McGill Battery which is also certain to give a good account of itself. Among other distinctions we have two VCs to our credit. So we are running Scotland hard in the race for honours'.

Inevitably, former pupils with a connection to Canada soon began to appear in the *Pro Patria Mortui* section of the school magazine. The first was William Gray, a thirty-two year old estate agent from Vancouver. Gray had not been not long in the trenches when he was struck by a bullet in the head and died instantaneously in April 1915. His brother David served in

France with the Canadian Mounted Rifles. He went missing presumed dead in March 1917. His body was never found. David Anderson, an agricultural student who had gone over to Canada to learn about new farming techniques there, was killed by a shell near Ypres in October 1917. A signaller, he had been trying to repair some broken wires near the forward lines. Hugh Anderson, an engineer in Montreal, died a similar death also near Ypres. He was hit in the chest by the explosive nose-cap of a high velocity shell, never regained consciousness and died an hour later.

Altogether at least nineteen Grammar FPs are known to have died in Canadian uniform. Of these, two are worthy of very special mention. John Shakespeare Watson was a vet student in London who went west to Canada in 1911 in search of his fortune. When he first attempted to enlist, he was turned down on account of his varicose veins. His solution to this obstacle was to have the offending veins removed and after a successful operation he donned the uniform of the Canadian Mounted Rifles. He was killed in a prolonged German bombardment during the Third Battle of Ypres on 2nd June 1917. The Canadians had suffered very heavily that day and lost a great deal of their equipment to enemy shelling. John Watson's obituarist recorded that the fight was an unequal one. The Canadians were outnumbered and outgunned but 'when they saw the enemy coming, they climbed from the trenches to meet them and charged magnificently but pitifully to their death, with no weapons but broken rifle butts, bits of entrenching tools and in some cases, their fists'. The correspondent concluded: 'I do not know where in war you will look for a more tragic or more thrilling episode'.

Robert Grierson Combe was born in Aberdeen in 1880 and was living at 24 Ferryhill Place when he entered the Grammar at the age of fourteen. He studied pharmacy and plied that trade before the war, in Aberdeen and then in Canada. Combe arrived at the Front with the City of Winnipeg Infantry in 1915 after successfully concluding the training in sub-zero temperatures mentioned earlier. He was invalided out of the front line in the summer of 1916 but returned to France in April 1917.

On 3rd May 1917, Combe and his company advanced towards the enemy lines in the face of sustained shelling. His men were under great pressure and took heavy losses. Combe however steadied his remaining men, attacked his company's objective and captured it with only five comrades remaining at his side. He then collected sufficient others from the chaos of battle to hold the position and transport eighty or so German prisoners back to the Allied line. As he was consolidating his control of the enemy trench and about to lead his bombers forward again, he was killed instantaneously by a sniper.

Combe was buried alongside his comrades in a temporary battlefield cemetery near Acheville in the Pas-de-Calais department in northern France. His grave and his body were destroyed in a later bombardment and he is therefore remembered on the Canadian National Memorial at Vimy, on land that is forever part of the territory of Canada. Combe was awarded the Victoria Cross for his 'most conspicuous bravery and example'. He was the only Grammar FP to be awarded the VC in the Great War. The medal was presented to his widow by the Prince of Wales in Regina, Saskatchewan in October 1918.

The most distinguished Canadian FP soldier was Lt Col William Rae, once of 2 Albert Street, and an apprentice lawyer who moved to Vancouver in 1907. Rae mobilised as a captain in the Seaforth Highlanders of Canada and arrived in Britain in October 1914 as part of the original Canadian Expeditionary Force. He saw much action in France and Belgium, ending the war as a member of the Allied Army of Occupation in Germany. Rae was in command of the Canadian detachment which recaptured four 4.7 guns that had been taken earlier by the enemy during the Battle of Second Ypres in the spring of 1915. He was wounded in July 1916 and in the latter stages of the war he served behind the lines at British and Canadian Headquarters. He received the DSO in 1916 and the French *Croix de Guerre* in 1919.

The most influential Canadian FP of the Great War period was probably Sir William Mortimer Clark, a pupil of the 'old Grammar' in Schoolhill and later a successful lawyer and businessman in Ontario. Sir William was appointed Lieutenant-Governor of Ontario in 1903. He was an ardent Empire loyalist and Vice-President of the British Empire League of Canada. During both the South African War and the Great War, he gave his unflinching public support to the view that Canada should defend the imperial motherland with all the power and resources at its disposal.

The Canadian colonial contigent was significantly larger than its antipodean counterparts. This reflects the fact that Canada had been an exceptionally attractive location for adventurous Scots in the decades immediately before the Great War. However Watt did identify a group of around twenty FPs who served in Australian units, most of them in non-commissioned ranks. Five of these men died in action or as a result of their service in uniform. The 'senior' military Australian FP was Major John McPherson who served in France as a Regimental Medical Officer with the Australian Imperial Force. A slightly smaller number of FPs, seventeen, are known to have served in units from New Zealand. Of these, six were medics. Two 'Kiwi' FPs died in action; John Ellis and John Hall were both killed in 1917, while another, Charles Tod, was twice badly wounded and then seriously gassed whilst serving in France.

More than twenty FPs fought for the Empire in South African units. Many were short term volunteers who returned to their homes once the Boer rebellion and the neighbouring German colony were quashed. However, a number stayed on in Botha's army and saw further service in the long East African campaign. Seven South African FPs also saw service on the Western Front. James Allan, once of Ferryhill but by 1914 an ostrich farmer in Oudtshoorn in the Western Cape, served first in South West Africa then in France where he died in the ranks of the South African Infantry in 1917. Newell Cran of the 2ⁿᵈ Rhodesian Regiment was taken prisoner in the black days of March 1918. Almost all the officers in this group were medics with the RAMC or the South African Medical Corps. The only decorated soldier in this group was Simpson Shepherd MC whose subterranean activities have been mentioned elsewhere.

A smaller group of FPs found themselves in South East Asia when the war began. Ten of these are known to have enrolled in local units such as the North Borneo Volunteer Rifles or the Singapore Volunteer Rifles. In due course, as the situation in that region stabilised, some of these men transferred to regular units elsewhere. Typical of these was Arthur Stephenson whose military experience began in the Malay States Volunteer Rifles. By October 1915 he was a Lieutenant in the Gordon Highlanders in France. He was killed in action at High Wood on the Somme in July 1916.

Around eighty FPs served in India and Ceylon, some in British-only volunteer contingents such as the Ceylon Mounted Rifles. Most however were professional officers soldiering in the Indian Army. Many of these FPs remained on garrison and police duties within the Raj for much of the war period. About a quarter of the group saw action on the North-West and Persian frontiers and about a quarter took part in operations beyond India, mostly in Egypt, Palestine, Syria, Mesopotamia and East Africa. Seven FPs spent part of their time in uniform within the Indian Expeditionary Force that served in France from September 1914 to March 1918. At one point over 130,000 strong, the IEF suffered from inappropriate equipment, difficulties in replacing manpower losses and cultural misunderstandings. Nevertheless it took its place in the imperial line and suffered over 9,000 casualties. In all, nine FPs of the Indian Army lost their lives during the war.

On the grounds that the original thirteen American states were once British colonies, a few lines about those FPs who served within the armed forces of the USA are included here. Mention has been made elsewhere of FP medics who rendered distinguished service to the US Army Medical Corps. Other 'American FPs' included Harold Scholle, once of Ashley Road but by 1917 a farmer in Manitoba, who chose to enlist in the US Army who trained him as a machine-gunner. His brother Otto, who also farmed in Manitoba, enlisted in his local Canadian regiment and was in France by April 1916 where he was wounded and gassed. Oswald Macdonald ended the war in the American Army Flying Corps while William McQueen of the Arizona Copper Company completed his service in the US Army Engineers as a Sergeant 1st Class. Another FP, John Harper, spent his war as a naval engineer working for the US Navy within the American ship-building industry.

Once the Great War was finally over, two North American Grammarians did some of the necessary 'tidying-up'. Lt Col Hector Brown DSO had enjoyed a varied life as a 'Mountie' and as a Canadian trooper in the South African War, followed by eight years exploring and mining in Africa. After doing his bit in France with the 4th Canadian Division, he was appointed Provost Marshal of Nova Scotia. One of his tasks in the immediate post-war period was to organise the transportation of tens of thousands of Chinese labourers. They had been stationed in Europe but were now being returned to their homeland on a long voyage westwards that included the trek across Canada by train.

Tidying up of another kind was undertaken by Armand Christen in 1919. Armand studied engineering at Durham in the Edwardian years, proceeded to a career in electrical engineering in New York, and once in uniform, spent the last year of the war undertaking research of an undisclosed nature in Paris and Switzerland. In 1919 he was posted to Tours where he was involved in the compilation [and manipulation] of the records of the US Expeditionary Force.

Chapter 25

Some Attitudes towards the War

'In the year before the war I travelled to Germany and felt that indefinable sense of latent hostility everywhere. In the dining-car between Cologne and Brussels some Germans were seated opposite me. They drank large quantities of hock before dinner and devoured roll after roll. Showers of crumbs shot from their mouths across the table in my direction. I barricaded myself behind a French newspaper, and somehow or other got through dinner. I was so glad when we got to the Belgian frontier that I went to the fruit-stall and said to the motherly French-speaking 'body' there - Thank God madame, I am out of the land of barbarians and back to civilisation again. Beaming with pleasure she insisted on filling my pockets with large black plums for which she would take no payment'.

German appetites deeply offended this anonymous FP who contributed an article to the magazine describing his pre-war experiences of travelling on the Continent. The North Sea crossing had been ruined by 'a lusty Teuton with large sausage-like fingers' who sampled 'everything on the generous menu card', continued eating long after everyone else had finished, and committed the ultimate dining-room crime of eating noisily like 'a modern Gargantua'. The writer's stay in Magdeburg was also ruined by the locals' habit of 'gargling the throat from finger-bowls and then squirting the water back into the bowl. In horror, I fled from Hunland'.

German over-indulgence also revolted the author when at Marienbad in Bohemia, the 'favoured resort of all the excessive beer-swillers of Germany' who travelled there in an attempt to reduce their 'elephantine bulk' and bring 'twenty-two stones of pendulous, flabby flesh' down to fourteen stones or so. A holiday in Spain provided no escape from *'their horrible table manners, their loud chomping noises as they stoked their food, and their hideous guttural German speech which grew louder as their faces grew redder under the influence of generous red wine'.*

In case any readers were willing to forgive the Germans their failings at the dinner table, the author clutched at a few more straws in his attempt to convince his audience of the frightfulness of the foe. Germans were eager to engage Britons conversation at every opportunity. This was not a sign of genuine friendliness, just their means of wheedling free English language tuition. A German botanist spotted near Loch Maree was perhaps a spy; 'What was in his vasculum - plans or plants ?' A German baron who had acquired a deer forest in the West Highlands was dismissed as 'no true Highland gentleman; he was just a usurer'.

This largely tongue-in-cheek article was the one sustained attempt in the wartime school magazine to generate some degree of animosity towards the enemy. There was much use of *Boche* and *Hun* in the magazine throughout the war but these terms had very quickly lost their original venom and become literary conventions. There is one mention of 'their frightful gas', one description of a German bombardment as 'their regular morning hate' and a reference to German troops sitting 'hating in their trenches'. The obituary of one FP killed in action portrayed his death as a sacrifice 'to save Europe from the yoke of Prussian despotism'; one of very few references to the causes and purpose of the war amidst the many pages of war-related material in the school magazine. Significantly, this comment was written by a civilian master at the school rather than an FP in uniform. Elsewhere, there is little sense of the war being fought specifically in a negative way *against* Germany, but rather of it being waged *for* positive outcomes such as the safety of the Empire.

There is in fact a remarkable lack of rancour in the pages of the magazine towards the enemy. Anti-German feeling was of course common, and at times very strong, throughout the civilian population of Great War Britain, and the recent official history of the Grammar School revealed the distress that this caused the Rector and his German wife. Anti-German sentiment was probably the reason why one pupil at the Grammar at this time, like his sovereign George V, felt the need to change his Germanic name. Hermann Carl Robert Gunther of 6 Forest Road was a pupil at the school from 1910 to 1919. In August 1916 he changed his name to the slightly more anglified Herbert Charles Thomson Gunter.

In contributions to the magazine written by uniformed FPs, the German armed forces were generally referred to with a considerable degree of respect. There are several expressions of sympathy for German troops about to be pulverised by an Allied bombardment. Instances of German kindness towards British prisoners and British wounded are duly recorded. Despite the many descriptions of battles at the Front in the magazine, there are relatively few mentions references to the killing of individual Germans. In one of the more explicit of these, written by a Canadian FP after charging a German trench, the writer seems bewildered by his actions; 'I accounted for one German. I was a little nervous before we charged, but when we got going and I saw a number of our fellows fall, I simply lost my senses and didn't care for anything'. Another rare reference to the act of killing appears in the MC citation for Archibald Spark who 'with all his officers wounded, covered the retirement and personally shot four of the enemy'.

To some extent, the real enemy in the war was not individual Germans or Turks but simply death itself. The graphic descriptions of death in what was a school magazine intended to be read by pupils and their families, still have the power to shock. The last moments of boys and men who would have been well known to many in the wider Grammar community are consistently described in the starkest terms: shot in the chest and face; struck by a bursting shell case; buried by an exploding mine; hit by the full blast of a hand-grenade; died of haemorrhage after his blood-poisoned leg was amputated. There is no attempt to dress up the reality of industrial war in sentimental niceties and this is clearly something that Theodore Watt intended.

In 1915 Watt found space to print a piece by the Reverend Robert Lendrum that looked beyond the war and stressed the importance of keeping the passions stimulated by war under control. Lendrum surmised that after the war 'everyone in Germany who says a good word for Britain will be regarded as a traitor, and even in Britain those who recall what is noble in Germany's past will be eyed with suspicion as if in defending Germany, they were disloyal to their native land'. He reminded Grammar readers of the advice of the great Victorian soldier Lord Roberts to avoid 'the unsportsmanlike habit of abusing our enemies', and 'to say all the good they could, of those whom duty has compelled them to fight to the death'.

The evidence in the Grammar magazine largely confirms the observations of many studies into the feelings and attitudes of the soldiery of World War One. Troops were often happier at the Front with their comrades, than back home on leave amongst a civilian population which had developed its own different perspectives on the conflict. Thus William Bruce, killed in France in April 1918, 'was home on leave last March and though he had had his due share of the experiences of those serving at the Front, was eager to be back'. Some troops felt guilty about enjoying leave while their comrades were left behind back at the sharp end where there were still important tasks to be done. William Smith died in January 1916 in the act of saving a wounded man. He should have been on leave back in Blighty, but had stayed at his post and written; 'What's the good of leave if you haven't done something worth while'.

There was at times resentment that not everyone in uniform was experiencing the same war, with too many pen-pushers enjoying 'cushy' jobs. Douglas Leith's ambivalent remarks about the comforts of life back at HQ well behind the lines have been noted. Staff Officers from GHQ or London who arrived to conduct brief fact-finding or inspectorial visits were the target of another magazine contributor. He struggled to hide his glee at the effort that the Hun put into giving one fleeting visitor a fiery welcome:

Our company had a three days' visit from a Captain who was sent out here to learn something about trench warfare. These officers are sent out by the War Office, spend three days in the trenches, get an idea of what the life is like, and return home to give lectures. I don't think the one who was attached to our company will have any desire to return. To give him a warm reception the Huns started shelling our line pretty fiercely. Next afternoon we were bombed by trench mortars and lost a few men, while on the third evening our friend was almost hurled out of his bunk by a mine explosion some distance away. For a couple of hours afterwards, artillery, machine guns, rifle fire, bombs and mortars made an infernal din, one which a newcomer would not soon forget. Altogether this Captain got his money's worth'.

Attitudes towards enlistment remained positive throughout the first half of the war: the senior school was certainly drained by the recruiting sergeant in the first initial phase of the conflict. By October 1914, classes in the upper school had already been 'much lessened in number owing to many Territorials being called away to serve their country' but the willingness to enlist was evident in the school section of the magazine for the next three years. Within the small world of the Grammar School with its deeply patriotic set of shared values, enlisting whilst still in the Sixth brought not just prestige but possible privileges: 'one or two of the Moderns have been sporting khaki armlets lately [a sign that they had joined up] probably in the hope that they would thus be immune from the indignity of further punishment. It certainly would not be the done thing for a master to use his strap on one of the defenders of our country'.

The class of 1916 was typical in its determination to fight for the Empire: 'our last session of School life draws to a close. Those of us who are old enough are counting the days until the time we shall doff mufti, don khaki and help Britain'. The following summer was the year of Third Ypres that culminated in the autumn slaughter at Passchendaele, described later by Lloyd George as 'the greatest disaster of the war...no soldier of any intelligence now defends this senseless campaign'. The reaction of the pupil editor to this catastrophe however remained faultlessly resolute: 'We have noted many School names in the casualty lists, which means there are gaps to be filled somewhere. And how can they be better filled than from the old School, which has sent so many of its sons to the fray?'

Comments expressing the impatience of young men to get involved were commonplace: in 1915 Dr Theodore Gray of Seacliff Hospital in New Zealand was 'doing all he can to find a man to take his place so he may get away to the Dardanelles'. Other examples amongst many include Hugh Wark, rejected three times by the University Company of the Gordons who cycled out to Banchory to join the local battalion there. And it was not just young men who were eager to see action. George Cruden was a retired advocate who had officered the 1st Volunteer Battalion in Aberdeen in the late Victorian and Edwardian era. Desperate to be involved in the war, the sixty-four year old Cruden rejoined the army as a private, served in France and Belgium and only settled back to civilian life in 1919.

That stories of this kind were fewer in the later issues of the magazine was probably due more to the establishment of conscription in 1916 than any war-weariness. Despite all the disappointments of the war, the spirit of the School remained positive and good-humoured. In the grim summer of 1916, one pupil editor leaving the Sixth was sent off to the army with the following ditty ringing in his ears:

Though you're shivering in a trench, never mind!
Though you're soaked and feeling blue, never mind!

For you're done with Maths and French
Latin, Greek and English too
And you're on the Roll of Honour, never mind!

In 1916 Watt discontinued his practice of recording the names of pupils and FPs who had volunteered for service. With the introduction of compulsory military service, he felt that the *raison d'etre* of the School Muster was no longer valid; 'it could no longer be regarded as constituting a Roll of Honour in the same sense as formerly'. In any case, so many Grammarians of military age were in uniform that he felt 'it would probably be a simpler matter now to bring together the names of those who are not serving than of those who are'.

The sheer numbers of lads of all social classes who were now in uniform had a significant impact on civilian attitudes to the Armed Forces and the Army in particular. This shift in sentiment was eloquently described by Professor J M Bulloch, an FP and keen military historian. He noted that the nineteenth century regular army drew its manpower almost entirely from two classes, *'the Lords and Labourers, the two classes at the extreme ends of the social scale which have really far more in common with each other than with the intervening classes from which a school like the Grammar is recruited. To enlist in the Victorian army was to be lost, from which it can be understood that the Grammar School boy who 'jined the sojers' was almost unknown. Well-to-do lads in temporary disgrace sometimes took the shilling but as a whole the Army was almost entirely recruited from the ranks of the manual workers, and of unskilled labour at that. Scarcely any civilian in the town except loafers were ever to be seen at the Castlehill Barracks. Not one citizen in a thousand had ever set foot within the square'.*

The Great War changed all that for now, as Bulloch noted *'everybody in Aberdeen, town and county alike, is poignantly interested in the Gordons. The word Gordon is graven tragically in many a civilian soul today, for thousands of lads have passed into the 92nd and hundreds of them will never return from the fields of Flanders and France. Grammar School boys who in the early part of 1914 were thinking of enrolling themselves at the age of seventeen as students of Arts must now become students of Arms. In 1914 the hope was for a Scarlet gown; in 1916 it is a Scarlet tunic, or rather its drab substitute, the khaki of wartime. No Grammar School boy of today will ever forget the Gordons'.*

Postscript

Then as now, local companies with a connection to the School loyally placed adverts in the Grammar magazine. By 1915 these were beginning to address the needs of FPs in the services, and the worries of their families. Adverts for military tailors '*Officers Uniforms a Speciality*' appeared regularly. Local jewellers advertised products that might prove useful to sons in the military such as luminous watches. WJ Milne, trading at 251 Union Street in those days, stocked rubber overshoes at two shillings per pair that men heading for the mud of France would certainly require, plus a range of woollen and sheepskin garments 'For Military Wear' to fend off the worst of a Flemish winter. John Dunn the shoe and boot-maker offered Rubber Cavalry Boots and guaranteed watertight Marching Boots in Black or Tan. Readers of the magazine were exhorted to 'Remember the Boys at the Front' by tobacconists offering to supply Tobaccos, Cigars and Cigarettes DUTY FREE to distant servicemen. The advert for Kennaway's Plum Puddings, Scotch buns and Shortbread similarly played on the guilt of readers at home: 'Have you friends abroad or at the Front? Are you sending reminders to them?' Other shopkeepers offered tinned ham, tea and other foodstuffs suitable for sending to 'our soldiers and sailors' to help supplement their government rations. The electrical contractors Claud Hamilton, previously known for their work as automobile engineers and domestic electricians, now advertised their willingness to work on Admiralty Battleships. Boys keen to prepare themselves for army life could 'Learn to Shoot with a BSA Air Rifle' from Alexander Martin Gunmakers of 128 Union Street and try them out before purchase at their underground rifle range. And *La Scala Photo Playhouse* in Union Street, later demolished to make way for the *Majestic*, offered all wounded servicemen free entrance to their shows.

Chapter 26

The Fortunes of War

For four years, the school magazine confirmed Napoleon Bonaparte's observation that 'war is a lottery' by detailing the conflicting fortunes of the Grammarians serving their country in uniform. Some FPs had what was once called 'a good war'. Many certainly held high office and were awarded high honours. Others suffered terrible fates. For some, the war was a brutally short experience. This chapter simply tells the 'war stories' of some of the 1914-1918 Grammarians; their experiences are typical of many others. Most of these men and boys have not been mentioned elsewhere in this book but their tales deserve a place on these pages.

James Hervey was 15 and completing his first year of training with Edmonds and Ledingham when war began. He immediately enlisted as a Bugler in the territorial RFA and served at various camps in Britain during the first two years of the war. In March 1917, still under the minimum age for service at the Front, he 'evaded the authorities and secretly landed at Le Havre'. Hervey saw action at the Third Battle of Ypres [Passchendaele] by which time he was a Signaller and Driver. In September 1918 he was struck by a shell and died instantly.

Malcolm Macleod enlisted as a trooper in the 1st Life Guards [Household Cavalry] in 1909. He served in France from August 1914 until the Armistice, transferring to the Machine Gun Guards in 1917. In 1915 he was awarded the French *Croix de Guerre* with palms. In June of that year he was recommended for the DCM for rescuing his troop sergeant who lay wounded in No Man's Land despite heavy shellfire. He died in London as a result of an accident on 29th June 1919, the first official day of peace.

Henry Butchart was one of five FP brothers and a captain in the Scottish Horse. He held senior posts in Egypt including spells with the Suez Canal Defence Section and the Intelligence Division. He transferred to France in 1918 when the Allies came under intense pressure in the *Kaiserschlacht*. Mentioned twice in dispatches, Lt Col Butchart was awarded the DSO in 1916 and the Star of Romania in 1919. His brother James, served in France and Belgium for almost all of the war, commanding a brigade in the RFA. He was awarded the DSO in 1917 and mentioned twice in dispatches.

George Alexander Smith, from near Leslie and an advocate in Aberdeen, mobilized as a Major in the Gordons and was wounded in France in 1915. Fortunately, 'his pocket book stopped a too penetrating shrapnel bullet which sought to end his usefulness at the Y wood near the Hooge chateau'. Smith later experienced a spell at General Headquarters. Preferring to serve nearer the Front, he joined the 5th Gordons which he commanded from March 1918. On 28th July, Lt Col Smith was on the brow of a small hill near Buzancy observing the progress of his battalion as it moved towards enemy lines. He was hit by a German shell and died several minutes later. Awarded the DSO in 1916 and mentioned four times in dispatches, Smith's Brigadier recorded that he had twice been recommended for the Victoria Cross.

Captain Robert Dunn, scion of the Aberdeen shoe-making family, was a keen hillwalker and chessplayer. He went to France in autumn 1915 and fought at High Wood and Beaumont-Hamel. At the start of an attack near Arras on April 23rd 1917, he was wounded in the leg just as he was climbing over the parapet. Quickly binding up his leg, he went on with his men but was killed by enemy machine gun fire directly in front of the German wire.

Major George Ledingham, the first FP to play rugby for Scotland [against France in 1913], was a civil engineer before the war and mobilized in the RE in 1914. He served in France throughout the first five months of 1915 until wounded in the knee by a bullet. He was mentioned in dispatches and awarded the MC in June 1915.

Frederic Connor was studying Agriculture when he was mobilised in the 4th Gordons. In 1915 he was commissioned in the Seaforths. On the early hours of the first day of the Somme, he was in the forward line, preparing to play his part in the Big Push when he bumped into a familiar face from the Grammar. This was Cyril Stuart, a junior officer in the East Yorks. They wished each other well in the day ahead. Connor died in action several hours later. Stuart survived the Somme but fell in the last spring of the war.

William Stephen, a merchant in the Fraserburgh herring trade, volunteered for service in 1915. An experienced Territorial officer, he held the rank of Captain in the 5th Gordons. In early 1916 he had the opportunity of a 'safe post' as a musketry instructor at a training base in Blighty but chose to go to the Front. On 13th November Stephen led his company over the parapet during the battle of Ancre. As they were closing on the foe, Stephen sustained the full blast of a hand grenade and died instantaneously.

Andrew Craig, a private in the 4th Gordon Highlanders serving near Arras, was posted as missing on 17th October 1915. No trace of him was ever found and in 1918 the War Office formally recorded that he was presumed killed in action. He was 21 when he disappeared.

Thomas Ogilvie began the war as a Major in the 4th Battalion of the Gordons. He served with them for spells in Britain and France until 1916 when his talents brought promotion to the key post of Administrative Commandant of the 4th Army Railhead. He was responsible for the organisation of all railheads in the sectors occupied by the 4th and 5th Armies until February 1918 when he was appointed 4th Army Labour Commandant. Colonel Ogilvie was awarded the CMG in 1915 and the CB in 1919 and mentioned five times in dispatches.

Alexander D Cruickshank MC was a 2nd Lt in the Machine Gun Corps and saw action at Gallipoli, in Sinai and in the first attack at Gaza in southern Palestine. He survived the sinking of the troopshp SS *Ivernia* off Cape Matapan in southern Greece on New Year's Day 1917. After hours drifting at sea, he had the good fortune to be picked up by an armed trawler from Aberdeen. Posted to France, he was slightly wounded in September 1918 and fatally wounded in October. He did not survive long enough to learn that he had been awarded the Military Cross.

Magnus Mowat RE had extensive experience of transport engineering before 1914, having worked in railways, docks and roads in Britain and India. He served in France until invalided out in November 1916. He then held a series of senior posts directly under the Chief Engineer ending the war as Director of Roads and Bridges in the War Office. He was promoted to Brigadier-General in 1919 and awarded the military CBE.

Charles Peterkin, an advocate in Aberdeen in 1914, mobilized as a Captain in the 4th Gordons. He undertook two spells of duty with the BEF in France and served with the British Army of the Rhine until his demob with the rank of Major in December 1919. He was mentioned twice in dispatches and awarded the CBE in 1919.

Alan Lumsden was a member of the School Company of the 4th Gordons but volunteeered for the Machine Gun Corps in 1915. Wounded in May, he returned to the trenches after a week in hospital. He was last seen on 25th September 1915 'running with others of his company to meet the on-coming Germans'.

Private Douglas Stephen of the Gordons was killed in action aged 18. He was scarcely a month in France. He went into the trenches near Epernay on 19th July 1918 and was killed by a French shell whilst on outpost duty five days later.

Sergeant James Brown, Signaller RE, won the Military Medal for his bravery at Beaumont Hamel in 1916. During the Spring Offensive, Brown was posted as missing on 12th April 1918. He lay in the open throughout that day but was taken to a house at night by two German soldiers who dressed his wounds and tended him for two days. They were forced to withdraw when the British shelled the house. He was found by British forces but died on 4th May.

Patrick Sangster was a professional soldier who had seen action in India in the 1890s with the Bengal Lancers before reaching the rank of Major in the Ferozepore Brigade. He held a series of senior appointments with the Indian Army in France from 1914 to 1918, before serving in Egypt and

Palestine in the final months of the war. He ended the war as Lt-Colonel, was awarded the DSO in 1916, CMG in 1919 and was mentioned in dispatches four times.

2nd Lt Campbell Lindsay Smith was an accomplished portraitist who studied at Gray's and exhibited his work at the Royal Academy and the Royal Scottish Academy. In October 1915 he was in Flanders with the 8th Battalion Gordon Highlanders. He was wounded during a reconnaissance for which he had volunteered and died of his wounds on 10th November 1915. He was buried at Kortevilde near Ypres.

George Rose 2nd Lt Gordon Highlanders was killed in action on 20th September 1918 aged 22. At Aberdeen, he was a founder member of the University's Peace Sociey and its first secretary and treasurer. When war broke out, he volunteered but was rejected due to defects in his vision. He was accepted at the second time of trying. On the day he died, he was commanding two platoons. He rallied his men under heavy fire, led them forward and died in hand to hand combat with the enemy.

Edward McGlashan was a probationary midshipman in the Royal Navy who served on HMS *Indefatigable* for the first sixteen months of the war. Fortunately he was transferred from that ship before it sailed for Jutland. The *Indefatigable* was sunk there with only two men surviving from its crew of 1,019. McGlashan served on destroyers in the latter part of the war.

William Smart mobilized as a Trumpeter in the Territorial Scottish Horse but was discharged in September 1914 when it was discovered that he was only sixteen. He re-enlisted in January 1915, transferring to the Dragoon Guards which whom he served from November 1917 until the end of the war. After demob, he went out to Perak in the FMS to learn rubber planting.

Goh Teik Sin was one of a number of Grammar pupils from families that originated in the Far East. Goh was a pupil at the school from 1914 to 1917 and immediately enlisted in the Lovat Scouts upon reaching military age. He died in the Central School Hospital in April 1917 aged 19.

Archibald Charles Spark of Glenbuchat served in the Gordons at the Third Battle of Ypres in 1917. A little before the battle, he told a comrade: 'I'll never go back to Scotland, lad.' He fell early on 23rd July. His company officer fell wounded but saw Spark 'carrying on through smoke and darkness' towards the enemy lines and his death at the age of twenty-one.

Ian McLaren was one of the pioneer Scottish skiers mentioned at the beginning of this book. He loved all forms of mountain sport, walking, climbing and skiing in Scotland, Switzerland and the Californian Sierras. One summer day before the war, Ian was one of a group of FPs who tackled the six major Cairngorms, 'returning to base as neat and unperturbed as when he had set out eighteen hours before'. A private in the London Scottish, he was killed instantaneously at the Somme in October 1916.

James Gillies was a founder member of the FP Club's motor-cycle section, its first Captain and keenest member. He not only planned and led the section's stravaiging through the Highlands but he wrote up the expeditions for others to enjoy in the magazine. A 'conspicuously capable officer and a born leader of men' he served as acting Major of his battalion in early 1916. He died in November 1916 of wounds incurred just before the capture of Beaumont Hamel as he and some of his men were clearing out a German trench. He was thirty years of age.

Major Harry Graham Simpson was the elder son of the Rector. On mobilization, he held the rank of 2nd Lt in the Grammar School Company of the Gordons. His knack for improvising on the hoof led to his rapid appointment as railway transport officer when his detachment left Scotland for Bedford. Harry saw action in France in 1915 at Hooge and at High Wood. In 1916 he was attached to the Machine Gun Corps and trained at Grantham where 'he developed such skill with the revolver - he could hit a penny at 20 yards every time' that he was appointed an instructor at the School of Revolver Practice. Harry was a keen inventor and developed two improved sighting devices in his time at Grantham. His practical skills, common sense and engineering background made him a useful man to have around when it came to everyday issues on the Front such as draining waterlogged trenches. In a front line trench with his company on 27th May 1918, Harry and his men were overwhelmed in the first wave of a major German offensive at Berry au Bac in Picardy. Harry was 23. His father never recovered from the loss.

Chapter 27

Armistice

On Monday 11th November 1918 at 8.11am precisely, the Rector addressed the School in the Hall and informed his pupils that the war had been suspended. One year later on the first Armistice Day, the school stood silently to attention for two minutes and then remained standing while Morland Simpson read out the names of the fallen, a long list that included his own elder son Major Harry Graham Simpson MGC.

The magazine issue after the Armistice contained references to the advent of peace, sad articles calculating the toll of casualties, mentions of FPs returning home, and the welcome arrival of normality to the life of the School. The war of course was not yet officially over. Thirteen thousand British troops were stationed in Germany as part of the Allied Army of Occupation. Amongst them were at least sixty-six FPs who included Lt Col Alexander G Nicol Smith DSO based at Allied HQ at Spa in Belgium and engaged in dispatches to the British Military Mission in Berlin. George Mair's crucial role in 'selling' the Paris Peace Settlement to the British and American public has already been noted. Thomas Johnstone had a more 'hands-on' involvement in the discussions at Versailles. A Field Surveyor with the Royal Engineers, he was wounded in 1915 and transferred to the RE Maps Section two years later. As a cartographic member of the British Staff in Paris, Johnstone was almost certainly employed in the production of the numerous draft maps of the 'difficult' national boundaries of the new European states that emerged from the peace treaties.

Cologne was the main posting for the British troops occupying Germany and one FP described the celebrations there when the peace treaty with Germany was finally signed on 28th June 1919, exactly five years after the first shots rang out in Sarajevo:

'It became known early that a salute of 101 guns was to be fired at Cologne when the news arrived that Peace had been signed. Three of us from the Highland

Division determined to be spectators of this historic event and accordingly made our way to the banks of the Rhine, where an immense throng had gathered. The Hohenzollern Bridge itself was dense with khaki, interspersed with the chasseur blue and the khaki and scarlet of the brave Belge. On the esplanade of the left bank of the river twelve field guns were drawn up, the battery commanders in place and the Brigade Commander studying his watch. By skilful manoeuvring, we found ourselves, twelve paces to the right of No.1 gun, about three minutes before the salute commenced. All about us were photographers with their cameras focused on the poor gun, and the remark was heard 'Fat price a misfire?' Otherwise the vast crowd was weirdly silent. Then a signal flag dipped, a sharp command 'No. 1 gun fire' and No.1 nobly responded amid a cheer of roaring. This was dying down when No.2 followed suit and the cheering broke out afresh. At regulation intervals the reports rang out down the line. The salute occupied about 25 minutes and during that time no one stirred - German, British, French, Belgian, American. There were even Russian and Portuguese soldiers in the crowd, and 'Tommy' gave a characteristic welcome to some Indian drivers perched on a lorry. At the cease fire the mass broke up and we hurried to the train station, hoping our luck would hold good in that the train would be late in starting. It was'.

The last guns in the Western war had finally been silenced, yet within weeks some FPs were again on the Western Front, not as servicemen this time but as tourists. There was immense public curiosity back in Britain about the battlefields of France and Belgium which companies such as Cook's were quick to appreciate. One FP described his trip to the battlefields in Belgium undertaken in September 1919. It vividly depicts, not just the post-war havoc, but the immense task of clearance and reconstruction that was already well under way.

The damage to the harbour at Zeebrugge, where the semi-submerged Allied blockships still lay, was the first point of interest for the writer and his companions. Then they hurtled inland by motorbus and car to see for themselves *'the horrors of war...villages that bore the brunt of bombardment...the solitary cemeteries crowded with wooden crosses...the fields studded with shell holes some full of water while in earlier shell holes long rushes were growing, interlaced with old, rusty barbed wire. Gangs of German prisoners were working, also numerous Chinese labourers, collecting old iron and levelling out the ground. There were miles of scrap iron selling, I understand, at £4 per ton and in one district, derelict tanks were prominent. One of these had suffered from a direct hit and been disembowelled.*

On reaching Ypres, what a scene! Absolute devastation! Not a single house standing! The fine old Cloth Hall and the Cathedral with hardly one stone standing on another were a melancholy sight, and to think that under these ruins the bodies of 700 of our men (200 of them, I understand, Royal Engineers) who were in the building when the steeple fell, are still there! As we stepped out of our car on arrival at Ypres, the first thing we noticed was an open cart, driven by an Indian. On the cart were four dead bodies with a Union Jack covering them. This gruesome scene goes on all day I was told, and can one wonder when there were 250,000 casualties round Ypres. We examined the ruins of the town and as I was keen on curios, I picked up a few. I could have got a dozen rifles but they were rusty and rather unwieldy to take away.

While all was devastation, it was not desolation. There are hundreds of tourists arriving, many with cameras, in motor-cars, motor bicycles and all sorts of conveyances, and there are wooden estaminets being erected along the streets to provide comfort and cheer for the inner man. In one of these an excellent lunch was served. We left Ypres in the afternoon and stopped at the roadside near Passchendaele. I picked up bits of shell, a fuse, a rifle etc but did not add to my collection a boot and its contents which I saw lying on the roadside. A visitor in our hotel, on the lookout for relics, found a German helmet lying in a field close to the road and picked it up. The interior of the helmet was ghastly! From Passchendaele we drove through the Forest of Houthulst where many a bloody battle was fought. Not a whole tree now stands; there are many stumps but all blasted by the fumes of powder and gas.

Dixmude was the next town and it was all in ruins. Here we had afternoon tea. We also examined the heavy concealed gun at Moere. This was the gun which the Germans concealed in a copse about 28 miles from Dunkirk that shelled that town daily. At 80 degrees it carried an immense shell into the town. The Germans' idea was to take Dunkirk, move the immense gun there and then take Calais. We arrived at Ostend in time for dinner, and a very good one too!

Our airmen had played dreadful havoc with the roads and consequently we tourists found travelling a bit uncomfortable. On the trip to and from Ypres my car had three punctures! We visited Bruges, had afternoon tea in Ghent and arrived in time for dinner at the Hotel Metropole, Brussels. The town seemed to be gayer than ever and there was little evidence of the Great War. From there to Antwerp, where we lunched, and visited the Cathedral etc. There was not much sign of destruction, although I noticed that the hotel in the square near the Cathedral at which we had stayed several times in pre-war days, had been blown to bits. That however was a small detail.

From Antwerp we motored to Louvain where the Germans did so much mischief *to many old and historic buildings including the world-famous Louvain Library with its priceless books. Thursday in Brussels, I read my Free Press which had been delivered at the hotel that morning, and next morning left for London, then Aberdeen having had a splendid time from beginning to end. The experience is unforgettable'.*

For some at least, the sorrows of war were receding and the Western Front was already established as a 'must-see' location. The war was quickly becoming safely distant history; the horrors and heroics of a few months before had begun their transformation into picturesque travellers' tales. Places that had been Hell for four years were now stops on a busy day's sightseeing before a spot of tea followed by a good dinner. One wonders how the ex-servicemen amongst the recipients of the March 1920 magazine responded to the article's breezy tone.

Life at the School was also returning to normality. The Literary and Debating Society had discussed the impending return to the pre-war school day and decided that it preferred the wartime arrangement with its free afternoons. The Serbian colony, a daily reminder of the reason for the war, left for home in June 1919. Long-absent members of staff were now returning from the ranks and the pupil editor of the School Notes wryly noted that they had brought back with them 'a touch of army discipline and vigour which their classes will no doubt appreciate'.

New faces appeared in the staffroom, none more influential than Duncan MacGregor, the school's first full-time Sports Master and an inspirational figure well placed to make best use of the school's new playing-fields. The pupil editor rightly noted that physical education 'had been rather neglected in our Scottish schools'. Army medical inspectors could confirm that observation. However the editor sensed that 'the War has brought home to all the importance of *mens sana in corpore sano*'. MacGregor brought 'a spirit of hustle and interest into our sports, and the whole school has been wakened up'. So many pupils turned up to witness his first appearance on the Rubislaw field that a crowd of puzzled passers-by congregated on Anderson Drive to observe the commotion.

Those first months of peace were not without their near-tragedies. The School Hall, Morland Simpson's Valhalla which housed all the sacred relics of Grammar History, nearly burned down. Some pupils, it was thought, had tampered with the stage foot-lights which burst into flames.

187

Fortunately the school jannie was on the scene and able to save the school's treasures for a later conflagration. Session 1918-19 was also interrupted by the flu pandemic and while there were no fatalities, the work and morale of the school was badly affected.

And there was a real tragedy for the FP community in the very first days of peace. William Bain Griffiths Minto was a qualified lawyer with a keen interest in things military who enjoyed a successful career in the Artillery Volunteers. At the start of the war he was a Major and the commander of the Torry Fort. He then led a battery in France at the taking of Beaumont Hamel in 1916 and at Arras the following year. Promoted to Lieutenant-Colonel, he was returned in due course to his home station of Torry. He was in command of the battery there in the summer of 1919 when it fired its salute over the city to celebrate the official signing of the Versailles peace treaties. Unfortunately a shell misfired and exploded, cutting down Minto who was standing nearby. This popular and dashing officer died of his wounds on 2nd July 1919.

But now at last the war was officially over. The survivors had time to reflect and remember happier times in their youth before the war when they had been, not warriors, but simply boys of the Aberdeen Grammar School:

'Our last scramble will live forever in my memory. After a hard walk, for the snow on the low ground was soft, the summit of Cairntoul was reached by way of Soldier's Corry. And our quartette, proud of the long and difficult day, rested for a few minutes with a couple of eagles for company, to admire the wonderful scene. And now I am alone this Christmas and the others, all Former Pupils of the old School, have made the supreme sacrifice'.

Chapter 28
Remembrance

The New Field was formally opened on Saturday 16th September 1916, a red letter day in the history of the School. The Grammar now took full possession of its magnificent asset, at twelve acres the largest school playing field in Scotland. Any doubts that the Good Lord above was himself a Grammarian were thoroughly dispelled by the magnificent weather, a bright blue sky with but a single drop of rain which set the 'beautiful sylvan scene to the west, still in full summer garb'. The banner of St Andrew of Scotland and of Scotland's ally Russia, waved gently above those of France and Belgium. In the centre of the field, the band of the Gordon Highlanders crashed out its melodies while a throng of 'naval and military uniforms of all ranks mingled with the gay colours of the dresses of our mothers, cousins and aunts'.

A sizeable contingent of those present were convalescents from the Front brought up to the Field from the many hospitals in and around the city by a fleet of volunteer cars organised by the genial FP Harry Holmes. For them, the seats of honour were strictly reserved although a special place was also found for the widow of James Esslemont and the wife of Alexander Cruickshank, the two FPs who, more than most, had pushed through the field scheme in the days just before the war. The required dignitaries from the School, the Club, the School Board, the University and the Town clustered to witness Mrs Cruickshank cutting the ribbon with a pair of silver scissors inscribed 'Opening of AGS Playfield, 16th September 1916'.

The Rector duly presented the scissors to Mrs Cruickshank and a clock bearing the same inscription to Mrs Esslemont. The games commenced with the ubiquitous Capt Hunter, once of Lodz but now based at Staff HQ Home Forces, acting as official timekeeper in the Field. Athletes entering the final straight of their race were spurred on by the hope of being immortalized on the moving film being taken of the day's events. The Sports Committee excelled at handling the larger-than-expected crowds on both days and at keeping the hordes of over-enthusiastic little boys sufficiently under control. It was a memorable weekend.

And yet the war hung over the whole affair. One witness (was it Watt himself who penned this anonymous piece?) keenly felt the absence of so many faces that should have been there enjoying the celebrations: 'who, strolling along the corridor of our School in these days of war can gaze unmoved on the photographs of the Cricket XIs or the Rugby XVs of the past twenty years? For almost everyone in the groups is serving his country. And over the names of so many we wreathe the proud sorrow, *mortui pro patria*. How small, how miserably small a thing by comparison seem all academic institutions. *Arma virumque canamus*. We paint the names of our intellectuals on the walls of our Hall. What shall we do for the names of our military heroes?'

The question of how to commemorate the School's Fallen had been troubling the Rector and the FP Club for some time. The new field however needed a pavilion. Might a subscription be raised to fund a pavilion as a permanent memorial to the FPs who had fallen in their country's service? The question was tentatively put to the School community in the June 1916 edition of the magazine and met with resounding approval. Although no formal appeal for subscriptions to fund a memorial pavilion was made, an encouraging sum had been donated to the Club by the time of Armistice.

A public meeting to discuss, but in reality approve, the scheme was called in the School Hall for Boxing Day 1918 at which the chief speaker was the Secretary of State for Scotland, the Right Hon Grammarian Robert Munro. At that meeting the plan to build a well equipped pavilion with dressing-rooms and other accommodation necessary for the effective running of games at Rubislaw was passed. The walls of the pavilion would be inscribed with a complete roll of the names of the fallen. The next four issues of the magazine contained long columns listing the names of subscribers and their contributions to the cause.

In June 1919, Charles Davidson, convener of the FP Memorial Committee, intimated that the appeal fund already totalled almost £2000, but this was still less than half of the estimated cost of £5000. He expressed his concern that there was a risk of waning interest attached to all schemes related to the War but he exhorted the school community to finish the task:

'the natural readiness to turn from the darkness of the past five years to the long-awaited dawn must not blind us to the fact that our duty remains unfulfilled until we have paid our tribute to the heroic self-sacrifice of those comrades who at so great a price bought for us this relief'. The fund stood at around £3450 in June 1920 but then subsided to a trickle despite being topped-up by a transfer of the remaining monies in the original Field Fund.

There was inevitably a degree of donation fatigue, as Davidson had feared. The School after all was also seeking subscriptions for the statue of Lord Byron and there were many other post-war charities in Aberdeen seeking help for their deserving objectives. The magazine editor encouraged readers of humble circumstances to send in their mite regardless: 'junior members perhaps feel rather shy at sending the small individual subscriptions that they are in the position to give but if all these junior members contribute, say, five or ten shillings, their united donations would amount to a goodly sum'.

If the total needed could not be garnered from donations, it would have to be earned; ticket monies from the annual gymnastics evenings in 1920 and 1921 amassed £34, an 'American Style' tennis tournament raised £2/16/0, the FP Dramatic Society performance of the Sherlock Holmes mystery *The Speckled Band* made a useful profit of £43/8/0, the sale of photograph portraits of the Rector brought in another £2/16/0, the reserves of the school's Sports and Games Committee were raided and with funds added by the Literary & Debating Society yielded a total of £26/9/0. Miraculously, the Lit & Deb found another £22/18/0 from somewhere. All of these contributions were gratefully received by the treasurer but made little impact on the shortfall of £1400 or so.

The details of all donations were printed in the magazine. The vast bulk of donations were received in 1919 and 1920. The name of each donor was recorded with their address and the size of their gift. Many gifts were named in honour of a lost family member or members. Other donations were dedicated to the memory of former classmates and/or comrades; 'in memory of three classmates who gave up their lives'; 'for the fallen members of the last Classical VI'; 'in memory of a pal killed at Beaumont Hamel'. Many donations were anonymous: 'From two who have served - 25 guineas'; 'From two present pupils - 1 guinea'. There were five donations of £100 and one donation of 100 guineas, considerable gifts at a time when the average weekly wage was around 30 shillings The smallest donation received was one shilling but the vast bulk of the approximately 1070 subscriptions were in the one to three guinea region. Numerous subscribers made additional donations and in many households, different family members made their own individual donations. Each of the five remaining members of the Rector's family living at Amatola, 448 Great Western Road made their own gift in memory of the family's lost boy Harry.

But still the money raised was simply not enough to meet the expected cost of the original project. At one point in 1921, the project seemed jeopardised by the rise in wages and prices that had resulted from the immediate post-war 'replacement' boom. The final sum needed seemed to be moving ever further out of reach but in 1922 the beginning of the long deflationary slump that lasted though the Twenties helped stabilise the purchasing power of the monies in the fund.

Donors were understandably impatient to see something tangible emerge from their generous gifts. Members of the FP Club's Memorial Committee were therefore delegated to meet with the architect to consider ways of pushing things on and perhaps paring the design back a little to make it simpler and bring it within the FP budget. The pavilion largely disappeared from the pages of the next few magazine editions and the readership's attention was instead directed towards the campaign to scrape together enough to pay for the Byron Statue. Then, at the FP Club AGM in Spring 1923, the long-awaited news was announced; plans for the pavilion had been agreed and 'in all probability building operations will be started in the coming summer'. The final plans were approved in June, the contractors' offers were accepted in July and work began in August. By late autumn much of the masonry work had been completed and the granite colonnade was taking shape. The structure was partly roofed and the distinctive red tiles of Rubislaw were soon to be in place.

Now that the project was nearing completion, money was also beginning to flow again. Three hundred and fifty pounds came from the much-harangued readers of the magazine. Two hundred was raised at the annual FP dinner led by the FP Provost of Huntly Alexander Christie who gifted £50 on the night. By June 1924, approximately £4,400 was available for the Pavilion. Then came the unexpected but welcome news from the contractor that the final cost would be less than feared, and possibly several hunded pounds below the estimated £5,000. The good old days indeed. When the final bills were settled in late 1925, the fund convenor Charles James Davidson, advocate with Lumsden and Davidson, personally met the final shortfall of £252, 15 shillings and 8 pence. This act of generosity brought Davidson's total donation to the Memorial Fund to well over £400, making him by some distance its most generous [known] benefactor.

The result was magnificent and a lasting symbol of the collective grief felt for the lost Grammarians of the Great War. The frontage measured 110 feet, dominated by the portico formed by four granite columns flanked by granite pilasters. The front façade was crowned with a granite entablature of cornice and frieze along its entire length. Each end of the frieze bore a Roman wreath in bronze, framing the inscription *Caesorum Comitum Memores* - Remembering our Fallen Comrades. The portico led on to the windowed central hall, lined in dark oak. Two oak mantelpieces at either end of the hall flanked a central tablet with the heraldic Arms of the School picked out in colour, the dates 1914-1919 and the words THIS PAVILION WAS ERECTED AS A MEMORIAL OF FORMER PUPILS OF THE SCHOOL WHO FELL IN THE GREAT WAR.

Some readers may remember the much-used pavilion at a point in its existence when it was tired, arguably delapidated in places and certainly quite obsolete. In 1924 however it was an impressive and state-of-the-art facility. Its wings housed dressing rooms and shower baths, a kitchen and a room for the games master. The upper floor contained a small flat for the groundsman, a 'ladies room' and a long gallery running above the portico, facing south across the open sward of Rubislaw. Modernised in recent times but not enhanced, the Memorial Pavilion remains one of the most distinctive buildings in a city rich in fine buildings and the central portion of this solemn memorial still reflects very well on its architect J A Ogg Allan. The Memorial Pavilion scheme had taken more than five years to reach completion. By then, two other memorial projects had been brought to fruition.

By 1921 a scheme for the embellishment of the School Hall was well in hand. Aberdeen Education Authority had decided upon a complete cleaning and re-painting of Morland Simpson's 'Valhalla'. The Authority had agreed to re-lettering the names that were already on the walls of the Hall, and to the addition of the names of the Great War fallen plus the

193

names of one hundred outstanding former pupils. There were also plans to purchase paintings and engravings of distinguished FPs and hang these in the Hall. Money had already been raised to buy a portrait of James Gibbs, architect of St Martin-in-the-Fields and much else. The Education Authority was keen to 'visualise the fame of the School and to create a pervading atmosphere of tradition within the building'. While the fund-raising for the FP plan of a Memorial Sports Pavilion at Rubislaw was temporarily stalled, the School found itself with a magnificent memorial in its inner sanctum, almost by default.

The refurbished Hall was opened, and the War Memorial unveiled, at a brief and moving ceremony on 8th May 1923. Admission was restricted to the close family of the Fallen, senior pupils, staff and platform guests. The address was given by the FP Lord Alness, Lord Justice-Clerk of Scotland. It touched on his belief in the League of Nations and his hope that the spirit of national unity forged in the war might be kept alive in peacetime. Alness unveiled the memorial, and a prayer was offered by the Rev D Bruce Nicol MC. Distant pipes played the *The Flowers o' the Forest* while two senior boys entered the Hall bearing a wreath which was laid beneath the Memorial. The *Last Post* was sounded from afar and the congregated body sang a benedictory hymn. While the pipers played *The Green Hills of Tyrone*, the boys of the School filed out one by one and saluted the names on the memorial as they marched past.

Theodore Watt rightly sensed that in this service the School had performed 'its own peculiar act of homage to the fallen'. As a result, it was later decided that no second ceremony of remembrance would be held at the Rubislaw pavilion and in the event, it was simply left open at the annual Sports for all to view and contemplate. Similarly, as the name of each one of the Grammar Dead had been recorded on the panels in the Hall, the oak panels at Rubislaw would now be left blank, a decision that explains their stark and effective contribution to the atmosphere within the pavilion's inner core.

The Great War Memorial in the School Hall consisted of nine panels painted in military grey grouped in three bays of dark, fumed oak. Each panel contained 27 names, making a uniform arrangement of all 243 names. Each name was inscribed in gold lettering. Beneath ran a regular gallery of 63 small panels containing brief biographical details of each of the men named above. The entire work contained almost 12,000 golden letters, inscribed by the craftsman Edward Garden under the supervision of Dr William Kelly ARSA. Above the names were the Arms of Scotland, a Saltire set within a wreath of holly and thistles, the Arms of Aberdeen in an ivy wreath, and the Arms of the School surrounded by flowers and laurel. Sadly, the Memorial's carefully composed and serene uniformity was disturbed within a generation by the need to add the names of the Grammar's losses in the Second World War.

The third commemorative element in the Grammar plan of remembrance was the Roll of Pupils, a work of almost 550 pages in all. Theodore Watt had in fact begun this monumental volume in 1908 and then, when almost ready to go to print in 1914, its publication was necessarily sidelined by the upheaval of war. By 1918, Watt had come to feel it necessary to undertake a major revision of his existing work in order to give full emphasis to the war service of the almost seventeen hundred FPs who had been members of HM Armed Forces. This was a massive task, complicated by the fact that much of the existing typeset work would have to be amended. Moreover, many of the Great War FPs had scattered to all parts of the globe following their demobilization, so gathering and collating information about their war service would inevitably take time.

Watt spent untold hours during the years 1919-23 exhorting and cajoling FPs to send in their biographical details so that he could ensure that the Roll would be as comprehensive and accurate as possible. The final Roll published in 1923 contains the names of more than 13,300 Grammar pupils and provides rich annotation concerning the 6,377 boys who attended the new school in Skene Street after 1863. The details are especially rich for the entries of the Great War FPs, giving as full details as Watt could gather. More comment is given about this uniquely valuable book in the following chapter. Suffice to say here, that in its attention to the war record of the Grammar' Great War cohort, it is the School's equivalent to the epitaph placed on the Greek burial mound at Thermopylae by Simonides:

'Tell it in Sparta, you that passeth by
Here, faithful to their charge, her fallen soldiers lie'

Chapter 29

Dr Theodore Watt

This book would not be complete without an appreciation of Dr Theodore Watt, a man of immense energy whose efforts to record the achievements of the Grammar School FPs are the foundation of this current work.

Watt had ink in his veins. After learning his trade, he managed the Rosemount Press in different capacities from 1914 until its merger with the University Press in 1932. He was joint managing director of the new company, the Aberdeen University Press, and enjoyed a high professional profile at national and international level. During the 1930s he was a pioneering president of the Scottish and British associations of Master Printers and he led the British delegation to the International Printing Congress in Budapest in August 1938.

Watt gave very generously of his time to his city, especially to bodies concerned with its educational life. He was an outstanding servant of the University and over several decades he made a major contribution to the success of the its alumnus association, and its journal the *AU Review*. After the Great War, he rendered 'invaluable assistance' to the production of the University's 1921 Roll of Service recording those students, graduates and staff who served and fell in the struggle. In 1935 the University published a roll of its graduates spanning the years 1860 to 1925 which Watt had compiled throughout the preceeding nine years. For thirty years he was a member of the Business Committee of the University's General Council and for the last four years of his life was an Assessor on the University Court. In 1938 he was awarded an honorary doctorate in recognition of his service to the University.

Watt's contributions to the educational life of Aberdeen were much wider and deeper than his university connection however. In 1923 he was elected to the Aberdeen Education Authority, then responsible for the city's primary and secondary schools. When the functions of that body were absorbed by the Town Council in 1929-30, Watt became a member of the new Education Committee. He also sat on the committee which regulated the work of the teacher training centre in Charlotte Street and its relationship with the 'demonstration' school in John Street.

He was a Governor of Robert Gordon's College and on the Board of Directors of the Aberdeen Royal Mental Hospital. He was a director of the Aberdeen Association for Improving the Condition of the Poor, a body which he served for over thirty years. A family man with five children, Watt also fulfilled several additional time-consuming duties such as Treasurer at St Paul's Street Congregational Church.

All this would have utterly exhausted most mere mortals but no mention has yet been made of his service to the city institution he loved above all others, Aberdeen Grammar School. Watt gave many thousands of hours to the School in many ways. He held various offices in the FP Club and was Club President in the year of his death. He was instrumental in setting up the Club Consul system and club centres in Edinburgh, Glasgow, Shanghai and Calcutta. He was much involved in the committee charged with fulfilling the Byron Statue project and he played a major part in the installation of the War Memorial in the School Hall. He was a director of the company that ran the school's boarding house in Queen's Road.

And then, in addition to all these other onerous responsibilities, he was editor of the Magazine from 1907 to 1946 and so effectively the archivist of the history of the school throughout that long period. His obituary explains the unique feeling which 'Watt's Magazine' provoked in Grammarians of the period. It recorded that 'tributes to the high standard and technical excellence of the Magazine under his editorship had come from all parts of the world and by many it was considered the finest School magazine in the country. In particular, the Notes on Old Boys forged a link at home and abroad that was probably unique. It was particularly appreciated during the two World Wars when, for many hundreds of FPs serving abroad, the magazine was one of the very few links with home'.

Lord Alness mused that how Watt 'found the time in a busy life to expend the meticulous care and whole-hearted devotion to this enterprise has always been a mystery to me. To Dr Watt this was a labour of love, pursued with characteristic modesty and characteristic competency'. Sir Patrick Cooper emphasised the impact that the magazine had on forming a unique Grammarian *esprit de corps*: 'He recorded the doings and achievements of Former Pupils in a manner probably never equalled in a school magazine. In all parts of the world he created the keenest interest in the doings of Old Grammarians'. The Rector Sir James J Robertson shared his insight into Watt's herculean labours: 'Many have praised the magazine but I suspect that only the few have ever fully realised how much it cost Dr Watt in time and thought...nothing but the rarest affection for the School would have made any man submit to such a burden for so long'.

The 1914-1918 issues of the magazine were the initial treasure trove plundered by the present writer. They are a fascinating source of information about the Grammar School community in the period and the ways in which the Great War impacted upon the city of Aberdeen. Yet the inexhaustible Theodore Watt still managed to find the time to produce an even richer lode, the Roll of Aberdeen Grammar School Pupils 1795-1919.

The factual details about the Roll are given in the previous chapter but one reviewer, Professsor Bulloch, understood the personal cost to Watt who had begun the task in 1908, almost finished it by 1914, but then felt obliged to take it up again to include the Great War Grammarians:

'I have some knowledge of the labour it has entailed. The difficulty involved will come home to everybody who has tried to name the figures on some faded photograph displaying one's class-mates, but instead of groups of a score or more, Mr Watt has had to tackle more than 13,000 names and in the case of nearly 7,000 he has had to find some identifying facts. Think of the endless correspondence in the appeals to people who were more or less indifferent; of the unanswered letters, then of the careful marshalling of the data on a well-thought system; and last of all, the intense drudgery of checking the material in print. Looking back on these fifteen years of preparation, Mr Watt himself is probably amazed at what he has managed to get through. Had he known in 1908 what he knows in 1923 he might never have tackled it'.

The present writer suspects that Bulloch was probably wrong, and that such was Theodore Watt's commitment to his old school, he would have embarked on the vast task nonetheless. The Grammar Roll is a rich historical archive that contributes much to our understanding of life in Aberdeen and Northern Scotland throughout the nineteenth and early twentieth centuries. It should also be an early port of call for any historian with an interest in the Scottish contribution to the building of the Empire and Commonwealth, for Watt carefully recorded the achievements of Grammar FPs in all the parts of globe that were then coloured pink, and most of the other bits besides. It is especially valuable as a record of the boys and men who fought in the Great War for these were the Grammarians that Watt knew best; in many cases his own school contemporaries and friends, their brothers and cousins. He fulfilled his debt to them by making sure that to the best of his ability and knowledge, the contribution of every Grammar FP was recorded for posterity.

This present publication would not have been possible without the Magazine and the Roll, the great fruits of Theodore Watt's archival labours and his lifelong affection for the Grammar School. The present writer fully acknowledges that, to paraphrase Isaac Newton, he has been standing on the shoulders of a giant.

Chapter 30

Appendices

a) The Grammar Cohort

In 1919 and 1923, Theodore Watt provided several tables that summarized the overall FP effort in the Great War. He was aware that these were probably incomplete but noted that they were still useful as they gave a reasonably accurate indication of the scale of the AGSFP contribution. In that spirit, some of Watt's figures are reproduced below.

Watt recorded a total of 1,688 FPs who served in HM Forces at some point in the war. Ninety-four served in the Royal Navy. The number who served in the Army totalled 1,474. Those serving in the RFC and later RAF came to 120. In all, 1,092 FPs were commissioned officers. Of the Army FPs, the largest contingent were in the Gordon Highlanders. The pupil roll suggests that 356 Grammarians served in the Gordons at some point in the war and that around sixty per cent of these FPs [214] spent all or most of their time in uniform in the North East's 'own' regiment. The majority of FPs served in the 4th Territorial Battalion. For many in this group, their time in the regiment was only their introduction to military life and a significant number of these men were among the 142 FPs who later transferred from the Gordons to other units in the course of the war, often to hold commissions. Of these, twenty-one transferred to the Royal Engineers, twenty to the RFC and RAF, eighteen to the artillery formations, and thirteen to the MGC. Of the remaining seventy transferees, thirteen went to other Scottish Regiments and twelve to serve in English units.

Watt always took great interest in the Grammar School Company of the Gordon Highlanders [D Company of the 4th TF Battalion] and in the first edition after the Armistice, he included a note on the numbers serving in this unit that were known to him at that point in late 1918. Although Watt acknowledged that it was an incomplete tally, he felt it was of sufficient interest to merit publication and it therefore also appears here as it gives a clear impression of the company's war record. Seventy-seven FPs served in D Company. Of that number twenty died, killed in action or later from wounds. Five were taken as POWs. Seven were discharged. Eight members of the Company won the Military Cross, one with Bar. Fifty-four of these men were in due course commissioned in other units; five in the Royal Engineers, eleven in Artillery formations, two in the Machine Gun Corps, one in the Tank Corps, six in the RFC/RAF, four in the Indian Army and twenty-five in other infantry regiments.

In all, a total of 226 Grammarians served in Scottish units other than the Gordons. The largest FP cohorts were in the Scottish Horse [35] and the Seaforths [33] followed by the Cameronians [26], the Black Watch [25], the Royal Scots [23], HLI [23] and the Argylls [21]. Smaller contingents included the Scots Guards [7], the Scottish Rifles [7], the Royal Scots Fusiliers [5], the Highland Cyclists [5] and the Lovat Scouts [4]. Eight FPs served in the Scottish county Yeomanry units. Three FPs in the KOSB and a lone member of the Royal Scots Greys complete this grouping. Almost 150 FPs served in English and Welsh units, of whom twenty-nine served in the London Scottish, while four fought in Irish regiments.

After the Gordon Highlanders, the next largest FP contingent was the group of over 280 men who served in the RAMC. Fourteen other medical FPs served in the Indian Medical Service and a similar number filled the ranks of the medical services of the Royal Navy. A number of FP medics also figure in the records of the Canadian, Australian and New Zealand Expeditionary Forces. Several FP medics were also engaged in the various African campaigns.

Over 185 Grammarians served in the artillery formations [the RFA, RGA, HAC and RAOC] while 152 FPs filled the ranks of the Royal Engineers. Thirty-three FPs served in the Machine Gun Corps. Ninety FPs served in the Indian Army, almost all as officers. Around eighty FPs are known to have served in the Canadian Expeditionary Force although as noted elsewhere, a number of FPs returned from Canada to serve in British units. Twenty and seventeen FPs served in the Expeditionary Forces of Australia and New Zealand respectively. Seven served in the armed forces of the USA while approximately twenty-five are known to have enlisted in the various colonial volunteer units such as the Ceylon Planters' Rifle Corps whose principal function at the start of the war was to help maintain order in Britain's possessions.

Two other significant groups were the 64 FPs in the ranks of the Army Service Corps, many of whom were attached to the ASC's Motor Transport section, and the nineteen FPs who [mostly] held command roles in the Labour Corps.

Over 900 Grammarians were involved in the Western Front at some point in their period of service. Over 320 were engaged in the campaigns against the Ottoman Empire in Gallipoli, Egypt, Mesopotamia and Palestine while sixty-two served in Salonika and the Macedonian Front facing the Turk's Balkan allies. Other significant cohorts were the sixty-five FPs who served in the African campaigns and the thirty-three who fetched up on the Alpine Front in north-eastern Italy. [Please note that uniformed chaplains have not been included in the above figures but are mentioned elsewhere.]

b) The Decorated

Grammar FPs were awarded three hundred and nine honours for their services during the war. Non-commissioned FPs won a total of twenty-seven decorations. Four won the Medal for Distinguished Conduct in the Field [DCM], nineteen won the Military Medal [MM] and three won the Meritorious Service Medal [MSM]. Arthur Forbes won a Bar to his Military Medal in 1917. William Forbes, Sapper in the RE Signals with the 51st Highland Division, won the Military Medal in March 1918 and the MSM three months later.

Two commissioned naval FPs, William Mackintosh and Peter Shaw, won the Distinguished Service Cross. One hundred and twenty-one FPs were awarded the Military Cross, twelve with Bar. Two Grammarian aviators won the Distinguished Flying Cross. Forty-three FPs were made Companions of the Distinguished Service Order [DSO]. Three of these held the DSO with Bar. Forty FPs were decorated with the newly-created Honours of the British Empire. Two were awarded the MBE, thirty-three were awarded the OBE and five were awarded the CBE. Nine Grammarians were admitted to the older chivalric orders. Sir William Watson Cheyne was made a Knight Commander of St Michael and St George [KCMG]. Thomas Ogilvie was made a Companion of the Bath [CB] and a Companion in the Order of

St Michael and St George [CMG]. Two other FPs were made CB, and five CMG. Robert Grierson Combe was the sole Great War Grammarian to win the Victoria Cross.

Grammar FPs were awarded a total of forty-eight decorations by foreign governments. Twenty FPs were decorated with the *Croix de Guerre* while James Lawrence Smith and Godfrey Power Geddes were admitted to the *Légion d'honneur* as Officier and Chevalier respectively. Eight FPs were decorated by the Belgian monarchy. FPs also received honours from Britain's other European allies Serbia, Italy, Roumania, Portugal, Greece and Tsarist Russia. Two FPs were decorated with the Order of the Nile by the administration in Egypt while James Webster received the Order of the Striped Tiger from the Chinese Republic.

A number of FPs were awarded multiple honours. Major Alexander Donald Fraser RAMC, a son of the manse at Alvah, can be said to be the most decorated Great War Grammarian. He won the MC in 1916 and the DSO and *Croix de Guerre* the following year. His fourth decoration was a Bar to the DSO in February 1919. Fraser served in France for most of the war with spells in Mesopotamia and the North Russia Expeditionary Force. James Noel Thomson, of Rubislaw Place and the RFA, won three 'gongs': the MC, the DSO and the French *Croix de Guerre*. He was 'mentioned repeatedly' in despatches. Donald Fasken Stevenson, of Polmuir Road and the RFC, won the MC in September 1917 and a Bar to the MC the following month. He added the DSO to his collection in July 1918. Godfrey Power Geddes won the DSO and the French *Croix de Guerre* in addition to his membership of the *Légion d'honneur*. In all, twenty-six FPs won more than one decoration.

Several pairs of brothers appear on the list of the Grammarians honoured in the war. The exploits of Major-General Andrew Skeen CMG, KCIE and Oliver Skeen DSO have been given due attention earlier. Major Henry Butchart, who later served as a notable Secretary to the University of Aberdeen, won the DSO and the Star of Roumania [Officer Class]. His older brother James who served in the Artillery rose to the rank of Lt Col and received the DSO in 1917. Ernest Ewart [Boyd Cable], once of 39 Osborne Place, served in the Artillery and then in the RFC/RAF. Demobbed with the rank of Lt Col, he received the OBE in December 1918. His older brother John Knox Ewart rose to senior rank in the Army Service Corps and was awarded the DSO in January 1918 and the Belgian *Croix de Guerre* in December that year. He was mentioned several times in despatches. [A third Ewart brother, Frederick, served in the RFA and the Ministry of Munitions]. Archer and William Irvine-Fortesque were both decorated, Archer with the DSO and William with the MC and Bar.

Alfred and William Lumsden, of Albyn Terrace, were both professional soldiers before the war. William enjoyed a successful war in military administration which took him to GHQ British Army of the Rhine by 1920. He received the DSO in 1917. His older brother Alfred also received the DSO that year. He was acting Brigadier-General in Feb 1918 but killed by a stray shell in June. Other Grammarian brothers-in-arms who were both decorated include; Lt Col Alexander Nicol Smith DSO and French *Croix de Guerre*, and Capt Norman Smith of the Northumberland Fusiliers and Royal Engineers MC; Major Thomas Milne of the 55th Coke's Rifles who was awarded the DSO and Order of the Nile and his brother Herbert S Milne RAMC MC and Bar; Capt George R W Stewart MC and his older brother Capt James S Stewart RAMC MC; the Riddoch brothers, John Louis and William Joseph of Forest Road who both served as NCOs and both won the Military Medal; Major John Rae RE MC and Lt Col William Rae DSO and French *Croix de Guerre*; and Michael and Theodore Ritchie who both joined the RAMC in the early Edwardian years. Michael rose to the rank of Major, was mentioned five times in despatches and was decorated with the DSO and OBE. Theodore, also Major was mentioned four times and awarded the DSO in 1917.

Several decorated FPs were not yet adults in the eyes of the law when decorated. This group includes Maxwell Campbell Wright and Allan Hendry, both Gordon Highlanders, who were both little more than twenty when they were awarded the MC. The youngest decorated FP seems to have been William Grenville Irvine-Fortescue of the Royal Engineers who was nineteen when he won the MC for 'exceptional coolness and gallantry when constructing a bridge under very heavy enemy fire'.

c) The Fallen

The names of 243 Grammar FPs are recorded on the School War Memorial. The largest contingent amongst the Grammar Fallen were FPs serving in the ranks of the Gordon Highlanders at the time of their death. They numbered sixty-eight in all, although two other FPs may be added to this figure. They had been discharged from the Gordons before the end of the war but died from medical conditions contracted while in uniform. Another thirty of the Fallen were serving in Scottish regiments, of which the largest number were those serving in the Seaforth Highlanders [ten], the Cameron Highlanders [six] and the Royal Scots [four]. Five died while serving in the London Scottish. Twenty four Grammarians died in the ranks of eighteen English and Irish regiments. Fifteen Grammarians died while serving in the Royal Engineers, thirteen in the Royal Army Medical Corps, ten in the various Artillery formations and five in the Machine Gun Corps. There were eight FP fatalities in the Royal Navy and its branches such as the Royal Naval Reserve. Nine Grammarians died as members of the Royal Flying Corps and the Royal Air Force.

The largest loss of life amongst 'colonial ' FPs was in the Canadian contingent who suffered twenty-one fatalities. Members of Australian military units accounted for another five deaths; FPs serving with New Zealand units accounted for another three. Six FPs died while serving in African units and one died as a Singapore Volunteer. A total of ten FPs died whilst serving in the Indian Army, mostly on service on the north-western frontiers of the Raj or in the Middle East. One FP met his death whilst serving in the Mesopotamian Police. The seven FPs who died while serving in the Merchant Navy bring the total to 243.

Thirty-five of the Grammar dead lost their lives in 1914 and 1915 ie the first seventeen months of the war. The figure rose sharply in 1916 to fifty-eight. This was the result of the increased scale of the war overall and the heavy British casualties incurred in the Battle of the Somme which lasted for four and a half months in the summer and autumn of 1916. The fatality rate remained high in 1917 [68] and 1918 [67] with many dying in the Third Battle of Ypres [Passchendaele] which lasted for more than three months. The Ludendorff Offensive in spring 1918 took a heavy toll but so did the Allied counter-offensive that finally secured victory. Twenty-three FPs died in the *Kaiserschlacht* between March and May, and twenty-two in the Allied 'push' between August and November. Fifteen of the men recorded on the War Memorial died in the period 1919 to 1921 of wounds or conditions that resulted from their military service.

Analysis of the locations where FPs died illustrates the overwhelming significance of 'the Big Show' on the Western Front in terms of the men and effort that it consumed. Of the 243 fallen Grammarians, 169 died on service in France and Belgium. Twenty FPs died back in Britain and a number of these expired as a result of wounds sustained on the Western Front. A total of thirty FPs died in the theatres of operation that might be termed 'Eastern', ie those areas of military activity that stretched from the Eastern Mediterranean through the Middle East to India and South East Asia. Seven FPs died in the various African campaigns. One FP died in the Allied Intervention in Northern Russia in 1918-19.

One hundred and forty two FPs were recorded as killed in action. To these must be added the eleven Grammarians who were recorded as missing in action presumed killed, and two who were killed at the Front by enemy snipers. Five were lost at sea as a result of enemy action. Thirty two were recorded as dying from illesses contracted while on duty. These ranged from diseases such as malaria and cholera, and ailments such as dysentery or the effects of exposure and exhaustion. Several men died as a result of influenza pandemic of 1918. Three FPs died from accidental injuries.

In terms of age, the largest group amongst the fatalities were FPs in their twenties. Sixty-nine FPs in their thirties and twenty men in their forties lost their lives. Four Grammarians over 50 appear on the list, the oldest being James Walker Beattie RAMC who died at Southampton in July 1918 aged sixty-five. Almost 40 Grammar FPs died before they had reached their twenty-first birthday, in those days the generally accepted age of reaching adulthood. Three of the fallen were only eighteen; Douglas Stephen, William Sellar and William Ledingham Watson who was the youngest of the Grammar Dead. A private in the Gordon Highlanders, he arrived in France in February 1915 and was killed on the 30th May. He had celebrated his eighteenth birthday just three weeks earlier.

The last FP to die on active service prior to the Armistice was James Reid of the Royal Engineers who died on 6th November 1918 of an illness contracted on service, but he died at Archangel in northern Russia where the conflict continued into the following year. On the Western Front, two FPs who died on October 23rd 1918 were probably the last of the Grammar's fatal casualties in that theatre of operations. Captain William Millar of the RAMC, who may have contracted malaria in Salonika, died in hospital at Dieppe on that day. Alexander Cruickshank MC of the Machine Gun Corps also died on the 23rd at Le Cateau. He was the last Grammarian to be killed in action before the Armistice.

d) Sources

Mabel D Allardyce [ed], University of Aberdeen Roll of Service in the Great War, 1914-1919, AUP 1921

Brian R W Lockhart & Arthur L McCombie, Bon Record, a History of Aberdeen Grammar School, Birlinn Press 2012

Theodore Watt [ed], The Aberdeen Grammar School Roll of Pupils 1795-1919, The Rosemount Press, Aberdeen 1923

Theodore Watt, The Aberdeen Grammar School Magazine, 1900-1946

David Yule, 1256 and all that, AGSFP Club 2006

A large number of websites were also used to dig behind the initial information in the School records. The following are only a small sample of the more helpful:

www.wrecksite.eu

www.cwgc.org

www.bac-lac.gc.ca

www.1914-18.net

www.national archives.gov.uk

www.iwm.org.uk

www.awm.gov.au

www.ww1battefields.co.uk

Index of AGS
Former Pupils

General Index